The Welfare Trait

The Welfare Trait

How State Benefits Affect Personality

Adam Perkins

Lecturer in the Neurobiology of Personality, King's College London, UK

First published 2016 by
PALGRAVE MACMILLAN

Palgrave Macmillan in the UK is an imprint of Macmillan Publishers Limited, registered in England, company number 785998, of Houndmills, Basingstoke, Hampshire RG21 6XS.

Palgrave Macmillan in the US is a division of St Martin's Press LLC, 175 Fifth Avenue, New York, NY 10010.

Palgrave Macmillan is the global academic imprint of the above companies and has companies and representatives throughout the world.

Palgrave® and Macmillan® are registered trademarks in the United States, the United Kingdom, Europe and other countries.

ISBN 978-1-137-55528-1   ISBN 978-1-137-55529-8 (eBook)
DOI 10.1057/9781137555298

This book is printed on paper suitable for recycling and made from fully managed and sustained forest sources. Logging, pulping and manufacturing processes are expected to conform to the environmental regulations of the country of origin.

A catalogue record for this book is available from the British Library.

Library of Congress Cataloging-in-Publication Data
Perkins, Adam, 1972– author.
    The welfare trait : how state benefits affect personality / Adam Perkins.
       pages   cm
    Includes bibliographical references.

    1. Personality and occupation.   2. Public welfare—Psychological aspects.   3. Welfare recipients—Psycology.   4. Welfare recipients—Attitudes.   5. Personality change.   I. Title.
    BF698.9.O3P46 2015
    155.9′2—dc23   2015020341

Contents

List of Illustrations   vi

Acknowledgements   viii

Preface   x

1   What Is Personality and Why Does the Welfare State
    Matter?   1

2   The Employment-Resistant Personality Profile   18

3   The Lifelong Impact of Personality   40

4   The Influence of Benefits on Claimant Reproduction   54

5   Childhood Disadvantage and Employment-Resistance   79

6   Genetic Influences on Personality   97

7   Personality as a Product of Nature and Nurture   112

8   A Model of How the Welfare State Leads to Personality
    Mis-Development   122

9   Further Evidence for Welfare-Induced Personality
    Mis-Development   140

10 What Next?   175

References   186

Index   197

Illustrations

Figures

2.1 The personality-filtering process triggered by the implementation of the welfare state   32

2.2 Employability as a function of the combined scores on conscientiousness and agreeableness in 2,532 UK adults   38

4.1 Distribution of antisocial personality traits in a sample of 514 US residents   61

4.2 Distribution of antisocial personality traits in a sample of 638 UK residents   62

4.3 Childhood self-control and reproduction in a British cohort born in 1958   66

4.4 Childhood self-control and reproduction in a British cohort born in 1970   67

5.1 The rate of return of childhood versus adult interventions   81

5.2 Children's quarrelling with parents by satisfaction with life overall, 2011–2012   84

5.3 Children's talk with parents by satisfaction with life overall, 2011–2012   85

8.1 Percentage of Perry Preschool participants who were unemployed at the age of 40 versus the average rate of unemployment for African Americans in 2004   125

8.2 Percentage of Perry Preschool participants who had served a prison sentence by the age of 40 versus the average rate of incarceration for African Americans in 2001   126

8.3 The distribution of questionnaire scores on conscientiousness in 2,532 participants from one of my own studies (dashed lines indicate one standard deviation)   132

9.1   Bar chart showing the average number of children
      under the age of 16 in working, mixed and workless
      households, April–June 2013, UK   158
9.2   Bar chart showing the average number of children
      under the age of 16 in working, mixed, workless and
      troubled households, April–June 2013, UK   159
9.3   Targeted annual expenditure on troubled families   161
9.4   Reactive annual expenditure on troubled families   162
9.5   Homicides in England and Wales between 1901 and
      2011   168
9.6   The relationship in the USA from 2000 to 2009
      between per-capita consumption of cheese and
      deaths due to tangled bed sheets   169
10.1 Bar chart showing the average number of children
      under the age of 16 in working, mixed and workless
      households, April–June 2013, UK   176

Tables

4.1   Average number of children under the age of 16 in
      working, mixed and workless households in England
      and Wales during April–June 2013   72
9.1   Employment status of individuals convicted of
      homicide in England and Wales from 2007/2008 to
      2012   165

Acknowledgements

Modern science is a matter of teamwork and this book reflects the influence of many people. First, I thank my parents Robert and Kathleen for endowing me – through the interaction of nature and nurture – with a thirst for knowledge, which is perhaps the most important asset of all for a scientist. They also gave me a belief that the status quo should be questioned as well as the benefit of a stable, supportive and loving childhood home, but without being a soft touch: my employment-resistant personality profile became apparent at an early age and my parents did their best to stamp it out. My sister Katie assisted with that process by setting an example of highly conscientious and agreeable behaviour, but I remain easily distracted and therefore must also thank my aunt and uncle, Barbara and Guy, who helped to save my sanity and this book by providing me with a quiet and internet-free place to write certain particularly difficult sections of the manuscript. The literary world is a complex and strange one to a scientific researcher and I was therefore lucky to benefit from the advice of Mike and Marian Shaw as well as their kind hospitality many years ago when I was a callow and near penniless warehouse worker, newly arrived in London. The bosses of that warehouse were decent enough to employ me for almost three years and at the same time taught me a lot about the world of work: thank you Paul and Anto. Once I entered the world of scientific publishing I was very lucky to benefit from the advice of the established scientific author Professor Tomas Chamorro-Premuzic, who provided many wise suggestions as to how to proceed. I thank the diligent and gifted staff at Palgrave Macmillan who helped to make *The Welfare Trait* into a book rather than just a series of chapters. In particular, I thank Paul Stevens for spotting the potential of *The Welfare Trait* as a Palgrave Macmillan book and Nicola Jones for taking time out of her Christmas holiday to read the entire manuscript, a sacrifice that (I hope) was worthwhile, as she provided astute editorial analysis that did a lot to improve the book. Eleanor Christie successfully saw the book through the labyrinth of anonymous peer review – I am most grateful to her for undertaking this arduous task, as well as to the three anonymous reviewers whose criticisms were sometimes harsh, sometimes gentle but always useful. As a result of all these efforts, I think this book represents a true meeting of minds between author and publisher and is much the better for it. Before the manuscript was known to the publisher, it had already gone through four drafts – drafts that were scrutinised by a doughty group of test readers, namely Alex Douglas, Simon Brunton, Rosalind Arden, Atalanta Arden-Miller and Jonathan O'Muircheartaigh. I also thank all those with whom I have had inspiring discussions over the five and a half years it took to write this book, especially Rob Davis, Andy Davis, Emma Wright, Sophie Inchley-Mort, Tim Bates and David Gasston. Last but not least, I salute Professors Philip Corr and James Heckman who have provided me with much of my scientific inspiration.

Preface

As a personality researcher employed at public expense, I feel I have a duty to use my scientific knowledge to try to help improve the prospects of our society. In this book, I explore a topic that is dear to my heart, namely how discoveries from personality research could be used to help improve the welfare state. This topic is especially important to me because for several years before I became established in my scientific career, I worked in a range of low-paid roles and, in between jobs, I claimed unemployment benefits. I am therefore more interested than most academics in seeking to use scientific findings to ensure that the welfare state is there to look after future generations, like it was there to look after me. This book was also motivated by my frustration at ill-informed personality-related stereotypes of welfare claimants. For example, we sometimes see welfare claimants stereotyped as genetically hardwired to be unconscientious and disagreeable, shunning work for a life of idleness courtesy of the public purse. Conversely, welfare claimants may be portrayed as the helpless victims of capitalism, mere leaves blown around by the powerful winds of the global economy. As I am both a personality researcher and a former welfare claimant, I have a stake in both aspects of this topic and I can therefore see from my own experiences how important the details are. For example, as the data summarised in this book show, welfare claimants on average do possess a personality profile that is less conscientious and agreeable than that of employed citizens, but genes don't have much to do with this – the environment is much more important. The global economic situation of course forms part of our environment, but so does the welfare state and, as I hope to show, the latter factor has a crucial role to play in shaping the personality profile of the population.

1
What Is Personality and Why Does the Welfare State Matter?

In October 1833, a young English biologist travelling in South America mused in his journal about the factors that influence the success of a nation, concluding 'a republic cannot succeed till it contains a certain body of men imbued with the principles of justice and honour'. That biologist was Charles Darwin, and in his journal entry he touched upon a resource that is now recognised as exerting a significant influence on the prosperity of a nation, namely human capital. The notion of human capital is a broad one, encompassing a nation's stock of skills and knowledge. But its end result is narrower, being the capacity to carry out labour that produces economic value.

The welfare state has long been viewed as a threat to human capital, owing to concerns that providing unemployed citizens with a guaranteed income may discourage them from working for a living (Beveridge, 1942). Scandinavian economists have led the way in attempts to define these concerns. For example, almost 20 years ago, the eminent Swedish economist Assar Lindbeck warned that 'the supply of benefits creates its own demand. Indeed, moral hazard and cheating are, in my judgement, the weak spot of the welfare state' (Lindbeck, 1995, p. 2).

Lindbeck's fears have since been supported empirically by studies showing that generous welfare states do indeed erode the ethical standards of citizens, much as he predicted. For example, the Nobel

Prize-winning economist James Heckman summarised this literature as follows:

> Participation in generous welfare states leads to erosion of the work ethic and withdrawal from participation in the social compact. There is evidence of cohort drift in welfare participation. Those cohorts who have lived a greater fraction of their lives under the generosity of the welfare state come to accept its benefits and game the system at higher rates.
>
> (Heckman, 2008, p. 20)

The biological literature also urges caution: in his seminal 1976 book *The Selfish Gene*, Richard Dawkins described the welfare state as perhaps the greatest example of altruism in the animal kingdom but warned of its self-destructive potential. Viewed together with the economic studies conducted in Scandinavia, Dawkins' warning therefore provides credible grounds for believing that we need to be vigilant as to the self-destructive tendencies of the welfare state. However, in order to protect the welfare state from itself, we must first understand the mechanisms that cause it to erode human capital so that we can implement amendments that preserve its good points but ameliorate its weaknesses.

One potentially important discovery is that the welfare state can boost the number of children born into disadvantaged households. For example, research in the UK has shown that for every 3 per cent rise in the generosity of benefits, the number of children born to claimants rises by approximately 1 per cent (Brewer, Ratcliffe & Smith, 2011). Moreover, this association between benefit generosity and reproductive behaviour appears to be causal, because follow-up interviews found that claimants discontinued contraception in response to increased generosity of benefits.

The importance of this discovery to the human capital debate is that childhood disadvantage has been shown in randomised controlled experiments – the gold standard of scientific proof – to promote the formation of an aggressive, antisocial and rule-breaking personality profile that impairs occupational and social adjustment during adulthood (Heckman, Pinto & Savelyev, 2013). A welfare state that increases the number of children born into disadvantaged households therefore risks increasing the number of citizens who develop an aggressive, antisocial and rule-breaking personality profile due to being exposed to disadvantage during childhood. Because this personality profile impairs occupational and social adjustment, its proliferation constitutes a potent and direct mechanism by which the welfare state can erode the human capital of the population from generation to generation.

Children are the future of our society and so the possibility that the ostensibly altruistic institution of the welfare state can damage their personality development – and thus their human capital – is a worrying one. I am a personality researcher by profession, and in this book, I examine the scientific literature in an attempt to evaluate the capacity of the welfare state to damage personality development.

First, in the chapter entitled 'The Employment-Resistant Personality Profile', we shall see evidence that the type of personality profile which tends to be developed by childhood disadvantage – an aggressive, antisocial and rule-breaking predisposition – is the same personality profile that is associated with impaired occupational performance across most of the employment spectrum. In line with this finding, we shall also see evidence that people with this personality profile are over-represented amongst welfare claimants. For this reason, I have dubbed it the 'employment-resistant' personality profile and formalise it as consisting of significantly below average scores on the personality dimensions of conscientiousness and agreeableness. As we shall see, these dimensions are well established in the scientific literature and are used by modern personality researchers to measure individual differences in aggressive, antisocial and rule-breaking tendencies.

These data leave unanswered the question of whether the employment-resistant personality profile is the cause rather than the product of unsatisfactory occupational outcomes. For example, it might be the case that adverse occupational circumstances reduce motivation to behave conscientiously and agreeably, which in turn worsens the individual's chances of gaining and keeping employment. In Chapter 3 – 'The Lifelong Impact of Personality' – we address this issue by examining studies that record personality characteristics in childhood and then trace their effects on adult life, whilst controlling for the effect of other important variables such as intelligence and parental socio-economic status (SES). These studies suggest that the employment-resistant personality profile is indeed the cause rather than product of negative occupational outcomes because the less conscientious and agreeable a child's personality profile, the worse they tend to do as adults in the world of work, despite their intelligence or social background.

A key conclusion in Chapter 3 is that the employment-resistant personality profile doesn't just impair workplace performance – it also increases the frequency of behaviour that is likely to impair the life chances of the next generation (for example, teenage parenthood). This is a crucial finding because it suggests that individuals with employment-resistant personality characteristics not only suffer impaired life outcomes, but also transmit that difficulty to their children and thus risk damaging the life chances of the next generation. But what role could the welfare state play in this undesirable life trajectory?

In Chapter 4 – 'The Influence of Benefits on Claimant Reproduction' – we shall see that the number of children born to welfare claimants tracks the generosity of benefits, with increases in the generosity of welfare benefits being followed by deliberate increases in their rate of reproduction via altered contraception usage. Furthermore, we shall see evidence that this effect is likely to be driven primarily by claimants who possess the employment-resistant personality profile, since epidemiological studies show that this personality profile is, in general, associated with having more children. In this chapter, we shall also see evidence that the employment-resistant personality profile is associated with financial irresponsibility, since such parents do not tend to manage their welfare benefits conscientiously to improve the lot of their children, but instead tend to waste the money on unnecessary purchases.

In Chapter 5 – 'Childhood Disadvantage and Employment-Resistance' – we shall see that the disadvantage suffered by children of welfare claimants is not only a matter of financial irresponsibility but also a matter of parental style: despite having more free time, welfare claimants tend to speak to their children significantly less often than employed parents do. This finding suggests that the personality characteristics which make an individual an unsatisfactory employee also make them less likely to give their children the verbal and social investment that is required to develop a pro-employment personality profile. This finding is consistent with the notion that dysfunctional personality characteristics are transmitted from parents to offspring via an environmental route. However, the existence of individuals who grew up in privileged families with diligent, nurturing parents, yet nevertheless turned out to be adults with the employment-resistant personality profile, gives us a clue that the transmission of personality characteristics from parent to child cannot be explained by environmental factors alone.

In Chapter 6 – 'Genetic Influences on Personality' – we shall see evidence that the missing link in the transmission of personality characteristics from parent to child is genetic, as parents exert a genetic influence on the personality profiles of their offspring. Key evidence of this type is provided by experiments that show personality traits in populations of non-human animals can be significantly altered by selective breeding. These experiments point to a genetic basis for personality and are backed up by cross-breeding experiments which show that the offspring of two strains of animals with opposite behavioural tendencies will typically display behaviour that is intermediate between the two parental strains.

However, concerns exist that psychological models created using non-human animals (for example, rodents) are too simple to be valid in humans. The demonstration of a genetic influence on personality in non-human animals therefore does not necessarily apply to humans. Moreover, in practice, genetic effects will act in combination with environmental effects and so analysing genetic effects in isolation lacks realism. In Chapter 7 – 'Personality as a Product of Nature and Nurture' – we examine research aimed at comparing genetic and environmental influences on human personality and see evidence that the more closely related two people are, the more similar their personalities tend to be. This echoes the non-human experimental data on the genetic basis of personality and suggests that such data do, after all, have relevance to humans. However, we will also see that genetically identical individuals (monozygotic twins) do not have identical personality profiles, showing that both nature and nurture influence personality development.

Chapters 5–7 show that, because human personality is a product of nature and nurture (and their interplay), the children of employment-resistant welfare claimants are not only disadvantaged through a greater likelihood of being neglected, but also by a higher risk of inheriting the genes for the employment-resistant personality profile, compared to children born to adults with a pro-employment personality profile. Therefore, a welfare state which boosts the number of children born to claimants risks undermining human capital by causing an increased incidence of personality mis-development. More specifically, such a welfare state will cause proliferation of the employment-resistant personality profile via both environmental and genetic channels. I dub this idea the 'welfare trait' theory.

In Chapter 8 – 'A Model of How the Welfare State Leads to Personality Mis-Development' – I build on these foundations by using a statistical model to obtain a quantitative estimate of the scale of welfare-induced personality mis-development. This may seem to be an impossible task given the bewildering array of variables involved, but, due to what is known as the normal distribution, we can insert certain key numbers into this demographic model and obtain an estimate of the size of the transforming effect of a certain level of welfare generosity on personality, as well as its approximate monetary cost.

In Chapter 9 – 'Further Evidence for Welfare-Induced Personality Mis-Development' – I summarise evidence that is circumstantial but nevertheless consistent with the notion that the welfare state is changing the developmental trajectory of the personality profile of the population towards greater employment-resistance. For example, we shall see that the introduction of the welfare state amongst the nations of the Western world has been followed by a substantial decrease in work motivation and an upsurge in criminal violence. This rise in criminal violence that followed the introduction of the welfare state in the Western world could be coincidental, but it is what we would expect to see if the welfare trait theory is valid because criminal violence is associated with employment-resistant personality characteristics.

In Chapter 10 – 'What Next?' – I argue that to prevent the welfare state proliferating the employment-resistant personality profile, the generosity of benefits must be adjusted so that the average number of children in workless households falls to a level that is approximately equal to that in working households. But I also argue that the greatest obstacle to amending the welfare state so that it does not cause personality mis-development is not a lack of scientific knowledge: after all, much of the evidence upon which this book is based has been published for decades and the eminent biologist Richard Dawkins warned presciently in 1976 of the personality-related dangers of the welfare state. In my opinion, the greatest obstacle to correcting the welfare state is a lack of will amongst the governing elite in previous decades to face up to this issue. I conclude the book by tracing this lack of will to the tendency of the governing elite to live in geographically and intellectually sheltered enclaves that mean they are out of touch with life in ordinary neighbourhoods, where the ill effects of welfare-induced personality mis-development are most apparent.

However, before we launch into the empirical content of the book, I will finish this introductory chapter with a brief summary of some basic concepts in personality research, as well as some comments on the scientific method. This end piece is primarily for the benefit of readers who are not familiar with personality as a topic of scientific research, but also serves to put the theme of this book in its proper scientific context.

First, we need a definition of personality. Creating definitions of personality is a popular hobby for researchers, leading to a sometimes confusing plethora of terms and phrases. But what most of these definitions have in common is the notion that personality refers to patterns of emotion, thought and behaviour that represent stable and lasting differences between individuals. So if we have a colleague who is a worrier in job-related situations, they are also likely to be a worrier when it comes to their private life. Moreover, that person is likely to have been a worrier as a child and is also likely to be a worrier when they become a senior citizen. This definition of personality does not rule out dramatic changes in a person's disposition following a traumatic experience, as in the old joke that a conservative is just a liberal who has been mugged. But it means that, on average, when we trace an individual's habitual pattern of emotion, thought and behaviour over their lifetime, we are able to observe regularities; that is, their personality profile.

This leads us to a second key concept, which is that personality is measureable. This is essential, because in order to observe regularities in personality from year to year or to compare personality to applied criteria such as job performance, we must be able to measure it. This can be accomplished by observing behaviour during an experiment, or obtaining reports from people who know the individual (for example, parents, teachers or colleagues). But by far the most convenient and widely used means of measuring personality is the self-report questionnaire, in which the respondent is asked to say how well a series of items applies to them. These items usually consist of personality-related adjectives (for example, talkative) or phrases (for example, I like to attend lively parties) and the participant typically indicates how well the item applies to them using a numerical response scale (for example, 1 = not at all, 2 = slightly, 3 = somewhat, 4 = very much).

As a supplement for this book, I have created an online personality questionnaire that you can use to measure your own personality. The home page is www.measureyourpersonality.com and you can access the questionnaire by entering the study code 92556379. This questionnaire divides the domain of personality into five dimensions, which is the current industry standard model of personality, often known as the 'Big Five' (for example, Digman, 1990; Costa & McCrae, 1992; Goldberg, 1993). This does not mean that other models of personality are incorrect or that there are only five dimensions of personality – it simply means that for most practical purposes, five dimensions have been proven to provide a useful and valid approximation of human personality. The 'Big Five' dimensions of personality are extraversion, conscientiousness, agreeableness, neuroticism and openness to experience.

Extraversion reflects engagement with the external world, especially engagement with people. Individuals who score high on this trait (often labelled as extraverts) typically enjoy being with people, are usually full of energy and experience frequent positive emotions. They also tend to be enthusiastic, action-oriented individuals who are likely to say 'Yes!' or 'Let's go!' to opportunities for excitement. In groups, they like to talk, assert themselves and draw attention to themselves and so excel in occupations that require frequent face-to-face interaction with the general public. Extraverts do however run the risk of appearing somewhat overpowering and even irritating owing to their talkative manner.

Individuals who score low in the lower range on extraversion (often labelled as introverts) typically have a rich internal life and need less stimulation form the external world than more extraverted individuals do. Introverts therefore tend to come across as quiet, low-key, deliberate and disengaged from the social world. Their lack of social involvement should not however be interpreted as shyness or depression; the introvert simply needs less stimulation than an extravert does and thus usually prefers to be alone or with one or two other people. The independence and reserve of the introvert should not be mistaken as unfriendliness or arrogance, as although the introvert does not usually seek out others, he or she will usually be quite pleasant when approached. Introverts excel in occupations that require lengthy periods of concentration with few other people around, such as radar operation or writing.

Conscientiousness reflects the extent to which we focus on detail and manage our affairs in a self-disciplined manner. Individuals scoring high on this trait come across as careful, cautious, planning, dutiful and detail-minded. They are typically focused on achievement and are capable of working consistently and patiently towards long-term goals. High scorers on conscientiousness do not tend to rush into decisions or actions. This steady, meticulous persona means that high scorers on conscientiousness tend to excel in occupations, such as the law or accountancy, which require considerable attention to detail and an ability to make sensible decisions that require a sober and prudent deliberation of all the facts of a matter.

Low scorers on conscientiousness are typically impulsive and tend to skip over detail, preferring instead to focus on the bigger picture. They also tend to make quick and seemingly intuitive decisions, even on big matters such as which job to take or which house to buy. When attempting to learn a new skill, low scorers on conscientiousness will tend not to apply themselves in a steady, efficient manner and thus will usually acquire only a shallow, superficial grasp of the matter at hand. They may therefore appear careless, but can also excel at adventurous/entrepreneurial occupations that require a vision of the big picture and an ability to seize short-lived 'spur-of-the-moment' opportunities.

Agreeableness reflects individual differences in cooperation and social harmony. Individuals in the high range on agreeableness value getting along with others and generally appear easy-going, fair-minded and nice. They are, therefore, considerate, friendly, generous, helpful and will make a special effort to avoid causing trouble or difficulties for other people. Agreeable people also have an optimistic view of human nature. They believe people are basically honest, decent and trustworthy. Individuals with high levels of agreeableness are likely to excel in occupations that require a caring and friendly face, such as social work, but may also appear something of a 'soft touch' who can easily be exploited.

Individuals in the low range on agreeableness tend to put their own needs ahead of those of other people and generally come across as tough-minded, uncooperative and assertive. They tend to be quite sceptical about the motives of other people and so are not easily fooled. Low agreeableness will cause the individual to come across as a stubborn character and so is especially useful in occupations that require tough or objective decision-making such as soldiering, police work or science.

Neuroticism describes the likelihood of a person experiencing negative emotions in response to everyday situations. People who score low on this trait rarely experience negative emotion and tend to be calm almost all the time. Even when they experience a severely traumatic event, such as a bereavement, low scorers on neuroticism will return to a calm state sooner than most. Low scorers on neuroticism tend to excel in occupations such as medicine, police work or military aviation that require the individual frequently to deal with upsetting or scary situations but, as a corollary, can appear to be emotionally flat or detached in their personal relationships. Likewise, the serene mindset of a low scorer on neuroticism can hinder creativity. However, freedom from negative feelings does not mean that high scorers experience a lot of positive feelings, as the frequency of positive emotions is a component of the extraversion domain.

People who score high on neuroticism typically respond with strong negative emotions (for example, anxiety, fear and depression) to events that would not bother most people, especially when the event concerns their personal interests (for example, being criticised). This hyper-emotionality means that individuals who score high on neuroticism are more likely to interpret ordinary situations as threatening and minor frustrations as hopelessly difficult. These problems in emotional regulation can diminish one's ability to think clearly under stress, make decisions when time-pressured and cope effectively with adversity – they may even lead to obsessive or perfectionist behaviour. High neuroticism has however been displayed by many famous geniuses, suggesting that a tendency to brood and to experience negative emotion may boost performance in occupations that reward single-minded obsession, creativity and perfectionism (for example, science, music composition, art, politics and film-making).

Openness to experience reflects an individual's interest in imaginative or intellectual matters. People with high scores on openness to experience are intellectually curious, appreciative of art and sensitive to beauty. They tend to be aware of their feelings and to think and act in individualistic and nonconforming ways. Scores on openness to experience are only modestly related to years of education and scores on standard intelligent tests. Another characteristic of the open cognitive style is a facility for thinking in symbols and abstractions far removed from concrete experience. Depending on the individual's specific intellectual abilities, this symbolic cognition may take the form of mathematical, logical or geometric thinking, artistic and metaphorical use of language, music composition or performance, or one of the many visual or performing arts.

People with low scores on openness to experience tend to be interested in practical and down-to-earth matters. They prefer the plain, straightforward and obvious over the complex, ambiguous and subtle. They may regard the arts and sciences with suspicion, regarding these endeavours as foolish or of no practical use. Low scorers on openness to experience prefer familiarity over novelty; they tend to be resistant to change and rather set in their ways. Openness is often presented as healthier or more mature by psychologists, who are often themselves open to experience. However, open and closed styles of thinking are useful in different environments. The intellectual style of the open person may serve a professor well, but research has shown that closed thinking is related to superior job performance in police work, sales and a number of service occupations.

Personality researchers often also study intelligence (indeed it might be argued that intelligence is just another dimension of personality), so at this point, it is worth briefly mentioning my views. I consider intelligence to represent problem-solving ability and to be functionally different from personality. One analogy I use to help my students understand this functional difference is to compare a person to a car: that person's level of intelligence represents the horsepower of the car's engine whereas their personality represents the steering system of the car, determining the goals at which they direct the problem-solving power of their intelligence. This is a well-established idea. For example, in 1739, the Scottish philosopher David Hume wrote in his famous book *A Treatise of Human Nature* that 'Reason is, and ought only to be the slave of the passions, and can never pretend to any other office than to serve and obey them' (p. 416). Thus, if an individual combines high levels of conscientiousness and agreeableness with a high level of intelligence, it is plausible that their personality will cause them to use their intelligence altruistically, to benefit society, for example by becoming a doctor. In contrast, a similarly intelligent individual but with the employment-resistant personality profile (that is, relatively low levels of conscientiousness and agreeableness) is likely to use their intelligence in a less constructive way and may even become a menace to society (for example, a criminal mastermind).

These points merely provide a snapshot of the personality research literature but I hope it will be sufficient to provide readers who are not personality specialists with enough understanding of the topic to make an informed judgement about the validity of the welfare trait theory. Continuing with the theme of demystification, we will end this introductory chapter with some comments on the scientific method.

The first point to note is that science is not really about microscopes, or pipettes, or test tubes, or even Large Hadron Colliders. These are merely tools that help us to accomplish a far greater mission, which is to choose between rival narratives. Sometimes a crucial experiment (*experimentum crucis*) can tip the balance towards a particular narrative. For example, stomach problems such as gastritis and ulcers were historically explained as the products of stress. This narrative was challenged in the late 1970s by the Australian doctors Robin Warren and Barry Marshall, who suspected that stomach problems were actually caused by infection with the bacteria *Helicobacter pylori*. Frustrated by scepticism and by difficulties publishing his academic papers, in 1984, Barry Marshall appointed himself his own experimental subject and drank a Petri dish full of *H. pylori* culture. He promptly developed gastritis which was then cured with antibiotics, suggesting that *H. pylori* have a causal role in this type of illness. Opposition continued for a decade or so, but by the early 1990s, it had crumbled, and for their work on *H. pylori*, Warren and Marshall were awarded the 2005 Nobel Prize in Physiology or Medicine.

Other narratives, such as the principle of evolution by natural selection, or the welfare trait theory that is presented in this book, concern slow, large-scale processes that are unsuited to testing in a laboratory. In these cases, we take a bird's eye view of the facts of the matter and attempt to decide which narrative they best support. This book accordingly takes a bird's eye view of some facts about personality and the welfare state, in an attempt to decide which of the following three narratives they best support:

1. The welfare state should be retained without change.
2. The welfare state should be abolished.

3. The welfare state should be amended to take account of personality.

As we will see, the evidence for any of these three narratives is far from conclusive, but in my opinion, at this early stage in the scientific discussion of personality and welfare, the third narrative is the best supported. If this book prompts new research that shifts the balance of evidence towards another narrative, then so be it – at least the book will have succeeded in advancing our knowledge of personality and welfare, greater comprehension of which can only benefit humanity in the long run.

This brings me to a second point, which is that there is no qualitative divide between people like me, who are scientists by profession, and people who have other careers. We are all scientists in the sense that we are all trying to make sense of the world by appraising the facts of a matter and trying to draw conclusions from them, whether it is to do with deciding what part of a town to live in, what career to pursue or whether someone is lying. This idea is perhaps best illustrated by Albert Einstein's famous observation: 'The whole of science is nothing more than a refinement of every day thinking' (Einstein, 1936, p. 349). Based on my own experience of working as a professional scientist, I agree with Einstein's observation with one qualification: in my opinion, the only difference between a scientific argument and an ordinary argument in a pub or at a dinner table is that scientific arguments are based primarily on evidence obtained by scientific studies that have been written up and published in scientific journals or books.

This formal method of archiving scientific results allows scientists to be aware of what their predecessors discovered. Awareness of previous discoveries is known as 'mastering the literature', which is an unglamorous but crucial part of professional science because, if we haven't mastered the literature, we are likely to waste time trying to discover something that has already been discovered. More briefly stated, we will keep trying to reinvent the wheel. Mastering the literature therefore enables science to move forward, since it allows current scientists to build on the discoveries of previous researchers rather than starting from scratch in each new generation. I view professional science as baton-passing, with the baton being the understanding of a particular topic. The business of each scientist is to polish that baton before he or she passes it on and that is what I am trying to do with this book.

Peer review is the second specialist part of professional science. It is a form of academic quality control in which draft manuscripts are subjected to the scrutiny of scientists who are experts in the field in question but who were not involved in writing the manuscript being reviewed. The reviewers attempt to assess the scientific rigour of the manuscript and judge if conclusions drawn by the author/s are appropriate to the results. A key part of the peer-review process is that the publisher usually conceals the identity of each reviewer from the author/s in order to permit expression of critical opinions without fear of reprisals. The peer-review system is far from perfect as, for example, the identity of the author is usually known to the reviewers and so their reviews may be skewed by professional rivalry or personal animosity (or both). Sometimes the identity of the author/s is withheld from the reviewers by the publisher, but even this cannot eliminate bias, as experts in a topic area often recognise the writing style of their peers and therefore often can deduce who wrote a particular manuscript from its content. But, like democracy, we have yet to find a better system and so peer review remains a cornerstone of scientific rigour.

In order formally to test the scientific rigour of my welfare trait theory, it has undergone two separate rounds of peer review. It was first subjected to peer review (in condensed form) as part of a paper I published recently on personality and reproduction. It survived and was accordingly published in a leading personality journal (Perkins et al., 2013). This book presents a much more elaborate and advanced version of the welfare trait theory and so the publisher decided that it required a fresh bout of peer review. This was undertaken by a panel of three anonymous scientists who were selected by the publisher for their expert knowledge in various different fields connected to the topic of this book. I used the feedback from the reviewers to improve the book, enabling it to be accepted for publication. I therefore must express my gratitude to the reviewers for taking the time to scrutinise my work so thoroughly and in the spirit of constructive criticism.

Being published in a peer-reviewed journal or book is however only one step towards validating a theory: it must also stand the test of time. Thus, the validity of the welfare trait theory will only become apparent decades from now. Even then, some new findings could be made that counter it, so the most accurate intellectual stance to take is that theory validation never really ends. This sentiment was expressed elegantly by the young British neuroscientist Tom Schofield in his posthumous comment piece on the scientific method that was recently published in *Nature* magazine:

> Science is not about finding the truth at all, but about finding better ways of being wrong. The best scientific theory is not the one that reveals the truth – that is impossible. It is the one that explains what we already know about the world in the simplest way possible, and that makes useful predictions about the future.
>
> (Schofield, 2013, p. 279)

However, just like pub debates over who is the best footballer, science boils down to a matter of opinion as to which rival narrative is correct (or at least not as incorrect as the others). When reading the evidence presented in the following chapters, it is therefore particularly important to be on guard against one's pre-existing views distorting one's perceptions of the facts. It is not easy to do this, but it is worth the effort because it will bring one's intellect into line with the advice of such great thinkers as the philosopher Bertrand Russell, who said the following in a 1959 BBC TV interview:

> When you are studying any matter or considering any philosophy, ask yourself only what are the facts and what is the truth that the facts bear out. Never let yourself be diverted either by what you would wish to believe or by what you think would have beneficent social effects if it were believed but look only and solely at what are the facts.

The physicist Richard Feynman warned in a similar vein in the conclusion of his report about the Space Shuttle Challenger disaster in 1986 that 'For a successful technology, reality must take precedence over public relations, for nature cannot be fooled.'

Applied to the present topic, the advice of great thinkers such as Russell and Feynman means that to create a successful welfare state – that looks after unemployed citizens but does not encourage the development of the employment-resistant personality profile – we would be wise to face up to the facts on personality, even if it is politically incorrect to do so. After all, penicillin is a successful antibiotic not because a politician tells us that it is but because it obeys the laws of nature: why should the welfare state be any different?

When we are evaluating a theory, the more lines of independent evidence that support it, the more convincing it is. Thus, a theory that is based on a huge amount of data gathered by one or two researchers is less credible than a theory which is supported by smaller amounts of data gathered by scores of independent researchers. As will be seen in the following chapters, my welfare trait theory falls into the latter category, but judging whether data support a theory is, in itself, a subjective process. I have therefore supported my theory primarily with older studies and experiments, the results of which have stood the test of time. Thus, I hope to avoid the common trap of rushing to publish a theory based on trendy new research findings, only for those findings to be discredited within a year or two.

This cautious strategy I have followed does not mean my theory is valid – that is a matter of interpretation – but it does mean that my theory is based on respected, time-honoured scientific discoveries that cannot be dismissed as a flash in the pan. Clarity concerning my sources of evidence was accordingly a high priority for me when writing this book. Each study that I have used to support my theory is therefore cited in my text in standard academic style with the author's name or names followed by the year of publication (for example, Smith & Jones, 1960). Quotations are shown in quote marks with the page number listed after the year of publication. The publication details for each study that I cite are listed in full at the back of the book, in alphabetical order of the first author's name. This is so that any reader who wants to learn more about a topic or who thinks there is something fishy about a piece of evidence I have presented can then use these references as start points for tracking down other publications on that topic.

Last, but not least, it is important to acknowledge that the welfare state is a political hot potato and this book, despite its scientific nature and sober tone, risks being mischaracterised as an attempt to undermine the welfare state and/or demonise its claimants. I therefore must put on record that after completing my BSc, I found it difficult to obtain graduate-level employment. I spent years working in a variety of low-paid roles and, between jobs, I claimed unemployment benefits. This experience left me with great admiration for our welfare state, as well as the belief that most unemployed individuals are keen to work and only rely on the welfare state temporarily, as I did. Moreover, I realised that blaming welfare claimants who are work-shy for their attitude is pointless: we are no more responsible for our personality profiles than we are for our height or our shoe size. It is better instead to assess the causes of problematic personality characteristics in the same neutral way that we assess the causes of other biological phenomena, because that is what personality is – a biological phenomenon.

The latter point about viewing personality as just another biological phenomenon leads me onto a second likely criticism, namely that because my academic specialty is the neurobiology of personality, this book cannot contribute any insights into problems with the welfare state. Such a criticism does not stand up to scrutiny because it fails to take into account the cross-disciplinary relevance of personality research. For example, insights from personality research can be used to help address psychiatric, educational and occupational problems: why should problems with the welfare state be off limits?

A third likely criticism is that the relationship between personality and the welfare state is complex and requires much greater nuance, detail and balance in discussing it than is contained in this book. That would be a sensible point decades in the future when the scientific discussion of personality and welfare is well advanced and the nuances of the topic are ripe for discussion, but my argument is that, at the moment, there is no scientific discussion of personality and welfare. What this book is aiming to do is blaze a trail for that discussion – a trail that will no doubt be bedevilled by thorny topics, empirical quicksands and conceptual wrong turns, but one that I hope will be turned into a smooth highway by researchers far cleverer, more detail-focused and better qualified than me.

Bearing these three likely criticisms in mind, I can therefore reassure the reader that this book is not an attempt to dress up political motives as science or waste time on arguments about whether personality researchers should be allowed to comment on problems with the welfare state. I prefer instead to let the data speak for themselves whilst accepting, as George Orwell declared, that 'no book is genuinely free from political bias' and it would be presumptuous of me to suppose that this book is an exception to that rule.

2
The Employment-Resistant Personality Profile

In order to assess the credibility of the idea that the welfare state could undermine human capital by inducing personality misdevelopment in the domains of conscientiousness and agreeableness, it is first necessary to summarise evidence showing the importance of these personality traits in the world of work. That is the purpose of this chapter, which presents evidence from three different parts of the scientific literature. First, we shall review neurological case studies of people who have suffered injuries to the prefrontal area of their brains. These injuries are relevant to personality and employment because they do not necessarily alter intelligence but do tend to alter personality in a way that is consistent with a reduction in conscientiousness and agreeableness (for example, Blumer & Benson, 1975). Furthermore, a prefrontal brain injury will typically transform a person with a good work record into someone who is unemployable. Such case studies, therefore, provide evidence that conscientiousness and agreeableness play a causal role in determining the likelihood that a person will work for a living.

A second source of evidence linking low levels of conscientiousness and agreeableness to employment difficulties is provided by research with so-called problem families (now known as troubled families). This research compared the psychological characteristics of problem families with those of families who are matched on important variables such as neighbourhood and income, yet are sufficiently functional not to require the intervention of more than one social service agency. The chief psychological difference between these families lies in the domain of personality: the adults of the problem families, on average, display personality profiles that are significantly less conscientious and agreeable than those of the adults of the comparison families. These attributes contribute to the employment-resistant personality profile, as it was found that the adults in the problem families also had significantly worse work records than the adults in the comparison families had.

Further evidence linking low levels of conscientiousness and agreeableness to employment difficulties is provided by studies that correlate personality questionnaire scores with occupational outcomes. The importance of these studies to the present argument is that they show that both conscientiousness and agreeableness influence job performance in healthy, employed adults in a way that is consistent with findings relating to the more extreme cases presented by prefrontal brain-injury victims or by problem families. So we can see that even in people who are in employment, the lower the level of conscientiousness and agreeableness, the less satisfactory they tend to be as employees. More specifically, conscientiousness is positively associated with job performance (Barrick, Mount & Judge, 2001) whereas agreeableness is positively associated with non-contracted behaviours that benefit organisational cohesion (for example, being personable or helpful; Hogan, 2011).

Viewed as a whole, these occupational studies suggest that there is a gradient of personality effects on employability, all the way from extreme but rare clinical cases such as brain-injury victims, through problem families, to people with relatively normal personalities and reasonably normal work records. These occupational studies can therefore be used to counter the concern that the sheer rarity of prefrontal brain-injury victims and problem families means that conclusions concerning effects of their personality profiles on their work records are too atypical to be generalised to the majority of the population. In line with Albert Einstein's view that science is just an extension of everyday thinking, it is easy to observe in most workplace contexts that some people are difficult to work with/for and that personality has a big influence on that.

Agreement between formally gathered personality data and the anecdotal observations that we make in the workplace might sound trivial but, as we will see in later chapters, such agreement is valuable to science as it provides an important sanity check, helping to confirm our results are measuring something real and are not merely the product of a misplaced decimal point or a statistical blunder. There-fore, when you are reading this chapter, it would be valuable for you to keep in mind your own experiences concerning the effects of per-sonality on employability so that you can check the credibility of the findings described here.

Case studies of the personality effects of prefrontal brain injury

A rich, if rare and specific, source of causal evidence that conscientiousness- and agreeableness-related aspects of personality are key determinants of employability comes from studies of individ-uals who have suffered injuries to the prefrontal area of their brains. Prefrontal brain injuries are important in the context of this book because they typically result in a drastic reduction in employability, not through loss of intelligence or physical ability (both of which are usually unaffected by this form of brain injury), but by changing the personality of the sufferer in a way that approximates to a reduction of conscientiousness and agreeableness.

The most famous case study of this kind is that of Phineas Gage, a 25-year-old railway construction foreman who was highly regarded for his diligent and polite personality by his employers and also his subordinates. On the afternoon of 13 September 1848, Gage was tamping an explosive charge into a rock that had been drilled for blasting when the charge accidentally exploded, driving the tamp-ing iron (three feet seven inches long and 13 and a quarter pounds in weight with a finely tapered upper end) up through his left cheek and out of the top of his head. Gage was an exceptionally fit young man and was able to walk and talk within minutes of the accident, despite the gaping wounds in the top of his head through which he had lost much of the left prefrontal area of his brain. Despite the severity of this injury, Gage nevertheless made an amazing physical recovery, being pronounced healed within two months of the accident despite losing the sight of his left eye (owing to the path taken through his skull by the tamping iron). His powers of speech and basic intelli-gence were also unaltered by the accident, yet his personality was changed.

The exact effect of Gage's brain injury on his personality can-not be quantified precisely, as modern personality questionnaires that formally measure conscientiousness and agreeableness were not available at that time but, by any reasonable analysis, Gage displayed lower levels of conscientiousness and agreeableness relative to his pre-accident self. The most reliable and informative source of first-hand evidence is the account of Gage written in 1868 by his doctor, John Harlow:

> The equilibrium or balance, so to speak, between his intellectual faculties and animal propensities, seems to have been destroyed. He is fitful, irreverent, indulging at times in the grossest profanity (which was not previously his custom), manifesting but little deference for his fellows, impatient of restraint or advice when it conflicts with his desires, at times pertinaciously obstinate, yet capricious and vacillating, devising many plans of future operations, which are no sooner arranged than they are abandoned in turn for others appearing more feasible. A child in his intellectual capacity and manifestations, he has the animal passions of a strong man. Previous to his injury, although untrained in the schools, he possessed a well-balanced mind, and was looked upon by those who knew him as a shrewd, smart businessman, very energetic and persistent in executing all his plans of operation. In this regard his mind was radically changed, so decidedly that his friends and acquaintances said he was 'no longer Gage'.
>
> (Harlow, 1868, p. 277)

The precise details of Gage's employment history after he left the care of Dr Harlow until his death on 21 May 1860 from a convulsive condition (possibly brought on by his brain injury) are lost, leading to much debate amongst modern scholars over some facts of this case. We do know from Harlow's records that his employers refused to take him back because of the effects on his personality of his accident. Some accounts suggest he then suffered chronic employment difficulties for the rest of his life, drifting through various basic jobs (including working in a circus freak show; Damasio, 1994). Other accounts suggest that his personality problems gradually subsided after his accident as his brain repaired itself and that he returned to work, earning a living right up until a few months before his death when he began to suffer from increasingly severe convulsions (MacMillan, 2000). We will probably never know for sure what happened, but two photographs of Gage taken after his accident support the idea that he survived reasonably well, as they show a well-built, youthful and healthy-looking man with a handsome face and full, glossy head of hair holding the tamping iron that had injured him, with the only visible sign of the accident being a closed left eye. What we do know for sure is that in the meantime, Gage's sister had married a wealthy merchant and moved with Gage's mother to San Francisco. In 1859, Gage moved in with them as his convulsive condition became severe and he died shortly afterwards aged only 38 years old.

The medical significance of Gage's case at the time was mainly his miraculous survival after such a serious head wound but it also gradually came to be appreciated as important for showing, for the first time, that

> there were systems in the human brain dedicated more to reasoning than anything else, and in particular the personal and social dimensions of reasoning. The observance of previously acquired social convention and ethical rules could be lost as a result of brain damage, even when neither basic intellect nor language seemed compromised.
>
> (Damasio, 1994, p. 10)

In support of my hypothesis, Gage's case tells us an extra thing, namely that an injury-induced reduction in conscientiousness and agreeableness has the knock-on effect of reducing employability, even when physical fitness and intelligence are adequate.

Regardless of the uncertainty surrounding the details of Phineas Gage's employment record after his accident, this conclusion is backed up by modern studies of patients with damage to the prefrontal area of the brain. In almost all cases, a consequence of this form of brain injury is a drastic decline in the capacity of the patient to hold down a job despite not usually suffering any significant reduction in their intelligence level. For example, one well-documented case study of the effects of prefrontal brain injury is that of Patient A (Brickner, 1932). A 39-year-old stockbroker from New York, Patient A suffered extensive loss of brain tissue in both prefrontal lobes when having a tumour surgically removed. Like Phineas Gage, Patient A showed no loss of intelligence or physical ability following the brain injury but did suffer profound personality change. Before the brain injury, Patient A had been polite, considerate and modest, but afterwards he was highly disagreeable, prone to boastful, cruel and inappropriate behaviour, especially towards his wife, as well as verbal abuse of others when frustrated. His attitude to work was also changed: he lost his drive, spending much time drawing up grandiose plans that he never bothered to implement.

The case of Patient A predates the availability of modern personality questionnaires so it is difficult to quantify exactly the changes to his personality, but based on the descriptions of Brickner (1932), they can plausibly be summarised as a drastic reduction in conscientiousness and agreeableness. The harmful effect of the injury on Patient A's employability was even more severe than in the case of Phineas Gage, as Patient A never returned to work and spent the rest of his life in the care of his family. This aspect of the case illustrates that patients with prefrontal brain injuries typically show the 'Phineas Gage Matrix' of unimpaired intelligence but damaged personality (Damasio, 1994), even if there is usually some variation in outcomes (perhaps reflecting individual differences in the precise site and magnitude of the injury as well as the post-injury care).

This latter point is made clear in a third case study known as 'Elliot', who, like Patient A, suffered prefrontal brain damage as a result of a tumour (Damasio, 1994). After the tumour was removed, Elliot also underwent personality changes, but they had a somewhat different quality to those suffered by Phineas Gage and Patient A: whereas these two earlier cases showed a reduction in both conscientiousness and agreeableness, Elliot suffered only a reduction of conscientiousness, being no less agreeable than he had been before his brain injury. For example, prior to the tumour, Elliot was a successful businessman and a caring husband and father, acting as something of a role model for his colleagues and family. After the tumour had been removed, Elliot remained as intelligent, knowledgeable, diplomatic and polite as before, but lost his drive, tenacity and sense of responsible priorities: he needed urging to get out of bed and go to work. At work, Elliot now lacked a sense of overall purpose and would easily be distracted from a task, failing to manage his time properly and deal with interruptions. He would typically spend many hours on one unimportant facet of a task so that the overall aim was neglected.

Nevertheless, in conversation, Elliot remained intelligent, lucid and even charming, an impression backed up by intensive testing which revealed his IQ score to be significantly above average. He was also able to give many sensible answers to hypothetical dilemmas concerning tricky moral or social questions. Despite this impressive level of intellectual functioning and many attempts by colleagues and family to help him, Elliot's decision-making in real life was flawed and he lost his job. Unable to cope with the change to his personality, Elliot's wife divorced him, and a second marriage to a woman that all his family and friends regarded as unsuitable did not last long. Ignoring many warnings, Elliot lost his life savings in a manifestly foolish business scheme and ended up relying on welfare benefits.

The interim conclusion at this stage of the chapter is that people who suffer prefrontal brain injury also suffer personality changes that in most cases drastically reduce their employability. Although a personality profile acquired through brain injury will never be exactly comparable to one that arises through natural variation in brain function, these individuals nevertheless display an acquired form of what I have dubbed the 'employment-resistant' personality profile, a profile that approximates to low conscientiousness and agreeableness. The next step in my argument is to summarise research that investigated the relationship between personality and employment in families that were dysfunctional and then compared their characteristics to those of functional families in the same neighbourhood. This is important research because if the members of problem families show similar personality profiles to the victims of prefrontal brain injury, we can accept this as further evidence that the employment-resistant personality profile consists of low conscientiousness and agreeableness.

The personality characteristics of problem families

To the best of my knowledge, the most rigorous study of the psychological characteristics of problem families is a two-phase longitudinal research programme that was conducted by W. L. Tonge and colleagues in the English city of Sheffield during the 1970s and 1980s. They aimed to disentangle the effect of psychological factors on social adjustment of families from the effect of socio-economic or geographical influences and then track the effect of those factors in the adult offspring of those families. This study was a rigorous and detailed research programme with many different facets that are of relevance to the theme of this book. I therefore have cited it several times in different chapters, but the relevant results here are to do with personality and employment.

The researchers (Tonge, James & Hillam, 1975) began by profiling 66 families who lived in low-income districts of Sheffield. Half of the sample (33 families) were what we now know as troubled families, but at the time, they were labelled by researchers as 'problem families'. The problem families were selected because they had sufficient social and occupational maladjustment to be involved with multiple government social-work agencies. The 33 comparison families were selected because they approximately matched the problem families on important variables such as location and income, but nevertheless behaved as relatively solid citizens (at least to the extent that they required intervention from no more than one government social-work agency). In 1981, the accessible adult offspring of the original 66 families were then followed up in order to determine the extent to which maladjustment was transmitted from parents to children (see Tonge et al., 1981 for a summary of phase two).

In phase one of this study, the researchers compared the two groups of families in exhaustive detail, including making comparisons of personality and work records as well as demographic variables such as the number of children in the family. Since modern personality questionnaires that measure personality with five dimensions (extraversion, conscientiousness, agreeableness, neuroticism and openness to experience; Digman, 1990; Costa & McCrae, 1992; Goldberg, 1993) were not available to Tonge and colleagues, they measured personality using a mix of self-report questionnaire and observer ratings. Extraversion was measured by self-report questionnaire (the Eysenck Personality Inventory; Eysenck, 1968) and observer ratings were used to measure impulsivity/irresponsibility, apathy, paranoia and aggression. These latter characteristics were not rated by severity but by frequency of incidents in order to boost consistency between observers. In the technical jargon of modern personality research, impulsivity/irresponsibility and apathy approximate to the low end of the conscientiousness dimension whereas aggression approximates to the low end of the agreeableness dimension.

The personality analysis by Tonge et al. (1975) showed there were no significant differences between the families on extraversion or paranoia, but that the men and women in the problem families were significantly more impulsive/irresponsible, apathetic and aggressive than those in the comparison families. All these attributes are measured by the dimensions of conscientiousness and agreeableness and so this result is consistent with the problem families tending to possess lower levels of conscientiousness and agreeableness than the comparison families.

This finding is important for the present argument because it shows that the personality profile of the problem families only differed from the comparison families on the personality characteristics which other studies give us reason to believe have a particularly strong negative influence on employability and which tend to be deficient in prefrontal brain-injury victims. For example, Tonge et al. (1975) found that 23 of the 30 men in the problem families for which there were assessments displayed at least one incident of impulsive/irresponsible behaviour compared to 5 of the 30 men in the comparison families. Similarly, 17 out of 31 women in the problem families displayed at least one incident of impulsive/irresponsible behaviour compared to 1 of the 30 women in the comparison families. With regard to apathy, 23 of 31 men in the problem families displayed apathy compared to 5 of the 30 men in the comparison families. Tonge et al. also found that 22 out of 30 women in the problem families displayed apathy compared to 3 of the 31 women in the comparison families. With regard to aggression, 13 of the 30 men in the problem families displayed aggressive behaviour compared to 4 of the 30 men in the comparison families. Similarly, 9 out of 31 women in the problem families showed aggression compared to 2 of the 30 women in the comparison families. To give a flavour of the personality survey technique used in this study, an example of an aggressive display was reported in the write-up (it also gives a clear indication of the challenging nature of this type of research): 'Father very antagonistic. During the visit he stood throwing a flick knife at the kitchen door while telling me he thought I was nosey, interfering and generally "no good". Clearly, in his mind the kitchen door was me. I was frightened' (Tonge et al., 1975, pp. 98–99).

If this combination of personality attributes displayed by the problem families represents the employment-resistant personality profile, then problem families should also have had significantly worse work records than the comparison families. And they did: only 9 of the 33 problem families contained parents who had worked for more than 10 per cent of the previous three years, compared to 23 out of 33 of the comparison families. Note that these differences in work record cannot be explained away as a result of the comparison families living in more affluent areas with a more plentiful supply of jobs, as Tonge et al. (1975) took care to make sure that the two groups of families were matched by location. This is important because it fits with the idea that the employment difficulties of the problem families are primarily caused by a lack of motivation to behave conscientiously and agreeably, rather than a lack of job opportunities in the neighbourhood or some other material difference.

Personality and occupational performance

If the neurological case studies and problem family case-control comparisons that I have described are a valid guide, then relatively low levels of conscientiousness and agreeableness should exert similarly harmful, but less extreme effects on the employment records of people who are already in the workforce. Psychologists first began systematic research aimed at revealing the correlates of occupational performance in the early to mid-twentieth century, primarily focusing on studying effects of intelligence. This was as much a practical decision as a theoretical one, since it seemed obvious to them that intelligence should influence job performance and it so happened that reliable and inexpensive mass-administration intelligence tests had become available in the 1920s.

This was a result of the pioneering work by Lewis Terman and colleagues during the First World War, who created a paper and pencil IQ test suitable for group administration in order to help the US Army assign soldiers to jobs that suited their abilities. These factors combined to produce hundreds of studies in the subsequent decades that proved general intelligence (often labelled as IQ or 'g') is an important determinant of the 'can do' or maximal, ability-related aspects of job performance (Schmidt & Hunter, 1998).

However, it has long been suspected that IQ is not the whole story when it comes to the psychological determinants of job performance and that the negative effect of personality deficiencies cannot be compensated for by high intelligence. For example, in 1964, the British industrialist Sir Paul Chambers wrote in *Nature* magazine that:

> Some top-rank public schools and university colleges produce men of brilliant academic achievement who have poor judgement, no power of decision and no capacity to delegate work or to control men. These men can be the tragedies of industry because their deficiencies are not revealed in their academic record and are difficult to detect at a selection interview. They can get started on a promising career, but end in the wilderness of the unpromotable clever boys. On the other hand, the same schools and colleges can produce second-rate graduates who are first-rate men with all the characteristics I have listed.
>
> (Chambers, 1964, p. 227)

In other words, an individual who is highly motivated to work for a living, possesses sound judgement and can interact successfully with colleagues will, in a typical job, perform as well or better than a more intelligent individual with a less functional personality profile performs. This idea has been backed up by research in the USA by the Nobel Prize-winning economist James Heckman and colleagues that has investigated the life outcomes of people who drop out of high school but then go on to pass the general educational development (GED) test. The GED test is an examination that lasts for seven hours 30 minutes and is intended to give individuals who have dropped out of high school a second chance to prove they possess the knowledge they would have acquired if had they completed high school. What these studies have found is that people who pass the GED test are on average as intelligent as high-school graduates (who do not go on to college) but that GED recipients on average turn out to be less successful in the workplace than high-school graduates because of the same personality characteristics that caused them to drop out of high school.

According to Heckman and Rubinstein,

> Inadvertently, a test has been created that separates out bright but non-persistent and undisciplined dropouts from other dropouts. It is, then, no surprise that GED recipients are the ones who drop out of school, fail to complete college (Stephen Cameron

and James Heckman, 1993) and who fail to persist in the military (Janice Laurence, 2000). GED's are 'wiseguys', who lack the abilities to think ahead, to persist in tasks, or to adapt to their environments. The performance of the GED recipients compared to both high-school dropouts of the same ability and high-school graduates demonstrates the importance of noncognitive skills in economic life.

(Heckman & Rubenstein, 2001, p. 146)

Viewed as a whole, these results have been interpreted by Heckman and colleagues as showing that 'Although the GED establishes cognitive equivalence on one measure of scholastic aptitude, recipients still face limited opportunity due to deficits in noncognitive skills such as persistence, motivation and reliability' (Heckman, Humphries & Mader, 2010, p. 2).

In stark terms, these studies of GED outcomes support the idea that, in many cases, being persistent and motivated is more important for occupational success than being smart. In the context of welfare legislation, I argue that this finding by Heckman and colleagues means that, since there are jobs to suit many different levels of intelligence, a person who is highly motivated to work is likely to attain a solid employment record regardless of their intelligence level by simply rising up or trickling down to whatever level of job complexity suits their level of intelligence.

A poor employment record is therefore not so much the result of inadequate intelligence but more an inadequate motivation to turn up on time, do what the boss says, speak politely to colleagues, behave helpfully towards customers and so on. Likewise, in harsh economic times when good jobs are difficult to find, a highly intelligent person who is also highly motivated to work might well swallow their pride and take a job that is well below their usual intellectual level in order to maintain a continuous work record. In contrast, an equally intelligent person with weaker motivation to work may plead that they are over-qualified and fall back on claiming welfare instead of working.

In line with this idea, Daly, Delaney and Egan (2015) studied a sample of 16,676 UK citizens that had been measured on self-control during childhood. Self-control measured in childhood approximates to a measure of conscientiousness and agreeableness in adulthood and their results were telling: children with low levels of self-control went on to suffer the greatest increases in unemployment during economic downturns.

This brings us to a crucial point about personality and work motivation that needs to be emphasised at this stage in my argument. The point is that, whereas we cannot boost our intelligence level by being more motivated, we can choose to be more or less conscientious and agreeable than we usually are if we are given sufficient motivation to do so.

Another way of visualising this is to say that we analyse the costs and benefits of behaving in a particular way in a particular situation and can switch to whichever personality strategy gives us the biggest pay-off in a particular situation. For example, if a cold-calling salesperson telephones us at an inconvenient moment, it is plausible that we would react differently than if our boss did the same thing. We are equally annoyed in both cases at being interrupted, but the costs and benefits of showing our annoyance are very different in the two situations: when we are replying to our boss, the likely high cost of offending him/her (for example, being fired or being passed over for promotion) means it is probable that we would react more agreeably to him/her than to the salesperson, who has no hold over us.

But, and this is important to understand, our perception of the size of a pay-off provided by a given strategy in a given situation is itself influenced by our personalities. This might sound confusing, but all it means is that a person who scores relatively low on conscientiousness requires a larger pay-off to motivate him or her to behave conscientiously compared to a person who scores relatively high on conscientiousness. Likewise, a person who scores relatively low on agreeableness requires a larger pay-off to motivate him or her to behave in an agreeable, cooperative manner compared to a person who scores relatively high on agreeableness.

As an illustration of this point, here are some thought experiments. First, with regard to conscientiousness, imagine you can win £1 by correctly counting the number of grains in a 10-kg bag of rice. Now imagine the same scenario except that you will now win £1,000,000 for a correct answer. In the first scenario, it is easy to imagine that the average person would be unlikely to count the rice carefully, since the financial pay-off for all that hard work is so small. In the second scenario, we are likely to have much greater motivation to count every grain carefully, taking weeks if necessary, in order to ensure that the pay-off of £1,000,000 is obtained. The effect of motivation on agreeableness can also be illustrated with a thought experiment: imagine you have two colleagues in the same role as you, but they are both much less experienced than you are (for example, you are in a service-industry job involving the use of a specialist and very tricky-to-use computer software package). Colleague A is an easy-going, likeable person who has a good sense of humour, is fun to be around and who always behaves politely and respectfully towards you. Colleague B is a horrible person who is rude, humourless, bossy and uncooperative, and generally makes everyone's life a misery. Colleague A realises his lack of experience with the software is hindering his career and asks politely if you could spare a few hours during the weekend to coach him on the software. Colleague B also realises this, but instead of asking you politely for some coaching, he shouts at you across the work canteen: 'Hey Loser! Cancel your weekend plans – if you have any – because I need you to coach me on that software.' It is easy to imagine that most of us would be more inclined to agree to help Colleague A than Colleague B. Now imagine that you refuse to help the nasty colleague, only for him to return shortly afterwards to your office, make a grovelling apology for his obnoxious behaviour and explain that it is a reaction to his only child being desperately ill. He then offers you £1,000 cash in return for some coaching on the software. Would you soften your stance and agree to his request for help now?

If we apply these thought experiments, trivial though they may seem, to thinking about the effects of personality on work performance, we can see in very approximate terms that the higher a person's score on conscientiousness, the lower the extrinsic motivation they require to work conscientiously at a boring, detail-focused task like counting grains of rice. But also, our levels of conscientiousness in any one situation are open to manipulation by the pay-offs available. Thus, a hypothetical super-conscientious person may indeed count the grains of rice in the 10-kg bag carefully for a reward of only £1. But the offer of £1,000,000 for a correct count is likely (temporarily) to transform an average person into a super-conscientious rice-counter. Likewise, the higher a person's score on agreeableness, the lower the extrinsic motivation they require to be helpful and cooperative: a hypothetical super-agreeable person may indeed help the nasty colleague without needing an apology or a cash reward, yet it is plausible that the offer of £1,000 for a few hours work will temporarily turn an average person into a super-agreeable colleague.

The crucial point to realise here is that a person with relatively low scores on conscientiousness and agreeableness is able to behave diligently and cooperatively, but will only do so when subject to some suitable powerful extrinsic incentive, such as the fear of destitution. If a welfare state is implemented that removes the fear of destitution, it can be viewed as a noble thing, but it is also a personality filter, preferentially stripping the workforce of those individuals with low levels of work motivation who, in pre-welfare eras, would have bitten the proverbial bullet, suppressed their antisocial urges and buckled down to the challenge of working for a living. Figure 2.1 illustrates this process using a simple diagram.

The notion of the welfare state as a personality filter is corroborated by studies showing that individuals with aggressive,

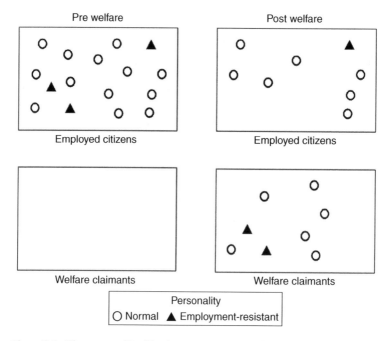

Figure 2.1   The personality-filtering process triggered by the implementation of the welfare state

antisocial and rule-breaking personality attributes that characterise the employment-resistant personality profile are over-represented amongst welfare claimants. For example, Markowe, Tonge and Barber (1955) analysed the psychiatric qualities of 222 British men registered as disabled for psychiatric reasons, 95 of whom were unemployed. The group of unemployed men contained significantly more individuals with a diagnosis of antisocial personality disorder (as defined by an interview with a psychiatrist) than the group of employed men, 26 versus 9. In a similar vein, New Zealand children with antisocial personality traits have a higher risk than average of turning out to be unemployed adults (Caspi et al., 1998).

Data from the USA tell a similar story: a survey of a large and nationally representative sample of 43,093 adults found antisocial personality disorder was associated with a significantly increased risk of claiming welfare support (Vaughn et al., 2010). This latter finding is backed up by more recent research by James Heckman and colleagues on the characteristics of GED recipients (high-school dropouts who have subsequently passed the GED high-school equivalency test). For example, when compared to high-school graduates, adults who dropped out of high school but then went on to pass the GED test were already displaying as children a significantly greater frequency of un-conscientious and disagreeable behaviours (for example, truancy, binge drinking, theft and criminal violence; Heckman, Humphries & Kautz, 2014a).

Importantly for the argument that personality affects employment prospects and thus welfare usage, follow-up studies show that GED recipients also tend to have significantly worse work records and a significantly increased risk of claiming welfare support compared to high-school graduates, despite possessing equal intelligence (Heckman, Humphries & Kautz, 2014b). The research on GEDs suggests that a personality-related deficit in work motivation, rather than a lack of intelligence, underpins the tendency to claim welfare benefits. It also suggests that the relationship between personality and employability differs sharply from that between intelligence and employability because intelligence is an ability rather than a strategy and so cannot be increased to maximise pay-offs. For example, if intelligence was influenced by motivation, then the huge financial and status pay-offs that accompany the very highest levels of professional performance in cognitively demanding jobs such as investment banking might be expected to enable success in people with low intelligence but high motivation to succeed. This is not the case, as studies show that the very highest levels of professional performance are only accessible to people with extremely high levels of intelligence. In other words, intelligence is a gift that keeps on giving, in that there appears to be no threshold effect on intelligence when it comes to aiding job performance: in jobs at the higher end of the complexity spectrum, the super-smart perform better than the merely smart, but are themselves outperformed by the 'scary smart' (Kell, Lubinski & Benbow, 2013).

If we now return to the occupational psychology literature, why was there a delay in studying personality effects in the workplace? As Barrick et al. (2001) wrote in their review of studies testing personality effects on job performance, there are two distinct phases to this form of psychology. The first ran from the early 1900s to the mid-1980s and essentially concluded that there is no effect of personality on job performance. The second phase has been running from the mid-1980s onwards and shows that personality has an important influence on our effectiveness in the workplace.

Barrick et al. (2001) cite many reasons for this, but the main reason was that personality measurement has only attained a mature state in the last 30 years or so: before this time, researchers seeking to test for effects of personality on job performance simply did not have adequate, easy-to-use measurement tools to accomplish their goals. All that was available was a plethora of poorly constructed and poorly validated personality questionnaires, often measuring hundreds of trivial, poorly replicated traits. These questionnaires typically showed little consistency, measuring personality constructs that had low reliability and confusing naming protocols. Nor were the questionnaires systematically validated using biological or physiological measures, with the result that researchers had little idea whether the questionnaire they were using really measured what it purported to measure, other than by the circular and uninformative process of correlating the scores with another questionnaire (Barrick et al., 2001).

This woeful situation began to change in the 1940s, largely due to the prescient work of Hans Eysenck, who advocated representing inter-individual personality variance with a handful of reliable, genetically and biologically-based personality dimensions (firstly extraversion and neuroticism; Eysenck, 1947, then psychoticism; Eysenck, 1952). Ignoring decades of ridicule by other psychologists who argued there were no such things as personality traits (for example, Mischel, 1968), Eysenck doggedly continued to construct questionnaires that reliably captured robust individual differences in underlying biological processes, arguing that whilst the three dimensions may not capture all the variance in personality, attempting to measure personality with hundreds of narrow, non-replicated, overly-detailed constructs (or not measuring it at all) was foolish.

Eventually, by the 1980s, most personality researchers had seen the wisdom of Eysenck's notion of capturing personality variation with a small number of fundamental dimensions, and began copying the Eysenckian dimensions of extraversion and neuroticism as well as refining psychoticism to form two sub-dimensions, namely conscientiousness and agreeableness (Digman, 1990; Costa & McCrae, 1992; Goldberg, 1993). As was mentioned in Chapter 1, this five-factor model of personality, usually known in the personality industry as the big five, has proved to be measurable by questionnaire and useful in studies attempting to probe the effects of personality on workplace performance.

Due to these advances in personality measurement, effects of personality (as measured by personality questionnaires) on occupational outcomes have been investigated in scores of studies over two decades now and show that conscientiousness is the heavy hitter in occupational settings, being positively correlated with performance in most jobs (Barrick et al., 2001). A statement of the obvious perhaps, given that it is difficult to imagine a job in which performance would be improved by being sloppy, unreliable and irresponsible, yet it is reassuring to have data to show this outcome.

Moreover, it seems that conscientiousness is already influencing an individual's employability before they even enter the workforce. For example, conscientiousness is positively correlated with academic performance (for example, Poropat, 2009) so it is plausible that high scorers on conscientiousness are primed for good job performance before they even arrive in the workplace, by tending to work harder at school and so be better qualified and skilled once they enter the workforce. As a caveat, it should be noted that there are a tiny minority of specialist occupations where high conscientiousness is likely to hinder performance: for example, it is plausible that an individual with the careful, rule-following, conformist, detail-focused attitude typical of a high scorer on conscientiousness will lack the off-beat, free-wheeling, 'big-picture' world view needed to be a creative genius. But the reality is that for society to function, we need far fewer creative geniuses than ordinary workers. Therefore, on the whole, we can accept that conscientiousness is crucial in boosting workplace performance.

Occupational psychologists have been slower to appreciate the importance of agreeableness in the workplace: it usually shows no significant relationship with direct measures of job performance or occasionally even a slight negative relationship (Judge et al., 1999). Indeed, it is easy to see that in some jobs, high agreeableness may be a disadvantage. For example, it is likely that a highly agreeable police officer will manage violent public disorder situations less effectively than a low scorer on agreeableness will. Likewise, a person at the high end of the agreeableness scale is unlikely to be effective as an officer commanding a platoon of infantry soldiers in combat. But for every leader there must, by definition, be many more subordinates who readily cooperate with the orders of their boss and the aims of the organisation, so for the vast majority of jobs, it is plausible that medium to high agreeableness is in general beneficial for workplace effectiveness.

This idea has been backed up by advances in occupational psychology that go beyond evaluating personality effects on individual measures of job performance, such as absolute sales figures or widgets produced, and instead test personality effects on behaviours that facilitate organisational cohesion. These thoughts have crystallised into an appreciation of what is known as organisational citizenship behaviour (OCB). This construct has been defined as 'individual behavior that is discretionary, not directly or explicitly recognized by the formal reward system, and that in the aggregate promotes the effective functioning of the organization' (Organ, 1988, p. 4). Within the overall construct of OCB, five major facets have been identified consisting of altruism, courtesy, conscientiousness, civic virtue and sportsmanship (Organ, 1988). Of these five facets, altruism, courtesy and sportsmanship plausibly relate to agreeableness. This idea has been backed up by studies showing agreeableness is positively related to organisational citizenship (Podsakoff et al., 2000).

The crucial point to understand with the altruistic component of OCB is that helping behaviours add up over time to the advantage of the organisation even if there is no measurable gain in every case of such behaviour (Organ, Podsakoff & MacKenzie, 2006). In a very simple form we see that high conscientiousness gives a benefit to what might be dubbed 'contracted' workplace performance (for example, turning up for work on time or sticking to procedures).

Agreeableness, in contrast, plays a key role in what might be labelled the 'non-contracted' aspects of performance that are less easily measured yet help an organisation to function (that is, the tendency to cooperate with co-workers and to help them do their jobs without being ordered to do so, taking care to avoid needless confrontations with co-workers or customers and so on).

Finally, recent research has shown that like conscientiousness, agreeableness may even be boosting our employability before we get into the workplace, as it is not only positively correlated with academic performance (Poropat, 2009), but it also helps us get hired (Hogan, 2011). In other words, it doesn't matter how conscientious we are, if we habitually display a confrontational, difficult or otherwise disagreeable manner, we may suffer in school and in the job interview situation, making the employer unlikely to choose to hire us.

Viewed as a whole, these three parts of the scientific literature allow us to visualise conscientiousness and agreeableness as coalescing to form a hybrid dimension of personality that could be dubbed 'employability'. At the high end of this dimension, we find individuals who score significantly above average on both conscientiousness and agreeableness (labelled as C+, A+ in standard personality notation). Individuals with this personality profile not only display strong intrinsic motivation to work diligently, but also to be polite, cooperative and helpful in their dealings with other people. These individuals therefore tend to be model employees in the workplace and solid citizens in the community.

At the low end of the hybrid dimension of employability, we find individuals who score significantly below average on both conscientiousness and agreeableness (labelled as C–, A– in standard personality notation). These individuals not only display weak motivation to work diligently, but are also relatively unlikely to cooperate constructively with others. They can therefore be viewed as possessing what I have called the 'employment-resistant' personality profile.

As a sanity check of studies showing that conscientiousness and agreeableness influence employability, it should be noted that Li Ka-Shing (Asia's richest person) emphasises both conscientiousness

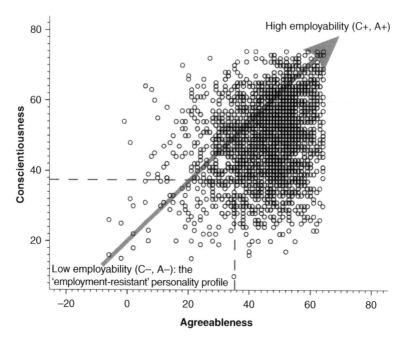

Figure 2.2 Employability as a function of the combined scores on conscientiousness and agreeableness in 2,532 UK adults

and agreeableness in his advice on how to succeed in the world of work: 'If you keep a good reputation, work hard, be nice to people, keep your promises, your business will be much easier.' Moreover, Ka-Shing's recipe for success is not hindsight, because in the 1960s, before he became famous in the wider world, he was already well known in the plastics industry as a particularly conscientious and agreeable man: 'When I did business with K. S. (Ka-Shing) we didn't need a contract. All it was was a handshake' (Alan Hassenfeld, Chairman of Hasbro).

To estimate the prevalence of the employment-resistant personality profile, Figure 2.2 plots questionnaire scores for conscientiousness and agreeableness in 2,532 UK adults from one of my own studies. The arrow indicates the hybrid dimension of employability. The dashed lines contain those who scored significantly below average on both conscientiousness and agreeableness (defined as scoring one standard deviation or more below the mean). These 103 people (four percent) possess the employment-resistant personality profile. It should be noted that all of the 2,532 participants whose scores are plotted in Figure 2.2 were volunteers and so the employment-resistant personality profile is likely to be under-represented in this sample, since volunteering to participate in a psychological study is itself an act of conscientiousness and agreeableness.

Conclusion

The evidence summarised in this chapter shows that the lower a person scores on conscientiousness and agreeableness, the less employable they tend to be. The employment-resistant personality profile can therefore be viewed as combining relatively low scores on both conscientiousness and agreeableness.

3
The Lifelong Impact
of Personality

The previous chapter showed that people who combine relatively low levels of conscientiousness and agreeableness tend to have unsatisfactory work records, irrespective of their intelligence level. These individuals can therefore be viewed as possessing the 'employment-resistant' personality profile.

A major question that stems from this conclusion is whether the employment-resistant personality profile is the cause rather than the product of adverse occupational experiences. For example, the arrow of causation might be bidirectional, with low levels of conscientiousness and agreeableness not only increasing the risk of unemployment, but also being a product of unemployment. Studies on this theme have found mixed evidence: for example, Specht, Egloff and Schmukle (2011) found no significant effect of unemployment on conscientiousness and agreeableness in a sample of 14,718 German participants. However, Boyce et al. (2015) studied 6,769 participants, also German, and found that although there were no direct effects of unemployment on conscientiousness or agreeableness, when sex was taken into account, a more complex picture emerged: agreeableness increased in men but decreased in women due to unemployment. The authors also identified a trend for conscientiousness to decline over time in unemployed men and, in women, they found a trend for conscientiousness to rise in participants unemployed for one and four years, whilst tending to fall in those participants unemployed for two and three years.

The studies of people who have suffered prefrontal brain injuries that we covered in the previous chapter go some way to supporting the idea that low levels of conscientiousness and agreeableness cause unemployment because victims of this sort of injury typically display a post-injury reduction in conscientiousness and agreeableness and at the same time display a reduction in employability. However, people with prefrontal brain injuries have suffered severe neurological trauma that means a causal role for conscientiousness and agreeableness in employability needs to be backed up by studies in non-brain-injured people. The programme of research on GED recipients that has been undertaken by James Heckman and colleagues hints that personality deficits cause later employment problems by showing that GED recipients display more antisocial behaviour as children and claim more welfare as adults, compared to individuals who go on to graduate from high school. But this research does not track the same individuals over time, instead taking a cross-sectional sample of data on the behaviour of children and the employment records of GED recipients, who are not the same people as those children.

To be sure that the employment-resistant personality profile truly is the cause rather than the product of poor occupational outcomes, we require so-called longitudinal studies that record personality characteristics in childhood and then trace the effects of these characteristics on subsequent outcomes in the same individuals during adulthood, whilst controlling for the effect of other important variables (for example, intelligence and SES). Studies of this type are rare as they are more difficult and expensive than cross-sectional research, in which we administer a personality questionnaire and measure the relationship between its scores and some easily procured measure of job performance (for example, supervisor ratings). Longitudinal studies are also rare because they take decades to do and so are not attractive to scientists, who usually want to do studies that provide quick results that can boost their career whilst they are still young enough to benefit. Few researchers are selfless enough to spend a lifetime tracking their participants only to die and have their glory taken by younger co-workers.

Nevertheless, longitudinal studies that record personality effects on life outcomes have been done, two of which are particularly rigorous and so are the focus of this chapter. First, I will describe Lewis Terman's study which from 1921 started tracking the lives of 1,528 Californian children born around 1910. Almost all of these children are now dead and so their full life trajectory is available for study, with follow-up surveys revealing that children with employment-resistant personality profiles generally turned out to have worse work records than average (for an overview of the entire research programme, see Friedman & Martin, 2011). Interestingly, the children with employment-resistant personality profiles also went on to have worse health, personal relationships and longevity than average children. Terman only enrolled highly intelligent children from middle-class or upper-middle-class families and so he eliminated intelligence effects, but this step also caused a limitation: the personality effects that were found in the Terman Study might just be quirks of the higher echelons of society. For example, conscientiousness effects on life outcomes may only be relevant in people who are intelligent enough to be eligible for high-flying jobs.

Second, I will describe a more recent investigation known as the Dunedin Study which has been following the lives of approximately 1,000 people born in the New Zealand city of Dunedin in 1972. The key innovation of this study is that it enrolled every baby born in Dunedin in that year and so the participant groups were not pre-selected on any variable such as IQ or social class. The cohort therefore contains a much wider and more representative sample of humanity than was found in the Terman Study. This study also used a different measure of childhood personality, namely the hybrid construct of self-control (which combines conscientiousness and agreeableness). Despite these differences, the Dunedin Study has so far backed up the results of the Terman Study: individuals with low levels of self-control as children go on to have less satisfactory life histories in almost every important domain, including work, compared to highly self-controlled children.

The Terman Study of the Gifted (often known as the Terman Study)

Born in 1877 in Indiana, Lewis Terman received his PhD in 1905 from Clark University then worked as a schoolteacher in California before, in 1910, becoming Professor of Educational Psychology at Stanford University. An expert on the measurement of intelligence, Terman subscribed to Francis Galton's view that intelligence is genetically based, but was concerned that the typical chalk-and-talk schooling methods of the time were not well suited to highly intelligent children and therefore might prevent them from reaching their full genetic potential as the intellectual leaders of the future (Terman, 1915). By this stage, the First World War had begun and the US Army asked Terman to assist with the creation of an intelligence test that could be used to help to assign recruits to soldiering jobs that were appropriate to their abilities. In response, he led the successful adaptation of Alfred Binet's famous IQ test into a mass-administration format, suitable for military job assignment.

After the First World War ended, Terman returned to his educational psychology research, where he began planning longitudinal research with intellectually gifted children. One question that particularly interested him was whether there was any truth in the stereotype that highly intelligent children have a tendency to develop into physically weak, sickly, socially inadequate and eccentric 'egghead' adults. He was also interested in what attributes predicted success. For these reasons, he initiated in 1921 a study in which schoolteachers in California were asked to nominate the most intelligent children in their class. Nominated children then had their intelligence confirmed empirically by being tested on the Stanford Binet intelligence test and were included in the study if their IQ score was 135 or greater. Children were added to the study on a rolling basis until 1928, yielding a final sample size of 1,528 (856 boys, 672 girls). Terman gathered an exhaustive range of data on the children and their family backgrounds upon enrolment, then followed them up every five to ten years to see how they turned out.

Lewis Terman died in 1956: in his lifetime, data on the participants were collected in 1921, 1923, 1928, 1936, 1940, 1945, 1950 and 1955. In 1960, further data were collected by Melita Oden. Robert Sears (who was himself a participant) collected additional data in 1972, 1977, 1982 and 1986. More recently, what is probably the final work on this project (since almost all the participants are now dead) has been done by Howard Friedman and Leslie Martin and colleagues, with their results being collated in a lively and fascinating book entitled *The Longevity Project* (Friedman & Martin, 2011) that is well worth reading for anyone who wants to know about the Terman Study in more detail. The first six chapters of the book report the effects of personality on longevity-related life outcomes and the remaining ten chapters describe the effect on life outcomes of external factors such as parental divorce and exposure to warfare.

In conducting their personality research, Friedman, Martin and their colleagues faced a tricky technical challenge that might best be described as psychometric archaeology: Terman recorded a detailed range of personality attributes, but did not have at his disposal the psychometrically polished personality questionnaires that are used by modern personality researchers. These modern questionnaires, as mentioned previously, typically boil down the variations of human personality into five fundamental dimensions of extraversion, neuroticism, openness, agreeableness and conscientiousness (Digman, 1990; Costa & McCrae, 1992; Goldberg, 1993). Nevertheless, Friedman and Martin reasoned that the impressions of personality gained from Terman's data should be broadly comparable to those produced by modern self-report questionnaires.

The first personality measurement in the Terman Study was done in 1922 by asking parents and teachers to rate the personality attributes of the participants on a variety of traits using a 13-point scale. Later research directly asked the participants about their own personality attributes by means of various self-report questionnaires. Although these early attempts at measuring personality are not directly comparable to modern personality questionnaires, Friedman and Martin nevertheless found that Terman's personality data were capable of being reanalysed to produce modern scores. This was determined by testing a new cohort of participants using the Terman personality measures, then asking the same people to complete a modern five-factor personality questionnaire (the NEO PI-R; Costa & McCrae, 1992). The results of the two types of questionnaire measurement were then compared statistically, allowing items in Terman's personality questionnaires that represented modern items to be used to create an approximately modern personality profile for the Terman participants. Of the five personality factors in modern representations of personality (extraversion, neuroticism, openness to experience, agreeableness and conscientiousness), only scores on openness to experience could not be recreated owing to a lack of suitable items in Terman's original research (Martin & Friedman, 2000). Since the focus of this book is conscientiousness and agreeableness, this is not a problem.

To cut a long, but fascinating, story short, based on their analyses of the whole lives of the Terman Study participants, Friedman and Martin conclude that conscientiousness is by far the most important personality variable with regard to life outcomes. Agreeableness was also a significant factor, but in a narrower way: it was positively related to happiness and good health but this appeared to be a product of a pleasant inter-personal manner aiding the formation of harmonious relationships with other people, rather than any direct causal relationship between agreeableness and happiness or health. This finding is nevertheless important for the theory advanced in this book because most jobs require social interaction. The data on agreeableness effects from the Terman Study therefore back up the occupational data summarised in the previous chapter that showed agreeableness relates to organisational citizenship behaviour: being unable to form harmonious relationships with colleagues or customers because of a disagreeable manner is likely to render a person less employable, and so increase their chance of ending up unemployed and claiming welfare benefits.

Conscientiousness, on the other hand, was found by Friedman and Martin to affect almost every aspect of life, directly and indirectly. Most clearly, highly conscientious children went on to live significantly healthier and longer lives than their less conscientious peers. This finding raises a rather important question, namely why should a phenomenon with so many contributing causal factors, namely death, be related to the tendency to behave in an orderly, responsible manner? Friedman and Martin found three main reasons. First, and rather obviously, is the discovery that highly conscientious participants engaged in more health-promoting behaviours and engaged in fewer death-promoting behaviours than their less conscientious peers. For example, they were more likely to obey rules on wearing seat belts in cars or follow instructions from the doctor concerning medicines and were less likely to smoke or abuse drugs. Friedman and Martin emphasise that this is not the same as being risk averse, but rather that 'they tend to be sensible in evaluating how far to push the envelope' (Friedman & Martin, 2011, p. 16). In the welfare trait theory advanced in this book, this attribute of being sensibly aware of risks is important: if the welfare system does indeed increase the proportion of individuals in the population who are not sensible in judging how far to push the envelope, then it is easy to see that it will damage human capital. This will happen due to the increased frequency of reckless, foolhardy behaviour that not only makes life less tolerable for the law-abiding, doctor-obeying, solid citizens who get caught in the crossfire, but also places a greater burden on the public purse expense, whether through increased insurance claims, or hospital bills, or prison costs.

A second and less obvious benefit of a high score on conscientiousness that Friedman and Martin found was the remarkable discovery that such participants are less prone to diseases that are unrelated to healthy habits. The causal mechanisms for this relationship are unclear but Friedman and Martin speculate that conscientiousness scores may reflect levels of neurotransmitters that also affect health-related behaviours and processes such as sleeping and eating. In other words, conscientiousness may be a proxy measure of the healthiness of a person's brain. Again, in the context of this book, this finding is bad news for nations with welfare systems that increase the number of children born to people with relatively low levels of conscientiousness: they not only have less healthy habits, they are also physiologically less healthy and thus will create more of a burden on the healthcare system. This finding has been confirmed by subsequent follow-up studies: in a study of thousands of contemporary US citizens, it was found that individuals with low scores on conscientiousness were more likely than average to smoke, suffer from affective disorders (anxiety/depression), have high blood pressure, and contract tuberculosis, diabetes, strokes or suffer from joint problems (Goodwin & Friedman, 2006).

Finally, Friedman and Martin found that conscientiousness influenced the tendency for a person to get into healthier job situations and social relationships: highly conscientious people tended to end up in happier marriages, more rewarding friendships and more suitable work than less conscientious people did. So, overall, highly conscientious people have healthier habits, healthier brains and healthier environments than their peers with low scores on conscientiousness.

If we allow ourselves to indulge in a thought experiment and extrapolate these findings by Friedman and Martin up to national level, it would seem plausible that a population containing predominantly highly conscientious and agreeable individuals will indeed be healthier, happier, more productive and longer lived than a population with the inverse personality profile. Crucially, they will not only be likely to pay more tax than the low scorers owing to their better employability, but will also be less of a drain on the public purse (for example, via lower expenditure on criminal justice or healthcare). This point strengthens the argument that a welfare system which proliferates the employment-resistant personality profile is a bad thing for both the economic and the social prospects of the nation. Since, as we will see in later chapters, personality runs in families for both genetic and environmental reasons, the findings of Friedman and Martin mean that children born to parents relatively lacking in conscientiousness and agreeableness are likely to resemble those parents, as would their children, and so on. This cycle of proliferation of personality dysfunction will therefore place an ever greater burden on the more functional citizens. On the other side of the coin, would an imaginary utopia populated solely by highly conscientious and highly agreeable 'solid citizens' be boring and bland, full of colourless, corporate drones who work hard, raise their children responsibly, wear seatbelts, do what the doctor says and pay their taxes yet lack any spark of the creativity or dynamism that makes society flourish? Not according to the Terman data: Friedman and Martin concluded that the most conscientious and agreeable children tended also to end up with what they viewed as the most exciting, creative and rewarding life trajectories.

The Dunedin Multidisciplinary Health and Development Study (known as the Dunedin Study)

One criticism that could be levelled at the Terman Study is that the participants were highly intelligent individuals from mostly Caucasian families with a relatively high (middle/upper class) SES. So it may be the case that, although the conclusions of researchers such as Friedman and Martin are rigorously supported and so are likely to be correct, they do not apply beyond that relatively narrow segment of society. Fortunately, this criticism does not apply to the Dunedin Study, which allows us to check the robustness of the findings of the Terman Study.

Perhaps the most carefully designed and controlled longitudinal investigation of child development ever conducted, this study has followed the lives of a complete birth cohort of children (totalling 1,037 individuals) born in Dunedin, New Zealand in 1972–1973. The participants are about 43 years old at the time of writing and, remarkably, 96 per cent of them have been retained in the study. Crucially in the present context, since all children born in Dunedin in that time period were enrolled into the study and almost all of them have remained in it, the participants' qualities are not skewed towards high IQ or any other individual differences or demographic variable. This has the benefit of providing results that are likely to be generally valid across the full spectrum of society, at least in countries with generic westernised lifestyles and democratic cultural values that are roughly equivalent to those found in New Zealand such as the USA, UK, Canada, Australia, Scandinavia and most of mainland Europe.

The key results from the Dunedin Study that relate to this book were those that were published in 2011 by Terrie Moffitt, Avshalom Caspi and colleagues that investigated the effects of self-control measured in childhood on health, wealth and criminality measured at the age of 32 years. Interest in the effects of childhood self-control on adult life outcomes has deep roots: perhaps the most famous experiment on the topic is the celebrated Stanford Marshmallow Experiment begun in 1972 by Walter Mischel. This used a delay-of-gratification design in which 95 children (53 girls and 42 boys) with an average age of four years and five months were presented with a marshmallow. The children were allowed to eat the marshmallow immediately if they wished, but were told that if they waited for 15 minutes without eating it, they would receive a second marshmallow. The children were followed up ten years later as adolescents and it was found that those who were able to resist eating the marshmallow for 15 minutes turned out to be rated by their parents as significantly more competent than the non-resistors (Mischel, Shoda & Peake, 1988). More specifically, it was found that 'their parents rated them as more academically and socially competent, verbally fluent, rational, attentive, planful, and able to deal well with frustration and stress' (Shoda, Mischel & Peake, 1990, p. 978).

In the context of this book, these results are important, as the children with high levels of self-control at age four go on to manifest as young adults precisely the kind of behaviour patterns that I would argue aid effectiveness in the workplace, as well as general solid citizenship. This latter impression is congruent with earlier work done by Mischel in Trinidad in which he found that children whose fathers had abandoned the family showed poorer delay of gratification than children from intact families, as if the tendency for a father to abandon his children is linked to lack of self-control in him that is then passed on genetically to those children (Mischel, 1958).

However, the studies by Mischel suffer from the same flaws as the Terman Study, namely that we cannot be sure the participants were representative of the general population but, reassuringly for the Dunedin Study, they do suggest that self-control measured in childhood is an important personality characteristic that goes on to influence employability and so is presumably related to conscientiousness and agreeableness.

Importantly for the generality of the Dunedin results, childhood self-control was not measured with a marshmallow. Instead, when the children were three and five years old, each of them was tested on a battery of cognitive and motor tasks. The participants were tested by examiners who did not know them. After the session, each examiner rated the child's self-control using the following trait labels: lability, low frustration tolerance, hostility, resistance, restlessness, impulsivity, requires attention, fleeting attention and lacking persistence.

Subsequent assessments then followed: at ages five, seven, nine and 11, with the self-control of participants rated by parents and teachers who completed the Rutter Child Scale (RCS) which includes items that measure impulsive aggression and hyperactivity. At ages nine and 11, the RCS was supplemented with further questions about the children's lack of persistence, inattention and impulsivity. Finally, at age 11, the participants were interviewed by a psychiatrist who rated them on hyperactivity, inattention and impulsivity. The component scores for all these separate ratings were then averaged to produce a single score of childhood self-control. In terms of the standard Big Five personality dimensions, a high score on childhood self-control primarily reflects high conscientiousness, but also to a lesser extent, high agreeableness and low neuroticism.

Conversely, low childhood self-control primarily reflects low conscientiousness and to a lesser extent, low agreeableness and high neuroticism. A low score on childhood self-control therefore is a plausible precursor for the adult employment-resistant personality profile that is proposed in this book. As found by Mischel and colleagues, it makes sense that a child with high self-control should go on to be an adult who is better suited to holding down most types of job than a person with low childhood self-control is. They should also be better able to look after their health and also are more likely to stay out of trouble with the law. But again, as with the Terman Study, data are needed to back up these educated guesses. The Dunedin Study data, as reported by Moffitt et al. (2011), support the validity of these guesses. Four hypotheses were tested by Moffitt et al. (2011): first, they asked if self-control as measured in the participants as children went on to predict their adult health, wealth and criminality similarly across the self-control range, from low to high. Second, they asked whether the Dunedin Study participants who moved up in the self-control range during the study showed improved health, wealth and reduced criminality. Third, they investigated whether children at the low end of the self-control range were more likely than average to make errors of judgment as teenagers that limited their subsequent success as adults (for example, dropping out of high school, smoking, abusing drugs, criminality, becoming a teenage parent). Moffitt et al. (2011) dub these mistakes 'snares' that trap the youngsters in lifestyles that damage their health and wealth as well as undermining the future safety and prosperity of society in general. Fourth, Moffitt et al. (2011) wanted to take advantage of the extremely comprehensive testing regime of the Dunedin Study and find out whether self-control scores at three years old influenced important life outcomes.

One concern in longitudinal studies of human development is whether the variable of interest (in this case self-control) is having a real effect and is not merely a by-product of the effect of another underlying variable such as intelligence or social class. Fortunately, the Dunedin Study also measured the intelligence and social class of the participants, allowing the influence of self-control on life outcomes to be separated from the effects of these other factors. This turned out to be important because preliminary analyses showed that self-control was significantly higher in children from higher socioeconomic classes and with higher IQ scores. Lastly, Moffitt et al. (2011) took advantage of sibling data gathered in a related British study (the Environmental-Risk Longitudinal Twin Study; E-Risk) that followed children up to the age of 12 years old, including measures of self-control taken at age five, and three important precursors of poor health, low wealth and criminality, namely smoking at age 12, poor school performance and antisocial behaviour. These data were used to determine if individual differences in self-control predicted differences in life outcomes, even in siblings who are raised together. This meant the role of a participant's self-control level in influencing life outcomes could be separated from other factors which differ between families.

To assess health in adulthood, the participants were given a battery of physical and psychiatric medical assessments at the age of 32. This process generated four health-related scores: physical health, recurrent depression, substance dependence and informant-reported substance problems. Low childhood self-control was generally associated with poor health. These associations persisted even when the influence of social class and IQ were removed. More specifically, participants with low childhood self-control were more likely to suffer from metabolic abnormalities, periodontal disease, sexually transmitted infections and inflammatory diseases. Childhood self-control did not affect the risk of respiratory disease or depression. Low childhood self-control was associated with a tendency to smoke cigarettes and consume illicit drugs but did not affect risk of marijuana use or alcoholism.

With regard to wealth, Moffitt et al. (2011) found that low childhood self-control was associated in adulthood with lower income, greater probability of single-parenthood, less financial planning and increased financial struggles such as credit card debts (whether self-reported or informant-reported). These effects of self-control on wealth were stronger than the effects of IQ or childhood social class. Finally, Moffitt et al. (2011) looked at criminality and found that 24 per cent of the participants had criminal convictions by the age of 32. They found that low childhood self-control was associated with a significantly higher risk of criminal offending, even when IQ and SES was taken into account.

Importantly, all three of these findings held true at all levels of the gradient of self-control in the participant cohort. Additionally, Moffitt and colleagues studied participants who moved up the self-control gradient by the time they had become young adults (as measured by self-report at 26 years old), finding that these individuals went on to show better life outcomes at the age of 32. This change implies that self-control has a learned component and so could be increased by interventions during childhood that aim to facilitate socialisation. This idea is congruent with the results of longitudinal studies of preschool training in conscientiousness and agreeableness which show that trained children went on to have better life outcomes than the control group who were not trained (for example, Heckman, 2006), as will be discussed in Chapter 5. With regard to adolescent mistakes, Moffitt et al. (2011) found that children with low levels of self-control were more likely to make mistakes in their teenage years that harmed their prospects of a successful life trajectory. More specifically, children with poor self-control were more likely to start smoking by the age of 15, leave school prematurely with no qualifications and to become teenage parents, even when taking into account the effects of IQ and socio-economic class. Interestingly, the effect of children falling into these traps did not fully account for effects of self-control on adult health, wealth and criminality: even amongst the participants who did not smoke, graduated from high school and did not become teenage parents, self-control still significantly influenced their adult life outcomes. This finding underlines the importance of self-control in determining the success or otherwise of an individual's life, suggesting that it would be more cost effective to introduce policies that increase self-control in the population rather than trying to target the surface symptoms of low self-control like smoking, teen parenthood and school failure. These results also add weight to the idea that welfare policies that increase the proportion of individuals with low levels of self-control are a bad thing for everyone – welfare claimants and workers alike. This is a crucial take-home point so is worth emphasising: *welfare policies that increase the proportion of individuals with low levels of self-control are a bad thing for everyone – welfare claimants and workers alike.*

The attempt by Moffitt et al. (2011) to test the effects of early measurements of childhood self-control (at age three) was successful: the scores predicted health, wealth and criminality at age 32, although the size of the effect was smaller than for the full composite score that incorporated all measurements of self-control up to age 11. Finally, by looking at a similar cohort study of siblings in the UK, Moffitt et al. (2011) aimed to test whether siblings with different scores on self-control showed different life outcomes. As predicted, it was found that at five years old, the sibling with lower self-control was significantly more likely to begin smoking when 12 years old, to behave in an antisocial manner and to perform poorly at school.

Conclusion

Putting the findings from the Terman Study together with the findings from the Dunedin Study, it is clear that children with personality characteristics reflecting a lack of self-control have an elevated risk of encountering occupational difficulties later in life. It is also clear that children with low self-control possess a personality profile that approximates to the employment-resistant personality profile (low conscientiousness plus low agreeableness). This means the employment-resistant personality profile is not a product of unemployment but increases the likelihood of becoming unemployed. Moreover, this effect of personality on employability is not a product of intelligence or social class, since the children in the Terman Study all possessed relatively high intelligence and social class, and the participants in the Dunedin Study were tested on IQ and for social class and had those effects statistically controlled when examining effects on life outcomes of personality. A secondary conclusion from these two studies is that the children with the employment-resistant personality not only went on to experience occupational difficulties but also difficulties in generally behaving like a solid citizen outside the workplace. These findings indicate that relatively low levels of conscientiousness and agreeableness play a causal role in promoting an unhealthy, work-shy, impoverished and criminal life trajectory and back up the epidemiological data in the previous chapter that showed individuals with the employment-resistant personality profile are over-represented amongst welfare claimants.

4
The Influence of Benefits on Claimant Reproduction

In Chapter 1, I raised the possibility that the welfare state can proliferate the employment-resistant personality profile by boosting the number of children born into disadvantaged households. This chapter is devoted to examining whether it is indeed the case that welfare claimants on average have more children than employed citizens and whether such differences could be driven partly by personality differences in reactions to welfare policy. To do this, I utilise the ecological theory that there are two opposing strategies for reproduction, the success of which depends upon the availability of resources. In conditions where resources are plentiful and competition for these resources is low, the optimal strategy is to produce as many offspring as possible but put little effort into their care. Conversely, when resources are scarce and have to be competed for, the optimal strategy is to produce fewer offspring but care for them conscientiously so that each offspring is itself capable of competing for resources.

The delineation of these two reproduction strategies has its roots in the work of Fisher (1930) and Dobzhansky (1950) but was more fully articulated by MacArthur and Wilson (1967) who labelled them as r selection and K selection, respectively. Since no organism exists in a perfect ecological vacuum, it is generally accepted that no species is completely r selected or K selected, but instead there is an r–K continuum upon which species are positioned according to the extent to which they favour offspring care over rate of reproduction. For example, insect species tend to be closer to the r selection end of the r–K continuum, whereas vertebrate species tend to be closer to the

54

K selection end of the *r–K* continuum (Pianka, 1970). Within species there may be individual differences in the tendency to lean towards *r* or *K* selection: in humans, *r–K* selection theory predicts that a reproductive strategy resembling *r* selection is optimal in environments where vital resources such as food and shelter are freely available, whereas in environments where vital resources must be competed for, a reproductive strategy resembling *K* selection is optimal (Geary, 2005). This analysis by Geary links *r–K* selection theory to the welfare state in two ways. The first link is that by granting claimants extra resources per child produced without requiring work in return, a welfare state eliminates competition for vital resources and swings the evolutionary advantage away from *K* selection and towards *r* selection. In the jargon of economics, the welfare state reduces the opportunity cost of each child born by reversing the usual pattern: in contrast to employed citizens, whose salaries are not linked to family size, welfare claimants gain financially from the birth of each child.

The second link is provided by studies that suggest the employment-resistant personality profile is associated with a preference for *r* selection, regardless of whether there is a welfare state. Historical evidence for this claim comes from a classic study by Julius B. Maller (1933), who analysed demographic data collected from the entire population of New York City in 1930, before the advent of the welfare state in the USA. In this study, Maller took advantage of the fact that the data were available separately for each of the health areas in New York City (at the time it was divided up into 310 health areas, each containing about 23,000 people). These health areas were small enough to provide separate sampling of different neighbourhoods, yet large enough to generate reliable average scores for each of the variables that Maller was interested in. By computing the average scores on the variables within each health area, Maller could therefore evaluate associations between different variables across the health areas.

This study predates modern concepts of personality and so the list of variables analysed by Maller did not include personality questionnaire scores. However, Maller did measure the rate of juvenile delinquency in each health area, computing this as the number of juvenile delinquents arraigned in that area during 1930 per 1000 children of court age (aged 6–15). Since juvenile delinquents on average score significantly lower on conscientiousness and agreeableness than non-delinquents (John et al., 1994), Maller's juvenile delinquency variable provides a plausible proxy index of the proportion of individuals in a particular health area who possess the employment-resistant personality profile.

Maller's results suggest that there is a link between the employment-resistant personality profile and rapid, irresponsible reproduction, since he found that juvenile delinquency was significantly positively associated with birth rate, death rate and infant mortality and significantly negatively correlated with school attendance and school progress. Furthermore, this finding has been backed up, using completely different methods, by modern research in the USA. For example, a study in 2006 that used modern personality questionnaires found that a preference for the r-selected reproductive style was positively associated with the following characteristics: 'impulsivity, short-term thinking, promiscuity, low female parental investment, little or no male parental investment, little social support, disregard for social rules, and extensive risk-taking' (Figueredo et al., 2006, p. 246). From this analysis, we can see the r-selected personality profile approximates to the employment-resistant personality profile.

Viewed as a whole, these data suggest that people who are already inclined by their personality characteristics towards r selection (that is, having lots of children and investing little effort in their upbringing) are also more likely than average – because of those same personality characteristics – to be less than satisfactory employees and thus end up unemployed and claiming benefits. When claiming welfare benefits, these people are then further encouraged to follow an r-selected reproductive strategy by a welfare state which provides extra resources for each child born.

Conversely, people who are already inclined by their personality characteristics towards K selection (having fewer children and looking after them conscientiously) are also more likely than average to be employed (due to being especially conscientious) and will therefore tend not to claim as many welfare benefits. Since salaries do not increase for every child born, workers are further encouraged by that financial reality to follow a K-selected reproductive strategy.

This is where the problem with the welfare state occurs, because we already know that the people who happen to have a personality profile that inclines them towards employment-resistance are not equally spread throughout the population, but instead are over-represented in the welfare-claiming sector of the population (for example, Vaughn et al., 2010). If we now accept that the employment-resistant personality profile corresponds to an *r*-selected reproductive style, we can see that it is likely that the welfare state will increase the number of children born into disadvantaged households because it is providing a financial incentive to have more children to people who are already inclined to behave that way in the first place. In colloquial parlance, the welfare state is pushing at an open door and, because being born into a disadvantaged household raises the risk of developing the employment-resistant personality profile (Heckman et al., 2013), we can see that the extra children that result from this concatenation of policy, personality and reproductive strategy are less likely than average to end up developing into conscientious, agreeable and economically productive adults.

To assess the validity of this hypothesis, this chapter summarises three sources of evidence. First, I describe associations between personality and reproduction in Britain prior to the introduction of the welfare state, as detailed in Greg Clark's 2007 book *A Farewell to Alms*. This seminal work uses biographical data (for example, last wills and testaments) to show that the unusually stable geopolitical nature of British society for seven centuries or so prior to 1800 meant that the most economically successful citizens typically raised twice as many children as citizens of average economic success and that the least economically successful citizens typically raised no surviving children at all. Clark was not able to administer personality questionnaires to his subjects but, since we already know from Chapter 2 that occupational success is positively associated with scores on conscientiousness and agreeableness, Clark's work allows us to infer that in pre-welfare state times, in the UK at least, these pro-employment personality characteristics conferred an evolutionary advantage. Equally importantly for the theory in this book, Clark's work also supports the more general notion that personality can evolve in response to changes in society.

Second, I summarise some studies that have measured associations between personality and reproduction in developed countries in the welfare state era (that is, from approximately 1945 onwards). These studies show that employment-resistant personality characteristics have gradually gained the evolutionary upper hand since then, with the result that people with employment-resistant personality profiles now produce significantly more children than average citizens do. This idea is supported by my own research on Australian and US citizens and also on US citizens by the research of Markus Jokela and colleagues.

Third, I summarise data on welfare and reproduction. To do this, I first cite government data from the UK showing that welfare claimants on average have significantly more children than employed citizens. Finally, I cite US and UK studies which indicate that the number of children born to welfare claimants tracks welfare generosity, with increases in welfare generosity causing them to have more children, and reductions in welfare generosity causing them to have fewer children.

These latter data are useful to my argument because they contradict the stereotype that large families are wholly a product of poverty or ignorance, instead showing the opposite: as financial benefits per child increase, so does the number of children born to claimants, in a dose-dependent manner and apparently through deliberate discontinuation of contraception. For example, in the UK, it has been shown that increases in the generosity of child benefit funding in the UK over the last decade of approximately 50 per cent per child have increased the number of children born to claimants by approximately 15 per cent (Brewer, Ratcliffe & Smith, 2011). Similarly, in the USA, less generous welfare payments per child beginning in the mid-1990s caused claimants to have fewer children through a decline in pregnancies rather than an increase in abortions (Argys, Averett & Rees, 2000).

More generally, in line with the notion that welfare claimants modulate their behaviour according to changes in welfare provision, it has also been discovered that spells on welfare support tend to be longer when welfare generosity increases, suggesting again that the citizens who claim welfare (despite being less conscientious on average than those who work) are nevertheless conscientious enough to monitor the generosity of government welfare schemes and tailor their economic decisions according to whether it is financially worth forgoing work for welfare (O'Neill, Bassi & Wolf, 1987).

I then devote the rest of this chapter to revisiting the study of problem families by Tonge et al. (1975) mentioned in Chapter 2.

These data are important to my argument because the exceptionally detailed nature of their study is capable of providing more information than census-style studies on the links between welfare and family size. The take-home message from their study is that it is the employment-resistant personality rather than poverty that leads to the reproductive strategy of having many children who are then neglected.

We know this because Tonge et al. (1975) focused on comparing the poverty of the problem families and the comparison families, and what they found was intriguing: whilst the problem families were relatively impoverished for the standards of the day, so too were the comparison families. Tonge and colleagues went as far as to describe the comparison families as strikingly underprivileged, with two-thirds of them being close to the poverty line and seven comparison families being below the poverty line. Yet despite these far from affluent financial resources, the comparison families managed their lives adequately, were mostly in employment and generally behaved as solid, capable citizens. Moreover, of crucial importance here, the comparison families had fewer children than the problem families and on average their children were better cared for. This finding means that any differences in the number of children between the problem families and the comparison families cannot be explained away as side effects of significant differences in affluence or social class, but instead reflect some other causal factor, such as possessing a personality profile that increases responsiveness to the perverse incentives of the welfare state.

A farewell to alms

Let's begin this section with a thought experiment: imagine that your country is populated entirely by individuals with the employment-resistant personality profile but you need treatment for cancer. Who are you going to turn to? Is it likely that an individual with the employment-resistant personality profile will conscientiously study to acquire the knowledge required to become a competent oncologist, let alone be capable of the smooth, cooperative team work required to treat you successfully? What about when an engineer is required to design and build a new sewer system for your neighbourhood? How about if a new medicine is needed to treat a neurodegenerative disease that is killing a beloved member of your family?

All these highly skilled jobs and thousands of others like them are vital for the effective running of the modern world. Yet they are unlikely to be performed adequately by people with the employment-resistant personality profile because, as we saw in Chapter 2, regardless of intelligence level, their personality characteristics impair their willingness to work diligently and cooperatively.

With these considerations in mind, it seems plausible that modern, developed democracies thrive because people with the employment-resistant personality profile are vastly outnumbered by people with diligent, cooperative pro-employment personalities who are predisposed to study hard at school, to work for their living and, equally importantly, pay the taxes that fund infrastructure development. We know this is true because of studies of the epidemiology of antisocial personality traits. For example, Neumann and Hare (2008) studied a stratified random sample of 514 non-incarcerated US residents between 18 and 40 years of age (196 men, 318 women) via an industry-standard scale which uses a structured interview format to tot up the number of antisocial personality traits displayed by each participant (the PCL: SV; Hart, Cox & Hare, 1995).

This analysis showed that approximately 70 per cent of the participants displayed fewer than three antisocial personality traits, well within solid citizenship territory. In this study, a score of 13 symptoms or more was used to indicate a possible diagnosis of antisocial personality disorder: only 1.2 per cent of the population reached this cut-off (see Figure 4.1). This scale records instances of antisocial acts that the majority of the population have never committed, so it represents what is called a half-normal distribution.

Similar results have been found in the UK. For example, a survey of a representative sample of 638 non-incarcerated UK residents revealed that 70.8 per cent of the sample (452 individuals) displayed no antisocial personality traits at all and were what could be called solid citizens. Eleven individuals (1.7 per cent of the sample) scored high enough to be rated as possibly displaying antisocial personality disorder and one person scored high enough to be rated as probably displaying it (see Figure 4.2). The UK population is approximately 63 million at the time of writing. Using the findings summarised in Figure 4.2 as a rough guide, we can estimate that there are about

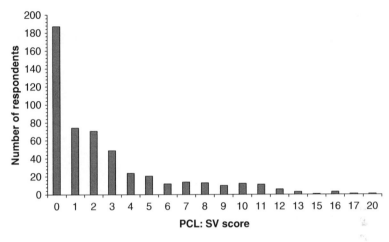

Figure 4.1 Distribution of antisocial personality traits in a sample of 514 US residents
Source: Neumann and Hare (2008).

100,000 people living in the UK (1 in 600 of the population) with personality profiles that are sufficiently antisocial to cause severe adjustment problems and about 1,000,000 people living in the UK (1 in 60 of the population) who are sufficiently antisocial to have some adjustment problems.

Overall, the findings shown in Figures 4.1 and 4.2 suggest that in the USA and UK approximately 70 per cent of the population are solid citizens, with only relatively few individuals distributed down the scale towards full-blown antisocial personality disorder. According to recent advances in economic history, it wasn't always this way: in his seminal 2007 book *A Farewell to Alms*, the leading economic historian Greg Clark challenged previous theories that the Industrial Revolution occurred in Britain in the eighteenth century because of the relatively sudden development of a stable society in Britain in the preceding century or so. According to Clark's research, compared to the rest of the world, Britain became unusually stable in political and economic terms from approximately AD 1100, much earlier than had previously been suspected. He argues that this much longer period of stability allowed a gradual, evolutionary change in the personality profile of the population towards greater cooperation

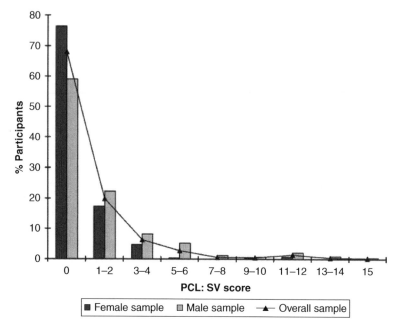

Figure 4.2 Distribution of antisocial personality traits in a sample of 638 UK residents
Source: Coid et al. (2009).

and diligence (in the jargon of personality research, that is higher scores on conscientiousness and agreeableness). It was this relatively slow change in personality that he suggested ultimately triggered the Industrial Revolution.

More specifically, Clark argues that the Industrial Revolution happened where and when it did because the increase in stability and peace of Britain from about 1100 significantly increased the economic pay-offs for cooperative, diligent and pro-social behaviour. Clark is not claiming that Britain from 1100 to 1800 was wholly tranquil but, in comparison to mainland Europe during the same time period, it was relatively sheltered from invasions, border changes, natural disasters and other agents of geo-political chaos. The sheltered and stable nature of British society from that time not only facilitated the accumulation of wealth through cooperative, diligent business endeavours but also the transmission of that wealth between generations via reliable pathways such as a legally binding system of wills and testaments, as well as reliable registers of property. Moreover, the stability of British society permitted increased scrutiny of the government by the people, as signified by such measures as Magna Carta, with the result that acts of despotism by the ruling elite (for example, imprisonment without trial and feudal payments) became progressively more difficult, further enhancing the opportunities and incentives for British people of that era to work steadily towards economic success.

As we saw in Chapter 2, some individuals are by chance particularly conscientious and agreeable. With the onset of a stable British society from approximately 1100, Clark suggests that these individuals began to out-compete economically individuals who were prone to impulsivity, selfishness and short-term thinking – what I have dubbed the employment-resistant personality profile. This differed from earlier, more chaotic eras in which it was maladaptive to plan for the future or work cooperatively because, in the absence of a stable society, any economic gains from behaving as a 'solid citizen' would easily be stolen or otherwise lost. Under those earlier conditions, Clark plausibly suggests that individuals with personality profiles inclining them to impulsivity, selfishness and short-term thinking would have had the upper hand.

Furthermore, by surveying a variety of relevant historical records such as wills and testaments, Clark found that economic success that highly conscientious and agreeable British people experienced between about 1100 and 1800 translated into greater reproductive success: the least economically successful people commonly raised no children at all and citizens of average income raised half the number of children compared to the most economically successful. Because the children of the economic elite tended to share, through both cultural and genetic inheritance, the diligent, cooperative personality profiles that had sprung their parents to success, solid citizen personality characteristics began to proliferate.

But, according to Clark, there weren't enough occupational niches at the top of society for all of the offspring of the economic elite, with the result that many of them filtered down to progressively more ordinary occupations. Clark calls this phenomenon downward mobility, with, for example, the offspring of wealthy landowners becoming farmers, their offspring becoming shopkeepers or teachers,

their offspring becoming farm labourers and so on. Since these down-
wardly mobile offspring of the economic elite tended to bring with
them to these lowly jobs the same pro-employment personality
characteristics that had caused the success of their ancestors, these
economically beneficial attributes became increasingly common and
thus boosted the overall economic effectiveness of society.

Eventually, by around the year 1800, Clark claims that this process triggered an economic and technological leap so enormous and
rapid, namely the Industrial Revolution, that it allowed Britain to
be the first country to escape the Malthusian trap. Other countries
with similar geo-political conditions to Britain followed suit rapidly,
so giving rise to the modern, developed world that we know today.
Crucially, Clark argues that, in parts of the globe with less stable
geo-political conditions, this personality moulding process favour-
ing conscientiousness and agreeableness has not occurred and so
attempts to impose Western-style industrialisation from outside have
generally seen little success because the average personality profile
of the population remains in a more employment-resistant state,
similar to the personality profile of Dark Age Britons. More briefly
stated, unless the solid citizen personality profile is prevalent in
the population, the seeds of industrialisation tend to fall on stony
ground.

For readers unfamiliar with the economic literature, the
Malthusian-trap concept explains why human societies up until the
Industrial Revolution stagnated economically and could not significantly increase their income. According to Clark's theory, the prevailing employment-resistant personality profile of the population
meant that the population in general was unable to work efficiently
enough to develop new technology at anything other than a slow
rate, so slow that it only ever boosted the efficiency of production
by a small amount and the resultant population increase consumed
the surplus. Average income then fell back to its former level, leaving
our ancestors trapped in a grim cycle of tiny improvements in living
standards followed by a rapid return to filth and squalor, fighting in
the mud for a less damp piece of sackcloth or a less mouldy piece of
turnip.

Viewed through the lens of personality research, Clark's findings
mean that the pro-employment personality characteristics that are
supposedly standard issue in the members of modern British society

(for example, turning up on time for appointments, working hard, doing what we are told, cooperating with our peers, looking after the weak, believing that one good turn deserves another) are by no means part of the typical human behavioural repertoire, but instead were moulded by natural selection in response to the peculiar environmental circumstances in the UK from about 1100 onwards that allowed particularly conscientious and agreeable people to prosper. Conversely, if circumstances change and employment-resistant individuals gain the reproductive upper hand – as I argue is happening due to the welfare state – then it is likely that the average personality profile of the population will swing back towards impulsivity, selfishness and short-term thinking with all the concomitant societal problems that will bring.

Personality and reproduction in the modern era

If it is true that the welfare state boosts the capacity of employment-resistant individuals to act upon their predisposition to r selection, we should find that, following the advent of the welfare state from the mid-twentieth century, there is an increasing tendency for the employment-resistant personality profile to be associated with relatively high rates of reproduction. Ideally, we should test this idea via longitudinal data, in which personality is measured in childhood and then compared to the total number of children that the participants have as adults. We saw in Chapter 3 that the Dunedin Study showed that childhood self-control is a proxy measure of employment-resistant personality characteristics: the lower the score on childhood self-control, the worse the individual tends to do in the world of work when they reach adulthood (Moffitt et al., 2011). We should therefore see evidence that relatively low levels of childhood self-control are associated with having relatively large numbers of children and that this tendency should become more pronounced in later cohorts as the welfare state becomes ever more entrenched in the culture of the nation.

In the UK there are two large cohort studies that are suitable for testing this idea since they both measured self-control in childhood and number of children, but crucially, the cohorts are separated by 12 years, meaning that they can be used to track changes over time in the link between personality and reproduction. In line with the notion that employment-resistant personality characteristics predispose individuals to having lots of children, both cohorts show a tendency for low levels of childhood self-control to be associated with having large numbers of children. But it is the increase over time of this effect that is important to the topic of this book. First, the National Child Development Study (NCDS) is following participants from their birth in one week in 1958, with the last survey point being at the age of 55 (7,219 participants provided full data). As can be seen in Figure 4.3, NCDS participants with five or more children scored on average 6 per cent lower on childhood self-control than participants with no children did.

Similarly, the British Cohort Study (BCS) follows participants from their birth in one week in 1970, with the most recent survey point being at the age of 42 (7,046 participants provided full data). Figure 4.4 shows that BCS participants with five or more children

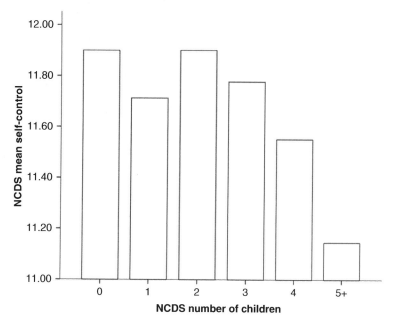

Figure 4.3   Childhood self-control and reproduction in a British cohort born in 1958
Source: National child development study.

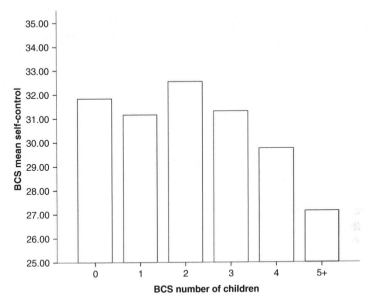

Figure 4.4 Childhood self-control and reproduction in a British cohort born in 1970
Source: British Cohort Study.

scored on average 15 per cent lower on childhood self-control than participants with no children did. This represents a doubling, in just 12 years, of the strength of the association between low scores on childhood self-control and having large numbers of children as an adult.

Viewed as a whole, the results of these two cohort studies – since they are 12 years apart, yet in the same nation – suggest that as the welfare state has become more entrenched in Britain, there has been a strengthening of the tendency for employment-resistant individuals to have large numbers of children. This finding could be a coincidence, but it is what we would expect to see if the welfare trait theory is correct. However, even if the finding is valid, both these cohort studies are based in the UK. It is therefore desirable to survey associations between personality and reproduction in other advanced nations that possess a welfare state in order to verify that this pattern generalises across nations and is not specific to British culture.

The study of personality and reproduction in humans is in its infancy but five studies have measured associations between number of offspring and personality questionnaire scores in advanced nations other than the UK. They can therefore provide some relevant insights into the topic. Three of these five studies support the notion that the reproductive fitness of the employment-resistant personality profile has changed since the era studied by Professor Clark, by finding that conscientiousness-domain scores were negatively correlated with reproduction. Jokela, Hintsa, Hintsanen and Keltikangas-Järvinen (2010) found that having more children was associated with low scores on persistence in 1,535 Finns. Similarly, in a sample of 8,373 US women, scores on conscientiousness were negatively associated with offspring number independent of educational level and parental SES (Jokela et al., 2011).

I have explored, with several colleagues, associations between reproduction and personality questionnaire scores in 4,981 women from four Australian samples. In two out of four of these samples, we found there were small but significant negative associations between reproductive fitness and personality measures in the conscientiousness domain (Perkins et al., 2013). In contrast, two other studies tell an opposite story, showing that reproductive fitness was positively correlated with social responsibility in 99 US women (Bogg & Roberts, 2004) and with conscientiousness in 2,900 Dutch women (Dijkstra & Barelds, 2009).

On balance therefore, the majority of these studies are consistent with the idea of a positive association in present-day developed nations between the employment-resistant personality profile and the tendency to have many children, but correlation does not necessarily indicate causation. In order to gain a more informative picture of the relationship between personality and reproduction, we require a study that measured the change in associations between personality and reproduction in different birth cohorts spanning pre-welfare state eras up to modern times.

Fortunately, another study by Jokela (2012) provides just such an analysis. This study used two major surveys that contained personality questionnaire scores and reproduction data in 10,253 US citizens with birth years that ranged from 1914 to 1970 (some of the same participants were studied in Jokela et al., 2011, so this study is not wholly separate from that one). Nevertheless, because it spanned successive birth cohorts, this follow-up study was able to reveal changes in personality–reproduction associations over time, showing that in women born in the 1910s and 1920s, reproductive fitness and conscientiousness were unrelated, but the negative association seen in modern studies emerged with increasing strength up to the final cohort of women who were born in the 1960s and 1970s.

Jokela (2012) hypothesised that this change is caused by the emancipation of the female labour force that began in the early part of the twentieth century which may have encouraged highly conscientious women to limit reproduction in order to build their careers. These data also fit the theory that the advent of the welfare state from the mid-twentieth century onwards may have progressively buffered the reproductive disadvantage of economic failure associated with low conscientiousness that, according to Greg Clark (2007), existed in pre-welfare eras.

Surveys by questionnaire of the type described above suffer from the limitation that they are voluntary and confer no material gain on the participant. It is therefore plausible that they reduce the effects of personality on reproduction, as they are more likely to be completed by citizens with relatively more conscientiousness and agreeable personalities, but miss data concerning people with the opposite personality profile, namely the employment-resistant personality profile that is the focus of this book. For this reason, it is valuable to turn to relevant data that are gathered under different circumstances, namely those where it is in the self-interest of the participant to complete the survey.

The second study in my publication that I reference above (Perkins et al., 2013) attempted to address exactly this question, since it used data from the Vietnam Experience Study (VES; US Department of Health & Centers for Disease Control, 1989) that gets round this problem of altruism skewing the results since participation in the study benefitted the participants. The reason for this was that the VES was initiated in response to growing public concerns in the 1970s and 1980s that the herbicide Agent Orange, which had been used in an attempt to make the location of communist forces easier by defoliating jungle in Vietnam, had damaged the health of US servicemen there.

The VES therefore compared the physical and mental health of US Army veterans who had served in Vietnam between 1965 and 1971 with that of veterans who had served during that same time period in territories where Agent Orange was not used (for example, Korea, Germany or the USA). A prominent concern relating to the use of Agent Orange during the Vietnam War was that it may have made the servicemen who were exposed to it less fertile. The VES therefore recorded offspring numbers. In addition, military discharge status and employment history after leaving the military were available for all participating veterans, making the cohort useful for the present research on the basis that participants with an employment-resistant personality profile would be less likely than average to receive an honourable discharge, and would go on to have a less satisfactory employment record. A key aspect of this data set was that failing to achieve an honourable discharge was rare. The vast majority of servicemen were honourably discharged (96.1 per cent), meaning that the non-honourably discharged servicemen can plausibly be seen as representing the extreme low end of the spectrum of employability rather than some slight tendency to be unreliable or difficult.

What we found was a pattern of results that supported the notion that the employment-resistant personality is associated with rapid, irresponsible reproduction. On average, honourably discharged servicemen fathered significantly fewer children than non-honourably discharged servicemen (1.79 children versus 1.98 children). The notion that the latter group of servicemen possessed an employment-resistant personality profile was backed up by the finding that despite around 15 years elapsing between leaving the military and being interviewed for the VES, in the three years before interview, the non-honourably discharged servicemen experienced an average of three times greater duration of unemployment compared to the honourably discharged servicemen (10.01 months unemployment versus 3.73 months). We went on to conclude that

> Since this finding persisted even when controlling for individual differences in cognitive ability, it points to an irresponsible personality profile amongst the non-honourably discharged men as, despite their seemingly chronic difficulty in holding down a job, the non-honourably discharged men nevertheless went ahead and

fathered more children than the occupationally more successful honourably discharged men.

(Perkins et al., 2013, p. 875)

This result fits the previous finding by Figueredo et al. (2006) that an *r*-selected reproductive strategy (rapid, irresponsible reproduction) is favoured by people with a personality profile that corresponds to my concept of employment-resistance. Moreover, although the VES did not include modern questionnaire measures of personality, it did obtain scores on the Minnesota Multiphasic Personality Inventory (MMPI-1; Hathaway & McKinley, 1940) for the subset of 4,459 participants who attended clinics to be studied in more detail for the VES. The MMPI questionnaire measures personality via ten clinical criterion-keyed scales that do not match the five-factor structure used in most modern personality questionnaires. Nevertheless, since it is plausible that clinical personality dysfunction will reduce employability, these MMPI data were examined with a view to providing a general assessment of whether men who failed to achieve an honourable discharge from the military had divergent personality traits in comparison to honourably discharged men.

In the 4,459 men in the VES with MMPI scores, those who were not honourably discharged scored significantly higher on seven out of the ten MMPI scales, most notably on the psychopathic deviate scale. This finding is important because the antisocial aspects of the employment-resistant personality profile mean it can be viewed as a mild form of antisocial personality disorder or psychopathy. This notion is backed up by the finding that individuals who have antisocial personality disorder are relatively lacking in both conscientiousness and agreeableness (for example, Lynam et al., 2005). It is further supported by our finding that servicemen who were not honourably discharged not only scored higher on psychopathic deviancy, but also had worse work records after leaving the military than those who were honourably discharged (Perkins et al., 2013).

Welfare and reproduction

The studies I have just summarised indicate that in the modern era, the employment-resistant personality profile is associated with having more children. This contrasts with pre-welfare eras when people who were economically unsuccessful – and thus presumably less conscientious and agreeable – tended to raise fewer children than average citizens (Clark, 2007). Since we already know that people with employment-resistant personalities are over-represented in the welfare-claiming sector of the population (Vaughn et al., 2010), this analysis suggests that we should see evidence that welfare claimants, on average, have more children than employed citizens. And we do.

For example, Table 4.1 summarises statistics on reproduction and employment in England and Wales for April–June 2013. These have the merit of measuring reproduction in three levels of reliance upon the welfare state: (a) working households, where every 16–64-year-old is employed; (b) mixed households, which contain both employed and unemployed adults; and (c) workless households, where all 16–64-year-olds are unemployed. This three-level measurement strategy shows that there is a positive linear association between reliance on the welfare state and average levels of reproduction in England and Wales: the higher the proportion of unemployed adults in a household, the greater the number of children (on average) that it contains. The implication contained in the data summarised in Table 4.1 is that a welfare state which provides a significant boost to household income for every child born is capable of boosting reproduction amongst claimants to a level higher than that of employed citizens.

However, raw, census-style data such as those shown in Table 4.1 take no account of confounding factors. For example, having an employment-resistant personality profile may indeed make a person more likely to claim welfare but it might also by chance be associated with biological characteristics that make reproduction easier (for example, the employment-resistant personality profile may be associated with more plentiful eggs in women or more vigorously

Table 4.1   Average number of children under the age of 16 in working, mixed and workless households in England and Wales during April–June 2013

	Working households	Mixed households	Workless households
Number of children	6,301,178	3,795,829	1,594,427
Number of households	3,877,455	2,181,509	872,757
Children per household	1.63	1.74	1.83

Source: Labour force survey household dataset.

swimming sperm in men). Alternatively, it may be the case that it is poverty in general rather than welfare claiming in particular that is the key factor in determining number of children, as it is widely accepted that since about 1880 in developed Western nations, poorer people tended to have more children than wealthy people, even when there was no welfare state (the so-called demographic transition; Clark, 2007).

Fortunately, these problems have been addressed by studies that explored effects of changes in welfare generosity on offspring numbers in welfare claimants and which show that increased welfare generosity increases the number of children born to claimants. This is the opposite pattern to that which we would expect if poverty increased reproduction. As an example, in the USA in 1996, the Personal Responsibility and Work Opportunity Reconciliation Act was introduced which ended the requirement for states to provide extra benefits to families who had additional children whilst on welfare, in an attempt to discourage families on welfare from having extra children (the so-called family cap). However, even before this act was signed into law, a number of states had received waivers from federal government that allowed them to cease providing extra benefits for extra children born to welfare claimants.

This situation created a natural experiment which was utilised by Argys et al. (2000) to compare the effects on reproduction of states with differing policies on the payment of financial benefits for children born to 1,168 unmarried women who reported receiving income from welfare during at least one year between 1979 and 1991. Argys et al. (2000) were also able to contrast differing levels of generosity between states that did pay extra benefits for each additional child born to a mother on welfare. For example, Argys et al. (2000) reported that in 1991, a mother in Mississippi would receive $101 on the birth of a second child whereas a mother in California would receive $178.

What Argys et al. (2000) found is that economic variables influence the reproductive behaviour of welfare-claiming women. The availability of incremental welfare benefits awarded for each additional child produced was positively and significantly associated with reproduction. This finding is congruent with those of other studies in the USA that show a similar tendency for increases in the generosity of welfare payments to be associated with increases in births amongst recipients (for example, Moffitt, 1998). However, Argys et al. (2000) additionally found that reductions in child-bearing in response to reduced welfare generosity were achieved by a decrease in pregnancies rather than an increase in abortions, concluding that: 'capping benefits will lead to a reduction in births by making women more efficient contraceptors as opposed to increasing abortions' (Argys et al., 2000, p. 584).

Overall these results suggest a willingness on the part of the women studied by Argys et al. (2000) to manipulate reproduction via contraception in order to maximise returns from per-child welfare benefits. The credibility of their findings is boosted by their congruence with earlier work showing that reproduction in general is sensitive to tax subsidies and universal child benefits (Whittington, Alm & Peters, 1990; Whittington, 1992; Milligan, 2005) and the general finding that spells on welfare support tend to be longer in response to increases in welfare generosity (O'Neill et al., 1987).

Evidence that welfare claimants tailor their reproductive behaviour according to whether it is financially worthwhile in terms of benefits claimed has also been found in the UK. In a bizarre coincidence, whilst the US government in the mid- to late 1990s was explicitly seeking to limit reproduction in welfare claimants by introducing the family cap, in 1999 the UK government boosted the generosity of per-child welfare payments by approximately 50 per cent in real terms. So generous were these welfare payments that the birth of a first child in a household in the bottom fifth of the UK income distribution would bring a cash benefit increase equivalent to a 10 per cent rise in net household income.

The effects of this change to UK welfare provisioning have been studied in detail by Brewer et al. (2011), revealing that reproduction is more sensitive to changes in welfare legislation than had ever previously been shown: not only did these increases in the generosity of per-child welfare in the UK in 1999 increase the number of children born to benefit recipients by approximately 15 per cent, but also this effect was nuanced according to the specific opportunity-cost circumstances of the individual women. Brewer et al. (2011) were able to show this because the increases in benefits were accomplished by increases in income support (for workless households) and the introduction of the Working Families' Tax Credit (WFTC), which resembles the US Earned Income Tax Credit (EITC) scheme, which was intended to increase financial incentives for welfare claimants with children to enter the labour force. Their analyses showed a bigger increase in births to women in couples than in single mothers, which reflected the effect of the WFTC rules that meant that mothers in couples whose partner worked 16 hours or more per week could leave the labour force altogether whilst nevertheless increasing their unearned income. Moreover, Brewer et al. (2011) found that the increase in reproduction in response was causally linked to the availability of more generous benefits, because they interviewed claimants and found that increases in reproduction were deliberately accomplished by discontinuation of contraception. This finding is in line with the earlier conclusion of Argys et al. (2000) that reductions in births in response to reductions in welfare benefits are accomplished by increased use of contraception.

These findings have been backed up by evidence from a different source, namely two recent analyses by the Office for National Statistics in the UK. First, a statistical bulletin released in July 2015 shows that there were 695,233 live births in England and Wales in 2014, a decrease of 0.5% from 698,512 in 2013. The bulletin proposed that the reduced fertility levels witnessed in 2014 could have been caused, in part, by the reductions in the generosity of welfare benefits that were implemented by the UK government in 2013. This analysis is congruent with the notion that welfare claimants voluntarily limit their fertility in response to reduced generosity of benefits. Second, it was found that women from 27 European nations who were living in England and Wales in 2011 on average had 0.34 more children than their compatriots at home. Furthermore, these data showed stratification according to the prosperity of the country of origin that is congruent with the idea that women from poorer nations who move to live in England and Wales are adjusting their birth rate upwards to take advantage of the more generous child benefit payments in the UK compared to their home nations. For example, women from nations with approximately similar levels of affluence to the UK who were living in England and Wales tended to have a similar number of children to women in their home country. For example, women from the Netherlands living in England and Wales in 2011 averaged 1.71 children and those living in the Netherlands averaged 1.76 children. In contrast, women living in England and Wales who came from much less affluent European nations typically had significantly more children than women who remained in their home country. For example, women from Romania living in England and Wales in 2011 averaged 2.93 children whereas those living in Romania averaged 1.25 children (source: Childbearing of UK and non-UK born women living in the UK – 2011 Census data; Office for National Statistics, 2014).

Viewed as a whole, these studies on reproduction and welfare seem to present two paradoxes. First, raising children generates work in its own right, so it might seem plausible that, instead of having extra children in order to increase welfare benefits, employment-resistant claimants should be deterred from doing so by the prospect of 18 years or so of childcare. Second, increases in household income due to greater welfare benefits should reduce disadvantage and therefore reduce risk of personality mis-development amongst the children of claimants.

Both these paradoxes can be resolved by remembering that in Chapter 3 we saw that children with relatively low self-control also turn out to have an increased risk of becoming teenage parents, suggesting that part of the employment-resistant personality is a lack of foresight. This suggests that employment-resistant claimants would indeed be more likely than average citizens to have extra children in response to welfare incentives, because their lack of foresight means they will focus on the short-term reward of increased child benefits and pay relatively little attention to the longer term reality that raising each extra child means 18 years of extra work.

The link shown in the Dunedin Study between the employment-resistant personality profile and rapid, irresponsible reproduction is confirmed by evidence from the study of problem families by Tonge et al. (1975). This showed that the problem families not only had significantly worse work records than the comparison families, but also had significantly more children. There were 200 offspring in the 33 problem families compared to 132 in the comparison families. More than 50 per cent of the problem families (17 families) had six or more children. In contrast, only nine comparison families had six or more children.

In the final chapter of their book, Tonge et al. (1975) listed the following four values as underpinning the maladjusted behaviour (including reproductive patterns) of the problem families: 1) rules were ignored; 2) discomfort was ignored; 3) long-term consequences were ignored; and 4) education was distrusted. The notion that the problem families were chasing extra welfare funds by having extra children, regardless of the long-term consequences, was echoed in the qualitative impressions of the researchers: for example, the researchers found that most of the problem families typically received sufficient welfare payments to cover the cost of such key necessities of life as food, clothing and heating. Yet instead of carefully husbanding their welfare money to ensure that their children were adequately provided for, the problem families tended to waste it on such needless items as expensive toys, luxury chocolates, cigarettes and alcohol, a spending pattern that typically left their children poorly fed, poorly clothed and in unheated houses.

This impression was supported empirically by the findings of Tonge and colleagues who compared the protectiveness of the mothers: whereas in the comparison families, 30 mothers were rated as normally or over-protective of their children, only ten of the problem family mothers gained this rating. In contrast, 20 mothers in the problem families were rated as under-protective or neglectful of their children, compared to just one mother in the comparison group. These data on protectiveness of mothers towards their children were backed up by the child mortality rates (per 1000 live births), which were 66 in the children of problem families and 39 in those of comparison families.

If we return for a moment to the ecological principle of r–K selection, this finding supports the notion that the employment-resistant personality profile biases the individual towards r selection (rapid, irresponsible, high-volume reproduction with little effort put into raising the offspring). Furthermore, by removing the need to compete for resources, the welfare state hands the reproductive upper hand to individuals who are biased towards r selection: individuals who, I argue, possess the employment-resistant personality profile. Additionally, the research of Tonge and colleagues suggests that simply throwing more money at the problem families would increase the frequency of unnecessary, impulse purchases (for example, electronic gadgets and luxury chocolates) but that the extra funds would not necessarily improve the situation of their children in any meaningful economic or social sense.

This pattern of irresponsible spending that is displayed by problem families is perhaps summed up best in a passage from Chapter 2 of their book, which addressed the challenge of finding the families:

At first glance it is difficult to single out problem families from others on the estates. All the houses are structurally similar, either terraced or semi-detached. They appear as endless rows of grimy brick and pebbledash, with doors painted in the colour chosen by the Public Works Department of the Corporation. On a grey day all merges imperceptibly with the horizon. On closer inspection the levelling effect of Corporation maintenance does not disguise everything. Here and there a front door knob is surrounded by black greasy marks, a window pane is broken or boarded up and curtains are half closed. Somehow the paint has weathered less well than on neighbouring houses and the front garden is characteristic. An overgrowth of natural flora competes with broken bottles, sodden cardboard and the rusting remains of once-expensive toys, prams, cycle parts and other scrap. A well-worn earth path leads from the dominant door to the pavement by the most direct route which involves a hole in the hedge or a section of shattered fencing.

(Tonge et al., 1975, p. 11)

Conclusion

Organisms can optimise their fitness either by having many offspring, but investing little effort in their raising (*r* selection) or having fewer offspring and conscientiously nurturing them (*K* selection). The utility of these strategies is influenced by resource availability: when resources are freely available, *r* selection is optimal, but when resources must be competed for, *K* selection is optimal. In humans, individuals with personality characteristics approximating to the employment-resistant personality profile are biased towards *r* selection. In pre-welfare times (at least when the geopolitical situation was stable, such as in pre-Industrial Revolution Britain), employment-resistant individuals appear to have been at a reproductive disadvantage owing to their problem of maintaining an income, but since then, the employment-resistant personality profile has gained the reproductive upper hand. I argue that one contributory factor to this shift in fitness from *K* selection to *r* selection in modern humans is the reduction in competition for resources that is brought about by the advent of the welfare state.

5

Childhood Disadvantage and Employment-Resistance

The next three chapters of this book summarise evidence on the transmission of personality characteristics from parents to children. This theme is important because, if it was the case that personality characteristics were not transmitted between generations, then a welfare state that boosts the number of children born to employment-resistant claimants would not affect the personality profile of the population. The child of a welfare claimant would be just as likely to become a conscientious and agreeable 'solid citizen' as the child of an employed person.

In the previous chapter, we saw evidence that individuals with the employment-resistant personality profile are especially likely to maltreat their children. In this chapter, we shall see evidence that child maltreatment is a significant cause of employment-resistant personality characteristics. Viewed as a whole, these two findings point to the existence of a trans-generational cycle of maltreatment, in which today's maltreated children become tomorrow's employment-resistant perpetrators of child maltreatment. More generally, it seems that employment-resistant personality characteristics can be transmitted from parents to children by a purely environmental mechanism, namely exposure to maltreatment as a child.

When considering the topic of child maltreatment, it is natural to focus on extreme, headline-grabbing cases, such as when a child spends years chained up alone in a darkened basement, or is used as a sex slave, or injected with heroin to quieten him or her down. These children would be expected to suffer personality mis-development,

79

yet such cases are thankfully extremely rare and cannot plausibly account for personality mis-development on a large enough scale to cause significant alterations to human capital.

In contrast, milder forms of maltreatment, such as parental neglect or inattention, are unlikely to make tabloid headlines and so may be overlooked as a cause of personality mis-development. Yet there is evidence that this milder type of maltreatment can impair child development. Moreover, as we saw in the previous chapter, research by Tonge and colleagues suggests that child maltreatment of the passive type – what I shall henceforth refer to as child neglect – is significantly more common amongst welfare-claiming, employment-resistant parents than it is amongst employed parents, even though the latter have less free time than the former. The first aim of this chapter is to summarise studies supporting these claims.

However, suggestions are not enough to prove a scientific point: the studies I have cited so far do not tell us conclusively that neglect has a significant role in causing children to turn out to be more employment-resistant than children who have not been neglected. Even if they could do this, these studies still cannot disentangle whether it really is child neglect that is driving this effect, as opposed to genetic inheritance. Nor can such studies eliminate the possibility that it is poverty that is driving this effect, rather than being a welfare claimant per se. To answer these questions we need to turn to research that combines a longitudinal design with proper experimental controls. In other words, we need to look at experiments in which disadvantaged children are randomly assigned to receive *in loco parentis* intensive preschool tutoring and then their life outcomes as adults are systematically compared to those of children who have not been given such tutoring.

Five experiments meet these rigorous scientific standards, four from the USA and one from Canada. These experiments show that disadvantaged children who received intensive preschool tutoring turn out to have significantly higher human capital as adults than non-tutored children because their personalities are on average less aggressive, antisocial and rule-breaking (that is, less employment-resistant) than those of the non-tutored children (for example, Heckman et al., 2013). Moreover, cost–benefit analyses comparisons of interventions aimed at boosting human capital strongly suggest that childhood experiences have a disproportionately large effect

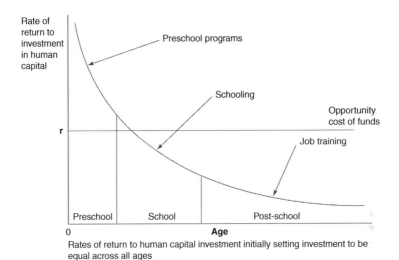

Figure 5.1 The rate of return of childhood versus adult interventions
Source: Cunha et al., 2006.

on the development of personality-related aspects of human capital (Heckman, 2013). This literature is summarised in Figure 5.1, which implies that adult interventions aimed at fixing a mis-developed personality are like attempts to add more eggs to a cake that has already been baked: difficult, costly and largely ineffective.

Effects of child neglect on personality development

The effect on offspring development of a form of neglect that is often dubbed 'parental inattention' has been studied extensively in non-human animals. For example, Liu, Diorio, Day, Francis and Meaney (2000) showed that mouse pups subjected to lower levels of maternal attention had worse cognitive development, even when cross-fostered to remove the effect of genetic inheritance. Weaver et al. (2004) found that differences in the level of maternal attention in mouse pups caused differences in DNA methylation that lasted into adulthood. In monkeys, maternal inattention causes impaired development via a similar mechanism (Provençal et al., 2012). Furthermore, environmental enrichment around puberty in mouse pups partially reversed the negative effects of maternal neglect on cognitive development (Bredy et al., 2003).

The effects of parental inattention on human development have been studied in detail with regard to language usage in different types of households, suggesting that welfare-claiming parents are less attentive to their children than employed parents are, despite having more free time. For example, Hart and Risley (1995) studied verbal interactions between adults and children in 42 families with a view to examining the effect of home experiences on child development. The families were observed for one hour per month for almost two and a half years, with the child participants entering the study at the age of ten months and leaving it when they were three years of age. Each family was assigned to one of three socio-economic groups depending upon the occupational level of the parents: professional, working class and welfare claimant. Importantly, this was not intended to be a study of child neglect per se, so only families rated by the experimenters as well-functioning were admitted to the study. This design feature meant any differences in language development between the groups could not be explained away as the by-product of gross parental dysfunction, such as might be caused by psychiatric illness or abandonment.

Nevertheless, what Hart and Risley (1995) found was relevant to this book. First, there were no significant differences between the children in the three groups of families in the age at which they began to speak, or in the structure and use of language. However, children from professional families heard an average of 2,153 words per hour, compared to an average of 1,251 words per hour for working-class children and 616 words per hour for the children of welfare claimants. Moreover, these differences in word flow from parents to children had significant effects on the development of the children. At three years of age, children in the professional families possessed a cumulative vocabulary of approximately 1,100 words, compared to 750 words for children from working-class families and 500 words for children from welfare-recipient families.

Since one avenue for moulding our behaviour patterns is via speech from parent to child (well done, do this, don't do that and so on), this discovery by Hart and Risley (1995) suggests that children of welfare claimants have a built-in disadvantage when it comes to acquiring adequate levels of social functioning, namely that their parents barely speak to them. Just how damaging this form of neglect can be was summarised in a recent OECD report on child development:

> Family disadvantage is poorly assessed by conventional measures of poverty that focus on family income, wealth, and parental education. The absence of parental guidance, nourishment, and encouragement is the most damaging condition for child development. Quality parenting – stimulation, attachment, encouragement, and support – is the true measure of child advantage, and not the traditional measures of poverty commonly used in policy discussions.
>
> (Kautz et al., 2014, p. 12)

The notion that parental inattention is a key ingredient in personality mis-development is backed up by research with GED recipients by James Heckman and colleague which shows that 'Compared to high school graduates, GED recipients are more likely to come from broken families with low incomes and have parents who invest less in their character and cognitive development' (Heckman & Kautz, 2014, p. 7). More specifically, Heckman and colleagues found that, relative to high-school graduates, GED recipients in childhood (up to age seven) had less access to books, magazines, toys, CD/tape players and musical instruments and were less likely to be read to, taken to cultural events and have meaningful verbal interactions (Heckman, Humphries & Kautz, 2014a).

Since we have already seen in Chapter 2 that GED recipients on average possess a personality profile that is less conscientious and agreeable than that of high-school graduates and also have worse employment records, these data on the family backgrounds of GED recipients provide credible support for the notion that parental inattentiveness promotes the development of the employment-resistant personality profile. Evidence for the importance of verbal interaction with parents in determining the quality of a child's life has also been found in the UK. For example, a study by the Office of National Statistics which was entitled 'Measuring National Well-being – Exploring the Well-being of Children in the UK, 2014', utilised data from the UK household longitudinal study (now known as 'understanding society'), which began surveying 40,000 households from the

UK in 2009 (approximately 100,000 individuals). These households will be surveyed regularly on a rolling basis, with a view to building a richly detailed picture of UK life. The adults in the survey are interviewed every year and 10–15-year-olds fill in a paper self-report questionnaire.

The key finding in the present context is that children who had relatively high satisfaction with their life in general also had better communication with their parents. For example, in 2011–2012, 69.7 per cent of children between ten and 15 years old who were relatively satisfied with their life quarrelled less than once a week with their parents. In contrast, 41 per cent of children who were relatively unsatisfied quarrelled more than once a week with their parents (see Figure 5.2).

It is unsurprising that frequent quarrels with parents reduce life satisfaction in children because quarrelling is a specifically negative form of communication. But the study also provides evidence that lack of meaningful parent–child communication in general is bad

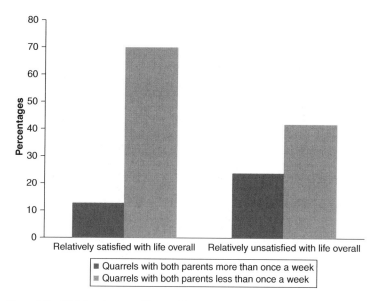

Figure 5.2   Children's quarrelling with parents by satisfaction with life overall, 2011–2012

Source: UK household longitudinal study, now known as 'understanding society'.

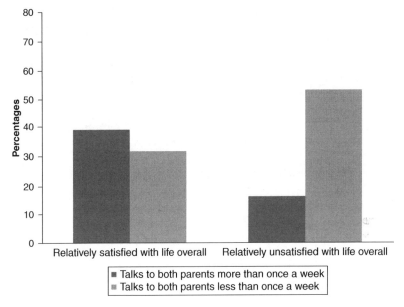

Figure 5.3 Children's talk with parents by satisfaction with life overall, 2011–2012
Source: UK household longitudinal study, now known as 'understanding society'.

for child well-being. For example, children who were relatively satisfied with life in general were approximately 2.5 times more likely to talk to their parents about important issues more than once a week than children who were relatively unsatisfied with life in general (see Figure 5.3).

These findings are correlational and so do not demonstrate causation, because low satisfaction ratings amongst children could be a product of impaired parent–child communication or they could be a cause of it, or they could arise from a third variable. But these findings are congruent with the notion that a lack of interest displayed by parents in their children is not only harmful to the vocabulary development of those children – as shown by Hart and Risley (1995) – but also to their subjective sense of satisfaction.

A specific link between parental inattention and the development of antisocial personality traits has been provided by a recent study of 213 children from the Liverpool area (Bedford et al., 2014). This study showed that lower levels of maternal attentiveness predicted higher levels of antisocial personality traits in girls, suggesting that parental inattention can promote the development of antisocial personality traits (at least in females).

In this study, children were not randomly assigned to mothers so the authors could not rule out the possibility that inattentive mothers possess antisocial traits that they pass onto their daughters via genetic rather than environmental means. However, despite this possibility, there appeared to be a genuine environmental effect of maternal inattentiveness upon antisocial personality development amongst daughters because the authors found that this effect remained significant even when maternal personality was statistically controlled.

Viewed together with the findings by Hart and Risley (1995) that welfare claimants talk to their children less often than employed parents do, the results of Bedford et al. (2014) suggest that this lower level of attentiveness risks promoting antisocial personality traits in their children (especially their daughters). This conclusion might seem absurd, since paying attention to one's children costs time, not money, and time is one resource that welfare claimants have in abundance compared to employed citizens. Yet my conclusion is echoed in the Sheffield problem family study by Tonge and colleagues (1975) cited in the previous chapter: the problem families in the Sheffield study, despite having higher rates of unemployment and thus more free time, were significantly more neglectful of their children than the more fully employed comparison families.

This finding suggests that the children of welfare-claiming parents are not only at higher risk of being ignored, but also of being under-provided with the necessities of life, despite the availability of welfare funds. The negative effects of this neglect were evident in the 1981 follow-up, since the children of the problem families turned out as adults to have significantly worse work and criminal records than the children of the comparison families (Tonge et al., 1981). Viewed together with the results of Hart and Risley (1995) and Bedford et al. (2014), the Sheffield studies therefore suggest employment-resistance is transmitted from parents to children and that child neglect is implicated as a key environmental factor in that transmission.

But the research in Sheffield did not allow a clean disentangling of genetic and environmental effects on personality development because, as Tonge and colleagues themselves observed: 'Psychopathic parents provide a psychopathic inheritance and a psychopathic upbringing, which includes both desertion and a failure to teach the values and norms of society' (Tonge et al., 1975, p. 37). In order to demonstrate the purely environmental effects of early childhood neglect on later life outcomes, it is necessary to turn to a group of five experiments in which children from disadvantaged families were randomly assigned to receive intensive preschool tutoring. These experiments come at the issue of child neglect from the opposite direction by using intensive preschool tutoring to counter the effects of neglect, then assessing the effects of this tutoring on life outcomes in adulthood.

David Weikart and the Perry Preschool Project

Born in 1931 in Ohio to parents who were social workers and teachers, David Weikart completed a psychology degree at Oberlin College in 1953 and then served as an officer in the US Marine Corps during the Korean War. Weikart started his PhD in education and psychology at the University of Michigan in 1956 and shortly afterwards began working as a school psychologist for the Ypsilanti public schools in Ypsilanti, Michigan. Through his experiences in this job, Weikart became concerned at the educational difficulties faced by children from disadvantaged African-American backgrounds and the apparent indifference towards these children by the local authorities. In response, Weikart and several reform-minded colleagues decided to test experimentally the possibility that disadvantaged children could be helped by intensive preschool tutoring programmes designed to increase intellectual maturity at three and four years old, in order to prepare them for a successful school career and a productive adult life. In order to find out if preschool programmes were effective, Weikart and colleagues hired four teachers to conduct intensive tutoring with the children in the experimental group and launched the Perry Preschool Project in October 1962, running until the spring of 1967.

The study participants were 123 children between three and four years old on enrolment, who were all from low-income African-American families in Ypsilanti and who were considered at high risk of school failure. These children were randomly assigned to either the experimental group (58 children) or the control group (65 children). Before the project began, the experimental- and control-group children were equivalent in intellectual performance and their demographic characteristics, with both groups being recruited from disadvantaged families. The experimental group of children attended the intensive tutoring classes for approximately three hours a day, five days a week, during term time for two years. The children in the experimental group also had a 90-minute home visit by the same teacher every week. The control-group children did not have the special classes and home visits.

Every year from the age of three to 11 the progress of both groups was assessed and follow-up assessments were conducted again at the age of 14–15, 19, 27 and 40. These follow-ups showed that the educational and life outcomes for the children in the experimental group were significantly superior to outcomes for the children in the control group. For example, in a review of the economic benefits of preschool intervention published in *Science Magazine*, the Nobel Prize-winning economist James Heckman summarised the Perry preschool results thus: 'In follow ups to age 40, the treated group had higher rates of high school graduation, higher salaries, higher percentages of home ownership, lower rates of receipt of welfare assistance as adults, fewer out-of-wedlock births, and fewer arrests than the controls' (Heckman, 2006, p. 1901). In the context of this book, these results mean the treated children turned out to be better adjusted than those who did not receive tutoring or, in other words, the preschool tutoring made their personalities less employment-resistant.

More specifically, in education, 77 per cent of the participants in the experimental group graduated from high school whereas only 60 per cent of the control participants did so and, in the females, the effect was even stronger with 88 per cent of the experimental group graduating compared to 46 per cent of the control group. In economic terms, at the age of 40, significantly more of the experimental group were in work (76 per cent) compared to the control group (62 per cent). The experimental group also had significantly higher median annual earnings at the age of 40 ($20,800 versus $15,300). Effects of the preschool programme on crime prevention were especially strong, with 55 per cent of the control group being arrested five times or more compared to 36 per cent of the experimental group. Similarly, by age 40, 28 per cent of the experimental group had served a prison sentence compared to 52 per cent of the control group. Finally, the preschool programme had a large beneficial effect on parenting in men, with almost twice as many of the males from the experimental group raising their own children (57 per cent) compared to the males from the control group (30 per cent; Schweinhart et al., 2005).

The economic relevance of the Perry Preschool Project has been confirmed by detailed follow-up analyses. These revealed that by the time the participants reached the age of 40, the Perry Preschool Project had returned approximately $16 for every dollar spent running it. Broken down into specific financial areas, 88 per cent of the benefit came from reductions in crime, four per cent from reduced costs of education, seven per cent from increased tax revenue due to higher earnings and one per cent came from welfare savings (Schweinhart et al., 2005).

The interesting finding in the context of this book was that the preschool programme did not permanently boost IQ. Early gains in the IQ scores of the experimental-group children were found during and for a year after the study, but these gains did not last and, from that time on, there were no significant long-term differences in IQ between the two groups of participants. This is unsurprising considering behaviour genetic studies have shown that IQ is more strongly determined by the individual's genetic make-up than personality and therefore likely to be less amenable to environmental influence (Plomin et al., 2008).

So if the preschool programme wasn't improving their IQ, what aspect of the children's psychological make-up did it improve? A clue can be found in its teaching content. David Weikart and colleagues had designed the preschool programme to build the children's skills in planning, executing and reviewing tasks and also in conflict resolution. This suggests that the programme served to improve the social adjustment of the children by training them to be forward-looking, dependable, cooperative and thus economically effective citizens. These characteristics at face value are associated with high scores on conscientiousness and agreeableness (McCrae & Costa, 2008) and form the pro-employment personality profile that I argue reduces likelihood of welfare dependency. This impression is backed up by a recent study, cited in Chapter 1, in which James Heckman and colleagues showed that the tutored children were better equipped to behave as solid citizens during adulthood because the tutoring caused their personality profiles to be, on average, less aggressive, antisocial and rule-breaking than those of their peers who were not tutored (Heckman et al., 2013).

The Abecedarian Project

The Abecedarian Project was designed to assess the benefits of a high-quality preschool tutoring programme starting at an earlier stage and lasting longer than the intervention delivered by previous studies such as the Perry Preschool Project. Like the Perry Preschool Project, the participants were children from low-income families and at high risk of school failure, but unlike the Perry Preschool Project, participants were typically enrolled within four months of birth and received the preschool teaching programme until five years of age. Running in North Carolina, the Abecedarian Project enrolled 111 participants between 1972 and 1977 and had good rates of retention, with 104 of the infants originally enrolled remaining in contact with the study administrators until 21 years old. Potential participants had been identified on the basis of 13 socio-demographic risk factors such as coming from an impoverished background, having an absent father and the mothers typically being around 20 years old, unmarried, poorly educated and unemployed. Participants were paired according to their scores on the 13 risk factors and then randomly assigned to the experimental group or the control group. In total, 57 infants were in the preschool experimental-intervention group (29 boys, 28 girls) and 54 infants (23 boys, 31 girls) were assigned to the control group.

The preschool intervention consisted of a broad spectrum of educational games designed to accelerate language, cognitive, motor and social-emotional development. These started with basic adult–child interactions of the type that a normal mother would undertake without requiring government intervention, such as talking to the child, playfully showing them objects or pictures and allowing them to explore and react to the environment. The interventions then became more advanced as the child grew, increasingly targeting the development of language, conceptual and social skills. At all times, the programme was designed to give the child freedom to explore and express their individuality.

At the end of the preschool programme, cognitive test scores at 48 months were then used to pair each participant from the experimental group with a matching participant from the control group. Half the matched pairs were then assigned to receive further interventions in the first three years of primary school whilst the other half received no further intervention. This step created four final experimental groups: EE (participants who received preschool + primary school interventions), EC (participants with preschool intervention only), CE (participants who received primary school intervention only) and CC (participants who received no interventions). The participants who were allocated to receive primary school interventions were assigned a home-school resource teacher (HST) who liaised between the school and family and served to increase family involvement with the child's schooling. To assist this process, every two weeks, each participant received a curriculum pack prepared to match the child's individual learning needs, as assessed by the classroom teacher. Parents were encouraged to use this pack for 15 minutes a day.

Results of the Abecedarian Project participants at the age of 21 are broadly similar to those of the Perry Preschool Project, except that criminality was not reduced in the Abecedarian preschool group and a small IQ gain persisted in adulthood for the Abecedarian participants who received the preschool programme, possibly because the Abecedarian intervention started within a few months of birth and lasted twice as long as the Perry Preschool Project, giving it a greater opportunity to improve the brain development of the child. More specifically, the Abecedarian participants who received the preschool programme completed significantly more years of education than controls and showed better maths and reading skills. They also were significantly more likely than controls to have a skilled job. With regard to parenthood, the participants who had received the preschool programme were significantly less likely than controls to become teenage parents and even within the group of preschool programme women who had given birth by the age of 21, significantly fewer reported second or third births.

Interestingly, the preschool programme also benefited the parents of the participants, with teenage mothers of participants assigned to the experimental group making significantly better educational and employment progress than teenage mothers of control-group participants. Marijuana and cigarette smoking was significantly lower in the treated group of participants. Results suggested the school-age treatment programme helped to preserve the effects of the preschool-age programme, but the school-age effects were generally not as strong, suggesting that interventions aimed at boosting life outcomes in disadvantaged children are best implemented before the age of five, and preferably from birth (Campbell et al., 2002).

Cost–benefit analyses of the Abecedarian Project show that for every dollar spent on childcare approximately $4 was saved in later expenditure by the time the participants got to the age of 21. This is substantially smaller than the level of savings estimated for the Perry Preschool Project ($16 saved per dollar spent), but it should be noted that the full benefits for that study only emerged by the age of 40. When Perry Preschool participants were followed up at the age of 27, similar to the age of follow-up for the Abecedarian Project, the Perry Preschool Project saved a much more modest $7 for every dollar spent. Also, it should be noted that the Abecedarian Project implemented childcare from birth to five years, a longer and more costly intervention than the Perry Preschool Project.

The Abecedarian participants have most recently been followed up at the age of 30, demonstrating excellent retention (of the 111 participants who were originally enrolled as babies, 101 remained at the age 30 follow-up) and revealing that the benefits of the intervention are still persisting. For example, the treated participants on average completed a year more of education than the control participants and were four times more likely than the untreated participants to have earned a college degree by the age of 30. Furthermore, 75 per cent of the treated participants were in full-time employment, compared to 53 per cent of the untreated participants. Similarly, in the 89-month time window during which comparisons were made for the age 30 follow-up, the untreated participants were over six times more likely to claim welfare than the treated group were (Campbell et al., 2012).

More recently, researchers assessed the health of Abecedarian participants at the age of 30. This revealed that treated participants (particularly males) have significantly lower risk of cardiovascular and metabolic diseases. For example, on average, the systolic blood pressure in untreated males was 143 mmHg, compared to an average of 126 mmHg in the treated males. Furthermore, approximately 25 per cent of the untreated males suffered from metabolic syndrome, compared to none of the treated males (Campbell et al., 2014). The methodology of this study was unable to determine conclusively the mechanism by which preschool tutoring caused these later health differences, but the authors suggested that, as in the Perry Preschool Project, the Abcedarian interventions may have improved personality characteristics which then improved health-related behaviours.

Project CARE

The Carolina Approach to Responsive Education (also known as Project CARE) aimed to build on the Abecedarian Project by comparing outcomes for three different experimental groups: the control group (no intervention), family group (weekly home visits only) and the family plus centre group (weekly home visits plus daily centre-based childcare). In most other respects, Project CARE closely replicated the study design of the Abecedarian Project. Prospective participants were selected using the same high-risk index and the background variables such as family environment and geographical location were the same. The interventions given to the children were also very similar to those in the Abecedarian Project, including the continuation of treatment after the children began attending primary school.

Participants in Project CARE were born between 1978 and 1980. A total of 66 infants were enrolled, with 16 assigned randomly to the control group, 27 to the family group and 23 to the family plus centre group. As with the Abecedarian Project, retention was high, with 60 of the 66 participants being followed up in adulthood, at an average age of 22.5 years. The life outcome follow-up measures used on Project CARE were similar to those in the Abecedarian Project, but abbreviated. The participants were not tested on psychological attributes such as IQ but were thoroughly assessed with regard to important biographical variables such as educational achievement, employment history, parenthood, marriage and criminality.

With regard to education and employment, the Project CARE results showed the centre-based intervention was successful and in close agreement with the Abecedarian findings: compared to controls, participants who had received the experimental treatment were seven times more likely to be in some form of educational programme at the time of follow-up. The experimental group were almost twice as likely to be in skilled employment compared to the control group. Importantly, these benefits only applied to the participants who had received weekly home visits plus daily centre-based childcare. The participants who received only the weekly home visits showed no meaningful differences to the control group, suggesting that daily intensive teaching out of the home is required to offset the negative effects on education and employment of being born into a disadvantaged family.

Insufficient numbers of the CARE participants had got married or had children to provide any meaningful results on that topic, which is unsurprising considering they were 22 years old at time of survey. For health and social adjustment measures, the CARE participants who received the centre-based intervention were four times more likely to report an active lifestyle (for example, sports participation) than the control participants were. In contrast to the Abecedarian results, the experimental group of CARE participants smoked more than the control group did. Also there were no significant differences between the groups on law-breaking and also there was no effect of the experimental programme. Effects on life outcomes in Project CARE of the treatment programme after participants attended primary school were minimal, as was also found in the Abecedarian Project. Overall, therefore, the results of Project CARE suggest (a) that special centre-based treatment for disadvantaged children ideally needs to happen from birth until primary school and that interventions later in life are not nearly as effective; and (b) Project CARE confirms the Abecedarian finding that the key benefits of early childhood intervention are in making children more effective in education and in the workplace (Campbell et al., 2008).

The Chicago Longitudinal Study

The Chicago Longitudinal Study (CLS) began in 1986 to evaluate the effectiveness of the Chicago Child–Parent Center (CPC) programme, one of the longest running initiatives in the USA intended to boost preschool learning of disadvantaged children. This programme offered preschool teaching for three-year-olds or four-year-olds, beginning in 1967 with four centres and expanding to include some 25 centres to date. The CLS was notable in having far larger sample sizes than previous studies and for using a non-randomised cohort study design: in total, 1,539 participants were enrolled, with 989 completing CPC preschool and kindergarten and 550 children receiving kindergarten only. For the school-age part of the study, 850 children who had participated in the extended (school-age) intervention were compared to those who had non-extended intervention (689), irrespective of whether or not they had received preschool teaching.

The CLS results for the 15-year follow-up showed that participants who received preschool intervention had a significantly higher rate of high-school completion than control participants (49.7 per cent versus 38.5 per cent) and a lower rate of school dropout (46.7 per cent versus 55.0 per cent). Participating in the extended programme made no significant difference to later educational attainment. Participants who received preschool intervention had a significantly lower arrest rate than controls did (16.9 per cent versus 25.1 per cent). Participation in the extended programme had no significant effect on criminality. However, participants in the extended childhood-intervention program had lower rates of special education enrolment (13.5 per cent versus 20.7 per cent) and grade retention (21.9 versus 32.3 per cent) by their late teenage years (Reynolds et al., 2001).

The Montreal Longitudinal Experimental Study

The Montreal Longitudinal Experimental Study began in 1984 with the aim of assessing the impact on life outcome of an intervention programme during kindergarten (Boisjoli et al., 2007). At six years of age, 895 boys from 53 kindergarten schools in impoverished areas of Montreal were rated by their teachers on a social behaviour questionnaire, which included a measure of disruptiveness. The boys who scored above the 70th percentile on disruptiveness (250 boys in total) were assigned randomly to one of three groups: prevention (69 boys), attention-control (123 boys) and control (58 boys). The remaining 645 boys served as the low-risk group. The boys in the prevention group received training in social skills for two years (46 participated) from the age of seven to nine. Training took place at school in groups of four to seven children with a ratio of one disruptive boy to three pro-social children. The parents of the boys were also trained in effective child-rearing and the teachers received information and support concerning how to work with at-risk children.

The boys were followed up 15 years later, revealing that the social skills training intervention reduced criminality and increased academic performance. In both cases, the treated at-risk boys were closer to the low-risk boys, relative to the at-risk boys who were not trained. For example, 32.6 per cent of the untreated at-risk group (59 boys) had a criminal record, compared to 21.7 per cent of the treated at-risk group (15 boys) and 16.1 per cent of the low-risk boys (104 boys). Similarly, 32.2 per cent of the untreated at-risk group (56 boys) graduated from high school, compared to 45.6 per cent of the treated at-risk group (31 boys) and 53.4 per cent of the low-risk boys (340 boys).

Conclusion

Child neglect is the active ingredient in the environmental transmission of the employment-resistant personality profile from parents to children. This takes the form of a trans-generational cycle of neglect, since child neglect not only increases risk of personality misdevelopment, but also makes the victim more likely to perpetrate child neglect when they are a parent themselves.

6
Genetic Influences on Personality

This chapter summarises evidence for the genetic transmission of personality characteristics from parents to offspring. This topic might seem like a matter for debate or even controversy, but it isn't: long before the advent of behaviour genetics as a scientific discipline, farmers used selective breeding to mould the psychological as well as anatomical characteristics of their livestock. For example, sheep are docile and passive farm animals yet the wild sheep from which they are descended are feisty creatures. This change in sheep personality is not the result of education, but instead has been achieved by centuries of selective breeding for docility.

Charles Darwin's rural background no doubt gave him a head start when it came to understanding the power of selective breeding to alter psychological characteristics. He was certainly aware of it, as demonstrated by this bold statement in the final chapter of the *Origin of Species*: 'Psychology will be based on a new foundation, that of the necessary acquirement of each mental power and capacity by gradation' (Darwin, 1859, p. 458). I say this was a bold statement because psychology barely existed as a scientific discipline at the time and, indeed, the first psychological laboratory was not set up until 20 years later (by Wilhelm Wundt at Leipzig University, in 1879).

The theoretical framework for this chapter is therefore a well-known one, namely evolution by natural selection. It has been called 'the single best idea anyone has ever had' (Dennett, 1996, p. 21) and more words have probably been written about it than any other scientific theory. This might give the impression that it is difficult to understand. It isn't. As I intimated above, natural selection is just like selective breeding for docility by farmers, except that instead of a farmer selecting which animals get to pass on their genes, it is the environment in the broadest sense of the word (such as climate, other organisms and geological factors).

The twist on the theme of natural selection in this book is that the environmental change in question is the advent of welfare legislation which serves to boost the number of children born to claimants. Since we have already seen that the employment-resistant personality profile is over-represented amongst welfare claimants (for example, Vaughn et al., 2010), we can accept that the genes for employment resistance will also be over-represented amongst them. This suggests the genes in question could be proliferated by a welfare state, such as that in the UK, which can cause claimants on average to have more children than employed citizens (see Table 4.1). As I argue that welfare legislation is the driving force in the evolution of personality towards greater employment-resistance, we could dub the process 'legislative selection' rather than natural selection, but it means the same thing. Whatever its label, the idea of genetically-based, welfare-induced personality mis-development is not mine: it was first proposed by the eminent biologist Richard Dawkins in his 1976 book *The Selfish Gene*.

This brilliant book is deservedly famous for setting out the gene's eye view of natural selection, but it also contains a concise evolutionary analysis of the personality-changing effects of the welfare state:

> Individuals who have too many children are penalized, not because the whole population goes extinct, but simply because fewer of their children survive. Genes for having too many children are just not passed on to the next generation in large numbers, because few of the children bearing these genes reach adulthood. What has happened in modern civilized man is that family sizes are no longer limited by the finite resources that the individual parents can provide. If a husband and wife have more children than they can feed, the state, which means the rest of the population, simply steps in and keeps the surplus children alive and healthy. There is, in fact, nothing to stop a couple with no material resources at all having and rearing precisely as many children as the woman can physically bear. But the welfare state is a

very unnatural thing. In nature, parents who have more children than they can support do not have many grandchildren, and their genes are not passed on to future generations. There is no need for altruistic restraint in the birth-rate, because there is no welfare state in nature. Any gene for overindulgence is promptly punished: the children containing that gene starve. Since we humans do not want to return to the old selfish ways where we let the children of too-large families starve to death, we have abolished the family as a unit of economic self-sufficiency, and substituted the state. But the privilege of guaranteed support for children should not be abused.

Contraception is sometimes attacked as 'unnatural'. So it is, very unnatural. The trouble is, so is the welfare state. I think that most of us believe the welfare state is highly desirable. But you cannot have an unnatural welfare state, unless you also have unnatural birth-control, otherwise the end result will be misery even greater than that which obtains in nature. The welfare state is perhaps the greatest altruistic system the animal kingdom has ever known. But any altruistic system is inherently unstable, because it is open to abuse by selfish individuals, ready to exploit it. Individual humans who have more children than they are capable of rearing are probably too ignorant in most cases to be accused of conscious malevolent exploitation. Powerful institutions and leaders who deliberately encourage them to do so seem to me less free from suspicion.

(Dawkins, 1976, pp. 125–126)

Apart from proposing the groundbreaking idea that the welfare state has evolutionary effects, Dawkins' argument is also important to this book because for the first time it identifies welfare legislation as an agent of personality mis-development, by showing how the welfare state will be exploited by selfish individuals whose genes for selfishness will proliferate as a result. But if Dawkins' selfish gene theory is correct, it raises the interesting question of why haven't we all gone hog-wild at the trough of welfare? After all, if systematic, nation-wide welfare provision has been in place for over 70 years in many developed Western democracies, by now society should surely be over-run with genes for selfish, unrestrained reproduction, courtesy of the welfare state.

Dawkins gives us an answer on the last page of *The Selfish Gene*: 'even if we look on the dark side and assume that individual man is fundamentally selfish, our conscious foresight – our capacity to simulate the future in imagination – could save us from the worst selfish excesses of the blind replicators' (Dawkins, 1976, p. 215). Dawkins was referring to a process known as delay of gratification, in which we forgo a small immediate reward in order to achieve a desirable outcome in the longer term. This is thought to be beneficial to life outcomes in the long run (for example, Smallwood, Ruby & Singer, 2012).

In other words, even though the vast majority of us realise that welfare benefits represent easy money and are also an easy way of proliferating our genes, we possess sufficient foresight to see that in the long run it would be unsustainable, since the entire population refusing to work and having 15 or 16 children at the expense of the welfare state would lead to economic and social disaster. So instead of milking the welfare system to the maximum, millions of us instead work for a living and also opt to restrain our reproduction.

However, and this is the most crucial point in the whole book because this is where I add to Dawkins' work, this course of action is not sustainable either because, as we have already seen in Chapter 4, there are personality-based differences between individuals in the level of foresight that they possess. The lower an individual's level of foresight, the more likely he or she is to perceive the welfare state as a tool for obtaining extra money by having extra children, since they lack the foresight to see the long-term un-sustainability of this strategy. A side effect of this attitude towards the welfare state is the proliferation of the genes of the claimants in question; that is, a set of genes that includes those for low foresight.

This might seem a far-fetched claim, but the available data suggest that employment-resistant individuals cannot be relied upon to rein in their own higher than average level of reproduction because of a lack of foresight. For example, this quote summarises the attitude to the future of the Sheffield problem families that were studied by W. L. Tonge and colleagues:

This is a curious set of values. It adds up to a complete failure to plan for long-term action. It takes forethought to do all that these families failed to do: to take out motor insurance and TV licence, to accumulate household comforts, to limit family size; and education is above all a long-term endowment insurance. This is a style of life which shuts its eyes to the future.

(Tonge et al., 1975, p. 117)

An objection to this argument is that since most people have more foresight than the problem families studied by Tonge and colleagues, they would have been able to foresee the dangers of the welfare state being exploited by such people and thus have voted against it. The answer is they could have done, but when the welfare state was introduced (at least in the UK), it was marketed to voters as a reciprocal arrangement, with workers paying a flat rate of national insurance and in return receiving welfare benefits if they happened to fall on hard times (Beveridge, 1942).

This reciprocal system of welfare provision was sustainable in principle because only those who paid sufficient national insurance were able claim welfare benefits. But the welfare state in the UK had an Achilles' heel that made it vulnerable to exploitation by the type of selfish person mentioned by Dawkins. This Achilles' heel was known as national assistance and it was intended to take care of the small proportion of people who were unable to pay insurance through, for example, being paralysed. The architect of the UK welfare state, Lord Beveridge, was a smart man who was well aware that national assistance had the potential for exploitation and took pains to emphasise that it must be tightly controlled:

Assistance will be available to meet all needs which are not covered by insurance. It must meet those needs adequately up to subsistence level, but it must be felt to be something less desirable than insurance benefit; otherwise the insured persons get nothing for their contributions. Assistance therefore will be given always subject to proof of needs and examination of means; it will be subject also to any conditions as to behaviour which may seem likely to hasten restoration of earning capacity.

(Beveridge, 1942, p. 141)

Unfortunately, the politicians who implemented Beveridge's plan ignored his wise dictum that national assistance should be designed carefully so as not to unbalance the incentives for work. For example, at the inception of the UK welfare state in 1948 there were approximately 800,000 recipients of national assistance. Yet by the early 1990s, the view of the welfare state as 'something for nothing' had gained such a foothold in the culture of the UK that what Beveridge had intended to be a residual safety net had ballooned up to become the most-claimed form of welfare benefit, being utilised by more than 8,000,000 people (Timmins, 2001).

Just how badly the UK welfare state has lost its bearings was recently revealed by the implementation in April 2013 of new welfare legislation that aimed to curb welfare as a life choice by imposing a cap on the weekly benefits income of each workless household. However, the generous size of the cap has undermined its effectiveness because, at £500 per week, it means that welfare still pays much better than work for thousands of UK households. For example, £500 per week is almost £100 more than the median weekly take-home pay of UK citizens who were working full time in April 2013 (approximately £407 per week) and more than twice as much as the take-home pay of those UK citizens who work full time on the minimum wage (approximately £226 per week). This revelation means that in the modern UK, the fact that anyone persists with a job despite taking home less than £500 in wages per week is, in itself, a telling demonstration of the power of personality in guiding financial decision-making, since from a rational perspective, it would make more sense for such individuals not to work for a living and instead rely on state benefits. Despite its flaws, this capping process has inadvertently served a different purpose, in that it also created a census of workless households who had previously received more than £500 per week in benefits: as of May 2015 that number stood at 62,571 workless households.

Since a key means of reaching the £500 benefits cap is by having children (as of November 2014, 94 per cent of capped households contained dependent children), we can see that despite the benefit cap, the UK welfare state still provides a substantial financial incentive for having more children for welfare claimants who lack the foresight to see that unrestrained reproduction at the expense of the welfare state is unsustainable in the long term. Thus, since low foresight is part of the employment-resistant personality profile, we can see that the welfare state, in the UK at least, still has the potential to drive the personality profile of the population towards higher levels of employment-resistance by the standard principles of natural selection; that is, by genetic means alone.

This analysis is congruent with Dawkins' advice that the welfare state is only sustainable in the long term if contraception is mandatory for welfare claimants, to avoid the spread of selfish genes. Interestingly, despite their different scientific background, Tonge and colleagues came to the same conclusion in their study of Sheffield problem families: 'it would seem wise to take special care to help limit the fertility of families in difficulties' (Tonge et al., 1975, p. 122).

In order to provide background support for the notion that the welfare state can alter personality by proliferating the genes for employment-resistance, we shall now see direct experimental evidence that the personality profile of a population of non-human animals can be genetically altered by selective breeding. Such experiments are obviously not permitted in humans but, since there is much neural and genetic similarity between humans and other mammals (for example, Panksepp, 1998), these experiments can be regarded as useful models of the selective-breeding effect of the welfare state upon human personality.

Selective-breeding studies of personality: The Maudsley reactive rats

Selective-breeding experiments are a powerful tool for researchers investigating the genetic basis of behaviour. Perhaps the most famous example of a programme of selective-breeding experiments for personality is that started by Peter Broadhurst and colleagues at the research wing of the Maudsley Hospital, the Institute of Psychiatry, back in the 1950s and 1960s (for example, Broadhurst, 1960). In that era, the idea that human personality traits were real was not widely accepted by many academics owing to the prevailing political climate that maintained personality is a myth, with behaviour instead being determined by situational cues (Mischel, 1968). Thus, for a researcher such as Broadhurst to try to test experimentally the idea that personality is genetically based was brave and revolutionary.

Working for a PhD under the supervision of Hans Eysenck, in 1954, Broadhurst began selective breeding of rats that he had tested on a single behavioural measure of fear: the open-field test. In the open-field test, rats are placed for two minutes in a circular, white-painted arena 32¾ inches in diameter which is brightly lit and exposed to relatively loud white noise (78 dB). Rodents innately seek dark, sheltered, quiet areas, as these offer protection from predators and so the open-field arena is highly aversive to the average rat. The test is conducted four times on consecutive days, at the same time of day each time. Fear is indexed by the number of faecal boluses deposited during the two-minute experimental test: the higher the total number of boluses deposited during the four daily sessions, the more fear-prone the animal. Broadhurst selected defecation as a measure of fear because research on reactions to combat of US Army soldiers in the Second World War revealed that 21 per cent reported losing control of their bowels when under fire (Stouffer et al., 1950), suggesting that defecation in response to threat is an objective and face-valid measure of fear in humans as well as rodents. Broadhurst confirmed the validity of defecation in the open-field test as a measure of fear by preliminary experiments that showed defecation rate increased as light and noise intensity was increased.

Broadhurst then brother–sister mated the most frequent defecators (the rats with the most fearful personalities) with each other and did the same with the least frequent defecators (the least fearful rats). Within ten generations, the defecation rate of the least fearful rats (known as the Maudsley nonreactive strain) in the open-field test had dropped from an average of three boluses to zero boluses and remained there despite attempts to scare them more intensely by increasing light and noise levels in the open field. Conversely, the most fearful rats (known as the Maudsley reactive strain) in the same number of generations increased their average defecation rate from three to four boluses. Importantly, the differences in defecation rate between the two strains of rat were specifically related to threat and were not some general metabolic phenomenon of frequent defecation. This was found by measuring defecation rates when the animals were not under threat (when they were returned to their home cages). This study showed the reactive rodents defecated less than the nonreactive rats when not under threat (Broadhurst, 1975).

It is critical to note that this divergence in defecation rates between the two strains was seen in rats that had no experience of the open-field test before they were tested on it: the differences in defecation rate were wholly genetically determined. This was confirmed by Broadhurst's use of cross-fostering to control for effects of potential differences in maternal care between rat mothers of the two different strains. In brief, the cross-fostering entailed swapping half the pups at birth between mothers of the two different strains. So, half the pups born to reactive mothers would be given to nonreactive mothers and vice versa. The results of this programme showed that there were no significant differences in the defecation rate between cross-fostered pups and pups raised by their own mothers. In a very basic but elegant way, this aspect of Broadhurst's research indicates that the differences in fearfulness in the rats was genetically based and not a product of differences in maternal behaviour.

However, the real significance of Broadhurst's experiments was that the reactive and nonreactive rats showed a similarly divergent pattern of reactivity to other measures of fear that did not use defecation rate and also differed in non-behavioural measures of processes that could reasonably be thought to underlie fear (Eysenck & Broadhurst, 1964). For example, relative to the nonreactive rats, the frequently defecating reactive rats reduce their food and water intake under threat, show higher heart rate, run away faster and are less exploratory in novel environments (Broadhurst, 1975). Moreover, relaxation of selection from generation 16 onwards caused no reversion of the defecation behaviour of the two strains (Broadhurst, 1975). These follow-up studies indicate that what had been created by Broadhurst's selective-breeding process was not two strains of rats with odd toilet habits but instead two strains of rats with personalities that differ in their general sensitivity to threatening stimuli (fearfulness), of which their differing defecation rate is just one manifestation. The reactive rats have been likened to people with high scores on the personality dimension of neuroticism and the nonreactive rats to low scorers on the same dimension. Importantly, the two strains of rats also differ in the activity of their noradrenergic and serotonergic brain systems, systems that in humans are thought to influence susceptibility to anxiety disorders and depression (Gray & McNaughton, 2000).

Broadhurst's work is valuable for supporting the general idea that personality can be changed by selective breeding over only a few generations, but the personality construct of neuroticism is not the focus of this book: we are interested in factors that influence conscientiousness and agreeableness. In order to check that the latter aspects of personality are as sensitive to selective breeding as neuroticism, I will now summarise selective-breeding programmes that target work ethic (as a non-human proxy for conscientiousness) and tameness (as a non-human proxy for agreeableness).

Selective-breeding studies of personality: Breeding work ethic in mice

Arguably, the selective-breeding experiments that are most relevant to conscientiousness are those done by Theodore Garland and colleagues who have shown that work ethic in mice can be altered by selective breeding. In these studies, work ethic was quantified as the activity that each mouse displayed on an exercise wheel. Importantly, in this sort of research, each mouse is typically housed individually with an exercise wheel that they can run on whenever they want, so the amount of wheel-running displayed by each mouse provides a direct measure of willingness to expend effort. The willingness to expend effort is not a perfect analogue for conscientiousness in humans because it measures more than just our tendency to be a couch potato, but nevertheless individual differences in laziness are captured by conscientiousness in most major personality theories (often under somewhat more polite labels such as activity, industriousness, persistence or achievement-striving, for example, McCrae & Costa, 2008). This analysis means that willingness to run on a wheel in rodents can reasonably be seen as equivalent to laziness-related aspects of human conscientiousness.

A good example of research on selective breeding for work ethic in mice is a study by Swallow, Carter and Garland (1998), in which they examined the effects in mice of ten generations of selective breeding for high levels of voluntary wheel-running. Approximately 600 mice per generation (from ten families) were placed in individual cages with exercise wheels for six days and selection was based on the average number of revolutions on days five and six. From each of the ten families of mice in each generation, the highest-running male and female were mated. Six additional mice (three male, three female) were selected to breed in order to provide enough offspring to produce ten families in each generation. These additional mice were the second-highest runners in the highest-running families. Siblings were not permitted to breed with each other. In order to provide a comparison, mice were randomly selected to breed from a control population, who were not selected according to wheel-running behaviour.

The results of this study showed that by the time ten generations had elapsed, the selected mice were running on average almost twice as far as the control mice and also that the males were lazier than the females: the female-selected mice averaged 8,774 revolutions per day whereas the control females averaged 5,077 revolutions per day. The male-selected mice averaged 6,056 revolutions per day whereas the control males averaged 3,437 revolutions per day. By generation eight, the two strains of mice had already separated enough in their wheel-running behaviour that there was no overlap between them. By generation ten, there were no signs of a limit being approached and the authors concluded that increase in wheel-running could continue to respond to further selective-breeding efforts (Swallow, Carter & Garland, 1998).

Selective-breeding studies of personality: The Russian domestication programme

The experiments by Garland and colleagues suggest that aspects of personality in the conscientiousness domain are sensitive to selective breeding, but they tell us little about whether traits related to agreeableness can be altered by selective breeding. This is important because people with personality-related employment difficulties are not only relatively lacking in conscientiousness but also lacking in cooperativeness (Moffitt et al., 2011), which is characteristic of low scorers on agreeableness. It is therefore important to assess the effects of selective breeding on animal behaviours that plausibly relate to agreeableness.

Arguably, the selective-breeding experiments that are most relevant to the theme of agreeableness are those done in Russia. These show that tameness in foxes can be altered by selective breeding. This experiment was begun in 1959 by Soviet scientist Dmitri Belyaev at the Institute of Cytology and Genetics of the USSR Academy of Sciences in Novosibirsk, Siberia and was directed after his death in 1985 by Lyudmila Trut (for a review of this research programme, see Trut, 1999). Belyaev was interested in how dogs became domesticated and, more specifically, wanted to test his theory that physical features seen in domestic dogs but not wild canids, such as floppy ears, curly tails and piebald fur colouration, were the by-product of selective breeding for a single attribute, namely tameness. He wanted to attempt to replicate the domestication process under scientifically controlled conditions so he obtained 100 vixens and 30 male silver foxes from fur farms and began selectively breeding the tamest individuals with each other.

The 130 silver foxes that were the subjects of this study were already moderately tame and so were better suited to Belyaev's purposes than wild-caught foxes, which tend to have very high mortality and very low reproduction rates in captivity. The method of selection for tameness that Belyaev's researchers used with the fox pups produced by these founding parents was straightforward: once a month for six months (starting when the fox was one month old), a human researcher conducted a standardised tameness assessment by offering the fox a food item whilst also attempting to pet it. Since foxes reach sexual maturity at about seven months old, an overall tameness score would then be calculated for each fox after the final assessment. Based on their performance over the previous six months, foxes were then assigned to one of three classes of tameness: Class One foxes reacted in a friendly manner when petted by humans, whining and wagging their tails. Class Two foxes tolerated petting and handling by humans but without showing any emotional response. Class Three foxes fled from humans and attempted to bite when stroked or handled.

Foxes from Class One were allowed to breed with each other, as were foxes from Class Three. This process produced two rapidly diverging strains of foxes, one highly tame and the other highly aggressive. Videos of both strains of foxes in action are available online and are worth watching to see just how enormous the behavioural differences are between the two strains of foxes: whereas the tame foxes resemble friendly puppies, jumping up, whining and trying to lick the experimenter's hand, foxes from the aggressive strain are ferocious, growling, snapping their jaws and throwing themselves at the bars of their cages in an effort to bite the experimenter. The key point to note is that these different patterns of behaviour are the result of genetic influence and not training, because contact between humans and foxes was strictly controlled and limited to set 'time-dosed' periods to ensure that all foxes, whether tame or aggressive, received equal amounts of human contact.

Within a few generations, there was no overlap in behaviour between the two fox strains so a new assessment scheme was introduced in which pups from the strain of tame foxes were scored according to the intensity of their friendliness towards the experimenter whereas pups from the aggressive breed of foxes were scored on the critical distance between the fox and the human experimenter at which aggression is first demonstrated (the greater the distance, the more aggressive the animal). In order to verify that selective breeding can change tameness in species other than the silver fox, the researchers in Russia have also successfully domesticated the American mink, the river otter and the wild grey rat using the same selective-breeding methods.

The original aim of Belyaev's research programme had been to test his hypothesis that the typical physical characteristics of domesticated animals were produced by selecting for tameness. This hypothesis was strongly supported as the tamed animals showed many traits now found in domestic animals such as floppy ears, curly tails and piebald fur. Such results are not relevant to the theme of this book, although two less appreciated findings are relevant. First, the Russian experimenters found that approximately 35 per cent of the variation in the selectively bred foxes' behavioural reactions to humans was determined by genetic factors (Trut, 1999). As we will see in Chapter 7, the size of this genetic effect on the foxes' behaviour patterns closely matches the 30–40 per cent genetic effect on human personality characteristics that has been demonstrated by twin studies, confirming across species that individual differences in personality (for that is what genetically-based behavioural patterns are) have a substantial genetic component, and so genetic studies with non-human animals such as silver foxes can be used to inform our understanding of human personality formation. Second, if the rate of personality change seen in the selective-breeding studies summarised here is extrapolated to humans, it gives us an approximate indication that welfare legislation could significantly change human personality in about 100 years by genetic change alone. In practice, this estimate is an upper bound for the power of selective breeding to change personality because mating between humans is not under the control of an experimenter.

As a caveat, it should be noted that it is likely selective-breeding experiments of the type I have described in this chapter may over-estimate the genetic contribution to personality. We know this because of experiments in which genetically identical mouse embryos of one strain were transplanted into mothers of a second strain that is known to differ significantly in a range of behaviours connected to anxiety and learning. When tested as adults, the mice from the first strain that had been transplanted as embryos into foster mothers of the second strain (and were then raised by those foster mothers) behaved in a broadly similar way to the mice of the second strain who had been raised by their real mothers, showing that apparently genetically-based differences in behaviour between the two strains of mice were in fact a product of the combined effects of environmental differences before and after birth (for example, differences in blood chemistry when in the uterus and licking once born; Francis et al., 2003).

However, despite these findings, we can rest assured that there is indeed a genetic contribution to behaviour, because of cross-breeding experiments. These experiments show that when animals from two opposite behavioural strains are mated, the resulting offspring display behaviour that is intermediate between that of the two parental strains. The only difference between the offspring is their mixed genetic heritage; hence, we can see that their intermediate behaviour must have a genetic origin.

Perhaps the most famous demonstration of this phenomenon was by Dilger (1962), who cross-bred Fisher's lovebirds (*Agapornis fischeri*) with peach-faced lovebirds (*Agapornis roseicollis*). The lovebirds of the first strain carry nesting materials in their beaks whereas the lovebirds of the second strain carry nesting material by tucking it into the feathers of their flanks and rumps. The offspring were sterile but nevertheless attempted to breed. As part of their breeding efforts they displayed nesting behaviours and the key finding was that the strategy used to transport nesting materials was intermediate between that of the two parental strains. To start with, the hybrid birds tucked the nesting material into the feathers of their rump and flank in the manner of the peach-faced lovebirds. However, once the material was lodged in the feathers, they still gripped it with their beaks rather than letting go and so when they raised their heads, the material was pulled out again. This behaviour was repeated many times, but as the birds matured, they began to carry nesting materials in their beaks in the manner of the Fischer's lovebirds. The tucking ritual never wholly vanished and the birds would usually turn their head to their rumps.

This production of intermediate behaviours by cross-breeding two strains of animals is not specific to lovebirds and has since been replicated in other species, including rodents (Broadhurst, 1969; Wigger et al., 2001), deer (Endicott-Davies, Barrie & Fisher, 1996) and ducks (Faure et al., 2003). Viewed as a whole, these cross-breeding experiments allow us to accept that behavioural traits are indeed genetically influenced, since they control for differences in both the prenatal and postnatal environment.

Conclusion

Selective breeding for personality causes significant, genetically influenced changes in personality within as few as five generations. As a caveat, these experiments present extreme examples. It should be noted that there is more variation in human mating than in selective-breeding studies of the type cited here, so the rate of change in human personality due to welfare-related selective breeding will be slower.

7
Personality as a Product of Nature and Nurture

So far in the book we have seen evidence that low scores on conscientiousness and agreeableness constitute the 'employment-resistant' personality profile. We have seen that the employment-resistant personality profile is over-represented amongst welfare claimants. We have also seen evidence that welfare claimants on average have more children than employed citizens, as well as evidence that welfare generosity is at least partly responsible for this reproductive difference. If we accept that personality runs in families, then a welfare state that causes claimants to have more children on average than employed citizens risks proliferating the employment-resistant personality profile.

This is my theory of welfare-induced personality mis-development – what I label the 'welfare trait' theory – but it only holds true if personality is transmitted from parents to offspring. If personality did not run in families, then the children of individuals with employment-resistant personalities would be just as likely to turn out to be solid citizens as the offspring of solid citizens and vice versa.

We saw evidence in Chapter 5 that childhood neglect appears to be the active ingredient in the environmental transmission of employment-resistant personality characteristics. We saw in Chapter 6 that selective-breeding experiments in non-human animals demonstrate that personality characteristics can be transmitted genetically from parents to offspring. However, there are concerns that psychological models created in non-human animals are too simple to be valid in humans (for example, Matthews, 2008). The purpose of this chapter is to summarise evidence that human personality characteristics are influenced by genetic as well as environmental factors.

Circumstantial support for the idea that dysfunctional personality characteristics are transmitted from parents to children is provided by the existence of the concept of 'problem families'. For example, Sheffield, Wright and Lunn (1971) followed up the offspring of 108 problem families and estimated that at least 250 new problem families would be created by them. I have already described in detail some of the research on problem families by Tonge and colleagues (1975). I have also mentioned that in 1981 there was an attempt to assess transmission of problem family status by tracking down and assessing the work records and other important variables of the offspring of the 66 families whose comparison they had published in 1975. The researchers (Lunn, Greathead & McLaren; W. L. Tonge had died in 1976) managed to obtain complete information on 16 sons and 18 daughters from the problem families and 13 sons and 12 daughters from the comparison families.

Overall, this follow-up of the 1975 study revealed a pattern of results that fits the idea of transmission of personality characteristics from parents to offspring: six of the sons of the problem families were unemployed whereas none of the sons of the comparison families were unemployed. In the daughters, the pattern was similar but less extreme: ten of the problem family daughters were unemployed compared to five of the daughters of the comparison families. In keeping with the idea that the employment-resistant personality profile has an effect on social conduct in general, criminality was also far more common in the offspring of the problem group than those of the comparison group: the 19 sons of the problem families had 255 convictions between them compared to 34 convictions in the 18 sons of the comparison families. Likewise, the 26 daughters of the problem families had 58 convictions between them compared to 17 convictions in the 16 daughters of the comparison families.

Interestingly, these differences in criminality cannot easily be explained away as being caused by greater affluence in the offspring of the comparison families because affluence levels in the two groups of offspring were similar. For example, since the participants were reluctant to disclose their earnings, the researchers assessed affluence by noting the possession of a full set of major consumer goods of the era (a car, a telephone, a colour television, a washing machine and refrigerator). Using this measure, the researchers found that five out of 29 households of the offspring of the problem families possessed the full set of consumer goods compared to six out of 25 households of the offspring of the comparison families.

Studies of problem families such as those conducted by Tonge and colleagues are useful for providing background evidence that social and occupational maladjustment is rooted in personality. They also suggest that these maladaptive personality characteristics can be transmitted from parents to offspring by both genetic and environmental means. In order to confirm genetic involvement in human personality transmission, I shall now summarise evidence from behaviour genetic studies of personality, which compare the similarity of personality attributes of individuals with different degrees of relatedness, allowing genetic and environmental influences to be disentangled.

Before getting further into this topic, it is worth saying a few words on common misunderstandings in genetic research. The first point to note is that humans are very similar genetically, so when we say that identical twins share 100 per cent of their DNA, we mean exactly that, as they are clones, whereas when we say that non-identical twins or siblings share on average 50 per cent of their DNA, we mean they share on average 50 per cent of the part of their DNA that varies between individual humans, which is about 0.1 per cent of our overall genome. To put this in perspective, over 90 per cent of the total human genome can be matched with corresponding regions in the mouse genome (Mouse Sequencing Consortium, 2002) and humans, bonobos and chimpanzees show even greater similarity between the part of their genomes that can be aligned (around 98 per cent; for example, Prüfer et al., 2012). These results indicate that even physically very different mammals share the vast majority of their genes. It is also important to correct a common misconception concerning the meaning of heritability. Heritability does not indicate how much influence genetic variants have on a particular attribute in a single person, it indicates how much of a role genetic variants have in creating differences in that attribute between different people (Plomin et al., 2008). Therefore, for example, we can say that the tendency for humans to have two eyes has zero heritability, even though it is 100 per cent the product of genetic programming.

It is also important at this stage to mention a caveat concerning genetic influences on personality, namely that we know little about which genetic variants influence personality or how they do it. For example, two decades or so ago things were more optimistic as it was thought that personality traits are shaped by a small number of influential genetic variants (known as candidate genes). A rash of studies came out supporting this approach to understanding personality (for example, Lesch et al., 1996), only for them to turn out to be unreliable as, when other scientists tried to do the same study, they found different results.

Even attempts to find the genes for easily measured physical attributes that we know are almost completely genetically determined, such as height, have failed to identify important candidate genes. These failures have prompted a rethink, with the latest research suggesting that human quantitative traits are likely instead to be influenced by many thousands of genetic variants, each contributing a tiny amount of variance to the trait in question that is probably too small to measure even in samples of more than 100,000 people (Yang et al., 2012). If that is not complicated enough, the expression of those genes is affected by the environment through epigenetic changes, in which, for example, a process known as methylation switches genes on or off in response to environmental influences. How environmental factors connect with genes to alter their expression is not clear, but we know that they do (Spector, 2012). Nevertheless, for the purposes of the present argument, we don't need to get bogged down in these technical issues: all we need to know is that personality has a genetic component.

The workhorse of behaviour genetics research is the 'twin study', a method first suggested by Charles Darwin's cousin, Francis Galton: 'Twins have a special claim upon our attention; it is, that their history affords means of distinguishing between the effects of tendencies received at birth, and those that were imposed by the special circumstances of their after lives' (Galton, 1883, p. 155). As Galton surmised, twin studies have turned out to provide a handy way of teasing apart genetic and environmental effects on a trait because the vast majority of twins are raised together, minimising shared environmental effects, yet come in two forms with different degrees of genetic relatedness: monozygotic (MZ, genetically identical twins: that is, clones) and dizygotic (DZ, genetically non-identical twins who share approximately half of their segregating genes and so are no more related than ordinary siblings). The rationale underlying twin studies is that genetic similarity should lead to phenotypic similarity, so if genes were to influence a trait, the similarity on that trait between MZ twins is expected to be higher than between DZ twins because we can be confident that MZ twins, being clones, are genetically more similar to each other than DZ twins. Conversely, if genetic factors have no effect on a trait, similarity on that trait between MZ twins should be approximately the same as between DZ twins.

MZ twin siblings turn out to be more similar on almost all types of behaviour than DZ twin siblings and, consequently, show that almost all types of behaviour are genetically influenced (Turkheimer, 2000). However, it is important to note at this stage that behaviour genetics research also shows that the degree of heritability is not the same for all behavioural traits. For example, intelligence is one of the most heritable behavioural traits, with approximately 60 per cent to 80 per cent of the variance in intelligence in adults being explained by genetic factors (Deary, Johnson & Houlihan, 2009). Personality traits are also heritable but much less so than intelligence: for example, twin studies show that the personality traits which are the focus of this book, namely conscientiousness and agreeableness, are somewhere between 30 and 40 per cent heritable (Bouchard, 1994).

This point about personality being significantly less heritable than intelligence might seem tangential to the topic of this book – personality and welfare – but it is important to make in order to avoid this book being mischaracterised as just another version of the long-running argument that higher birth rates amongst individuals with low intelligence can cause genetically-based decreases in the intelligence level of the population. Since empirical tests of this latter (dysgenic) hypothesis usually show the opposite, namely that the average level of intelligence of the population is rising (the so-called Flynn effect; Flynn, 1994), critics might seek to tar the welfare trait theory with the same brush, on the basis that the heritability of personality is less than that for intelligence and so if intelligence is not suffering from dysgenic effects then personality is even less likely to do so.

But this is lazy thinking: apart from the obvious rebuttal that this book is about personality and welfare, not intelligence and welfare, the lower heritability of personality makes more room for environmental effects. It therefore makes more room for the personality profile of the population to be harmed by a welfare state which increases the number of children born into disadvantaged families. This fact means that my argument is not the tired old Social-Darwinist dysgenic one that has been offered many times before in intelligence-related debates, but rather hinges less on genetic factors and more on the crucial role of childhood disadvantage in forming the employment-resistant personality, as demonstrated by James Heckman and colleagues using evidence from randomised controlled trials (Heckman et al., 2013). No critics have been able to offer cogent evidence to contradict Heckman's finding – because there is none.

It should however be noted that twin studies have a variety of limitations. For example, they usually make the assumptions that mating is random, that identical twins are not treated more similarly than fraternal twins and that only one form of genetic mechanism is acting on a particular trait. There is evidence to cast doubt on these assumptions and thus on twin studies: for example, some studies suggest that mating is not random with regard to personality and that there is a slight trend in humans to mate with those whose personalities resemble our own (Le Bon et al., 2013).

To reject the results of twin studies of personality because of these issues would however be to throw the baby out with the bathwater. We know this because the results of twin studies are backed up by two other types of behaviour genetic experiment. First, in studies of personality in twins reared apart, we find heritability estimates for personality that are similar to those generated by studies of personality in twins that were reared together (for example, Tellegen et al., 1988). Second, twin study results are backed up by a new way of estimating genetic influences on traits, known as genome-wide complex trait analysis (GCTA). Pioneered by Peter Visscher and colleagues, GCTA allows an estimate of the variance in a trait that is explained by genetic variants that are in common between the people surveyed, even if those people do not come from the same family. Briefly stated, GCTA compares DNA profiles to estimate the degree of genetic overlap or relatedness amongst the participants. The degree of overlap is then related to the amount of overlap on some measured characteristic, such as height, weight or personality. The significance of GCTA is that it allows genetic effects on traits to be studied in any random sample of people, meaning that GCTA analyses don't suffer from the limitations of twin studies.

Importantly for the argument about genetic effects on personality, GCTA studies confirm twin study findings, showing that the more related two people are, the more similar they tend to be in their personality characteristics (for example, Verweij et al., 2012; Vinkhuyzen et al., 2012). As a caveat, it should be noted that GCTA studies only capture additive genetic effects on traits but are insensitive to non-additive effects. This contrasts to twin studies, which are a metaphorical dragnet and are able to detect all forms of genetic influence on a trait. Therefore, whereas twin studies indicate personality traits are approximately 30 per cent to 40 per cent heritable, GCTA studies provide lower estimates of personality heritability, in the range of four per cent to 12 per cent. For any readers unfamiliar with the meaning of the term 'additive genetic effects', it refers to when alternative forms of a gene (known as alleles) add up to influence a trait. For example, if the genes in question are additive, an organism with one gene for blue colouration and one for yellow would turn out to be green. When genes interact with each other or the environment to influence a trait, we see what is known as a non-additive genetic effect: GCTA studies are blind to this form of effect.

The advent of GCTA means that, even though there are limitations to twin studies, we can accept their basic message, namely that genes influence personality and that identical twins have personalities that are more similar than non-identical twins because of their greater genetic similarity. Furthermore, we can accept that this effect is real and not merely an artefact of some confounding factor such as non-random mating or the tendency for parents to treat identical twin pairs more similarly than non-identical twin pairs. If the picture still seems confusing, think about it like this: if personality was 100 per cent controlled by genetic factors, identical twins would have identical personality profiles (assuming zero measurement error) whereas non-identical twins would not. Conversely, if personality was 100 per cent controlled by environmental factors, then the personalities of identical twins would on average be no more similar than those of non-identical twins. What we find is something in between: identical twins do not have identical personalities, but their personalities are on average more similar than the personalities of non-identical twins, showing that there is a clear influence of genes on personality.

However, in order to pull together the research summarised in this chapter into a coherent whole, we must finish off by thinking more about what is meant by environmental effects on personality. As the studies summarised in this chapter showed, differences between individuals in personality attributes are significantly influenced by genetic variants, but they also showed that on average environmental variation shapes personality even more strongly, in a ratio of roughly 40 per cent to 60 per cent. However, the partitioning of environmental influence on personality is odd: despite being raised together, identical twins have personality profiles that are far from identical, suggesting that the shared/family environment seemingly has little or no effect on how our personality characteristics turn out.

As far as twin studies are concerned, non-genetic influences on personality appear to be almost all from non-shared environmental factors (plus measurement error; Turkheimer & Waldron, 2000). However, the preschool experiments also described in Chapter 5 contradict this conclusion by showing that if children from disadvantaged, welfare-claiming families receive intensive tutoring in pro-employment behaviours before the age of five (especially planning, executing and reviewing tasks and resolving interpersonal conflicts), they turn out to be significantly less employment-resistant in their personality profiles and also more successful as adults than children from similarly disadvantaged families that did not receive the tutoring (Heckman et al., 2013).

Moreover, the preschool studies showed that it is the shared/family environment influence that was doing the damage to the personalities of the deprived children, as it turns out that home-delivered special educational tutoring was not effective, in contrast to tutoring delivered in an education centre. Therefore, in order to have a good chance of developing the personality of a solid citizen, the child needs to be removed from their dysfunctional family environment and placed in the ordered, constructive environment of a special education centre. In other words, special educational tutoring, as long as it is delivered in a dedicated centre, is effectively stepping in and partially making up for the personality damage caused by growing up in a dysfunctional, impoverished welfare-claiming family with parents that themselves tend to possess mis-developed, employment-resistant personalities.

The twin and preschool studies summarised in this book therefore present a seemingly confused and contradictory picture of environmental effects on personality: twin studies indicate that the shared/family environment has almost no effect on personality, but preschool studies suggest that a disadvantaged family environment warps personality towards employment-resistance. How can they be reconciled?

One plausible explanation is provided by the observation that disadvantaged families rarely participate in twin studies (Turkheimer et al., 2003). Conversely, preschool studies do not recruit participants from middle-class families because the focus of this type of research is to understand disadvantage (Heckman, 2006). This difference in participant type between the two types of research is important to the theme of this book because parental effectiveness differs between families at different levels of the socio-economic ladder (Lykken, 1998). Briefly stated, in affluent middle-class families there is relatively little variance in parental effectiveness and so the vast majority of affluent middle-class children will have the opportunity to express whatever genetic tendencies they possess. For example, almost all children in affluent middle-class households will be taught to read, will learn mathematics, study science, take music lessons, play sport, debate the day's news over dinner and so on. Overall, this will tend to exaggerate the influence upon subsequent behaviour of genetic factors and unique (non-shared) experiences, but downplay the effects of the shared (family) environment.

In contrast, children who grow up in disadvantaged households tend to have a much more uneven exposure to these important developmental stimuli: some will be taught to read, some won't. Some will have access to a musical instrument, some won't. Some will get coached in sport, some won't. Some will be given a computer, some won't. This greater variation in parental effectiveness in disadvantaged households (relative to middle-class households) hypothetically means that individual differences in psychological characteristics are more strongly influenced by the specific family environment in children raised in disadvantaged households than in children raised in affluent, middle-class households.

This hypothesis is backed up by studies that show shared environmental experiences play a larger role in the variations in IQ in lower SES children than in high SES children (for example, Turkheimer et al., 2003; Hanscombe et al., 2012). The issue of SES modification has not been as widely studied with regard to personality, but results thus far are supportive. For example, Tuvblad, Grann and Lichtenstein (2006) investigated the moderating effect of SES on the family environment's capacity to develop antisocial traits in 1,133 Swedish twin pairs, aged 16–17 years. This study found that the more disadvantaged the family, the stronger the influence of the family environment on antisocial behaviour in the offspring. We would thus expect that family/shared environmental effects on personality would be minimal in twin studies but highly pronounced in the preschool studies, which is what we find.

This insight is important to the welfare trait theory because it counters the argument that welfare policy may indeed damage personality, but the size of the effect will be miniscule. More specifically, a critic might admit that there are detrimental upbringing effects on conscientiousness and agreeableness amongst the offspring of welfare recipients, but might then claim that such effects will be too small to worry about because twin studies show that family environment effects on personality development are small. Furthermore, a critic could argue that the effects of disadvantaged family circumstances on personality cannot be large because, if they were, the population-level link between personality and fertility would be much larger than the low levels shown in the studies cited in Chapter 4.

Because we now know that the more disadvantaged the family, the larger the effect of the family environment on antisocial traits in the offspring, we can see that these criticisms do not stand up to close scrutiny. Both the small size of family environment effects on personality development and the weak links between personality and fertility can be explained as artefacts of the tendency for middle-class families to participate in research projects (Lykken, 1998). As we have already seen, when researchers include disadvantaged families in their studies, they tend to find not only that there is a large effect of family environment on personality (Heckman et al., 2013), but also that there is a strong link between low conscientiousness/agreeableness and high fertility (Tonge et al., 1975).

Conclusion

Human parents transmit their personality attributes to their children by genetic and environmental means, with children in affluent families tending to display greater genetic influence and children in disadvantaged families displaying greater influence from the family environment.

8

A Model of How the Welfare State Leads to Personality Mis-Development

Up until this point in the book, we have primarily been preoccupied with laying out the evidential building blocks of the welfare trait theory: now it is time to assemble those blocks of evidence into a coherent model of welfare-induced personality mis-development, beginning by reminding ourselves of what this book is about. This book is about personality and the welfare state. It's about our attitude to work and the factors that shape that attitude. But most of all, it is about asking how the welfare state might alter the personality profile of the population to any significant degree.

As we know from our own experiences in the workplace, as well as decades of scientific research, our employment prospects don't just depend on how intelligent we are, but also on how keen we are to turn up on time at work, to do what we are told, to be polite to customers, to cooperate with colleagues, to obey workplace regulations and so on. In short, our employment prospects are influenced by our scores on two dimensions of personality that, in the jargon of personality research, are usually labelled as conscientiousness and agreeableness. Briefly stated, people with personality profiles that are relatively lacking in conscientiousness and agreeableness tend to do worse than average in the workplace (Barrick et al., 2001; Hogan, 2011). In line with this notion, people with this particular combination of personality characteristics – what I call the employment-resistant personality profile – are over-represented amongst welfare claimants (for example, Caspi et al., 1998). Studies suggest that part of this personality difference between welfare claimants and working citizens is likely to be a result of the demoralising effects of unemployment (for example, Boyce et al., 2015), but we know that part of it is caused by these personality traits themselves, since longitudinal research shows that low levels of conscientiousness and agreeableness as measured in childhood are predictive of unemployment in adulthood (for example, Moffitt et al., 2011).

In the previous three chapters, we saw evidence that personality characteristics are transmitted from parent to child via both environmental and genetic channels. The over-representation of employment-resistant individuals in the welfare-claiming sector of the population therefore suggests that a welfare state which increases the number of children born to claimants risks proliferating the employment-resistant personality profile, because these children will tend to take after their parents in personality terms for both environmental and genetic reasons. This seems like an unfortunate situation, but scarcely a reason for hitting the panic button, because thus far we have not estimated the size of the problem caused by welfare-induced personality mis-development. The primary purpose of this chapter is to estimate whether welfare-induced personality mis-development is likely to be a large enough problem to deserve the attention of policymakers.

We will begin by revisiting the Perry Preschool Project which we first examined in detail in Chapter 5. This time, instead of comparing the life outcomes of the two groups of Perry Preschool participants (tutored versus untutored), we will compare their life outcomes to those of average individuals from approximately the same sector of society (African Americans who were approximately 40 years old in 2004). Such a comparison is very much a blunt instrument, but it will allow us to obtain an initial, tentative estimate of the magnitude of the effects on life outcomes of childhood disadvantage in the population as a whole.

Next we will examine the size of genetic effects on personality because, although the genetic influence on personality is modest compared to other traits (for example, intelligence), it is real. Therefore a full picture of the scale of welfare-induced changes in personality can only be obtained if genetic factors are also taken into account.

Finally, we will end this chapter with the presentation of a model that provides a quantitative estimate of the scale of welfare-induced personality mis-development through environmental and genetic channels, as well as an estimate of its likely cost to the public purse.

The Perry Preschool Project revisited

As we saw in Chapter 5, the Perry Preschool Project shows that two years of intensive preschool tutoring from the age of three to five years old can significantly improve the life outcomes of disadvantaged children decades later. For example, at the age of 40, the children in the Perry Preschool Project who did not receive intensive preschool tutoring earned approximately 25 per cent less, had twice the rate of unemployment and were twice as likely to have been incarcerated as the tutored children (Schweinhart et al., 2005).

These facts provide a compelling argument for government investment in intensive preschool tutoring as a means of boosting the life chances of disadvantaged children. But not all children are disadvantaged, and so the Perry Preschool Project only gives us a partial picture of the scale of the damage to adult life outcomes that can be done by childhood disadvantage. To fill this gap, we need to compare the life outcomes of the two groups of Perry Preschool participants to the life outcomes of less disadvantaged children with a similar demographic profile. A useful start point for this exercise is to note that the intensive preschool tutoring only lasted for two years and so the tutored children remained disadvantaged compared to individuals who were born into families who provided adequate care from birth onwards. This insight allows us to conceptualise, as shown in Figures 8.1 and 8.2, that the untutored children in the Perry Preschool Project represent a high disadvantage group, the tutored children in the Perry Preschool Project a medium disadvantage group and the population average a low disadvantage group (average African Americans who were around 40 years old in 2004).

By comparing life outcomes across three levels of disadvantage, we can put the effects of both childhood disadvantage and intensive preschool tutoring into perspective and begin to get a sense of how much damage could be done to society by a welfare state that increases the number of children born into disadvantaged households. It should be noted that this exercise will only provide an estimate of the relative scale of effects of childhood disadvantage on life outcomes (threefold, fourfold, fivefold and so on) and not the

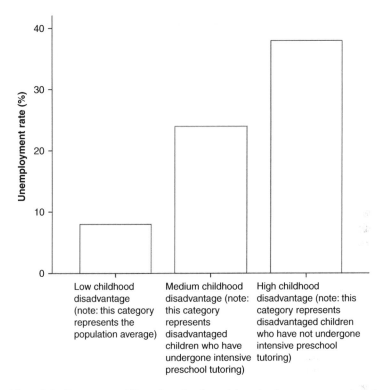

Figure 8.1 Percentage of Perry Preschool participants who were unemployed at the age of 40 versus the average rate of unemployment for African Americans in 2004

Source: US Department of Labor/US Bureau of Labor Statistics in column one and Schweinhart et al. (2005) in columns two and three.

absolute level, because the age 40 follow-up of Perry Preschool participants was published in 2005 and so absolute figures for annual income, unemployment rates and other such historical data are not especially meaningful now.

What we find is that childhood disadvantage has an approximately linear, dose-dependent effect on life outcomes. For example, Figure 8.1 shows that significantly fewer of the tutored children in the Perry Preschool Project were unemployed at age 40 (24 per cent) compared to the untutored children (38 per cent), yet their rate of unemployment was still almost three times higher than the average

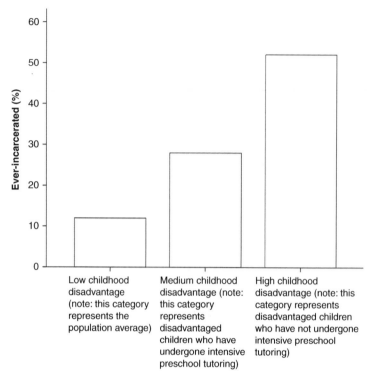

Figure 8.2 Percentage of Perry Preschool participants who had served a prison sentence by the age of 40 versus the average rate of incarceration for African Americans in 2001

Source: Bonczar (2003) in column one and Schweinhart et al. (2005) in columns two and three.

rate of unemployment for African Americans in 2004 (8 per cent; US Department of Labor/US Bureau of Labor Statistics).

A similar pattern occurs with criminality. For example, Figure 8.2 shows that significantly fewer of the tutored children in the Perry Preschool Project (28 per cent) had served a prison sentence by the age of 40 compared to the untutored children (52 per cent), yet their rate of incarceration was still more than twice as high as the average 'ever-incarcerated' rate for African Americans in 2001 (12 per cent; Bonczar, 2003).

Viewed as whole, the data presented in Figures 8.1 and 8.2 show that childhood disadvantage damages life outcomes in both employment and criminal domains but, more importantly in the context of this book, they also allow us to obtain an estimate of the scale of the burden that is imposed on society by childhood disadvantage. It should be noted that this will be a conservative estimate because the population average that represents the group with low levels of childhood disadvantage includes life outcomes for disadvantaged individuals: if they were stripped out of the data, the low childhood disadvantage group would have even better life outcomes.

The estimation process is a simple one: divide the number for the high childhood disadvantage category by the number for the low childhood disadvantage category. For example, if we look at Figure 8.1, we can see that 38 per cent of the high childhood disadvantage group were unemployed whereas only 8 per cent of the low childhood disadvantage group were unemployed. If we divide 38 by 8, we can see that the high childhood disadvantage group on average had a rate of unemployment that is 4.75 times greater than individuals in the low childhood disadvantage category. Similarly, Figure 8.2 shows that 52 per cent of the high childhood disadvantage group had served a prison sentence whereas only 12 per cent of the low childhood disadvantage group were former prisoners. If we divide 52 by 12, we can see that the high childhood disadvantage group on average had a rate of imprisonment that is 4.3 times greater than individuals in the low childhood disadvantage category.

A critic might dismiss these numbers as an artefact of the sampling differences between the low and high childhood disadvantage groups – after all, we must remember that the life outcomes of the low childhood disadvantage group are merely the population averages for African Americans who were aged about 40 in 2004, not those of a carefully selected experimental group as was the case of the Perry Preschool Project. But this is where the medium childhood disadvantage group becomes useful, because it acts as a sanity check for our estimate: as can be seen in the bar charts, the life outcomes of the putative medium childhood disadvantage group fall in between those of the low and high childhood disadvantage groups, suggesting that the differences between the low and high childhood disadvantage groups are not merely a fluke but instead are part of an approximately linear association between the severity of childhood disadvantage and the frequency of problematic life outcomes.

Based on these estimates, which are conservative for the reasons previously stated, we can now see that childhood disadvantage has a hugely damaging effect on life outcomes – in two key areas of life, namely employment and criminality, it causes a fourfold worsening of outcomes compared to average individuals. Moreover, by inspecting Figures 8.1 and 8.2, we can see that intensive preschool tutoring can only cancel out about half of that damage, because in every chart we can see that the life outcomes of the tutored children from the Perry Preschool Project are positioned approximately midway between those of the untutored children and the average for the population as a whole.

This insight leads us to a key finding of this book, which is that a welfare state which increases the number of children born into disadvantaged households risks imposing a significant per capita headwind on society, because each of those children will, on average, go on to create a burden for the welfare state and the criminal justice system that is four times larger than the burden imposed by average individuals. Bearing in mind that the average includes disadvantaged individuals, we can be confident that the real headwind is even stronger. Moreover, even if we lived in some utopia in which we could afford to give every disadvantaged child a place in a scheme for intensive preschool tutoring, we can see that this headwind cannot be fully cancelled out by remedial action: the tutored children still create a burden for the welfare state and the criminal justice system that is approximately two times larger than of the population baseline.

This quantification of a per capita headwind is key for later in the book because if we can next obtain an estimate of the numbers of extra children born due to welfare incentives, we can combine the two estimates to make an educated guess about the scale of the damage caused to a nation by a welfare state that increases the number of children born into disadvantage.

But this book is not just about disadvantage – it is also about personality. We now need to estimate the proportion of that headwind that can be attributed to personality. For example, it may be true that childhood disadvantage increases the rate of unemployment in adulthood, but if none of that effect is caused by personality deficits resulting from exposure to disadvantage, then welfare-induced personality mis-development is not worth worrying about.

Of particular importance is the already-cited study by James Heckman, Rodrigo Pinto and Peter Savelyev (2013), who used data from the Perry Preschool Project to show that childhood disadvantage blights life outcomes at age 40 by altering personality. More specifically, disadvantaged children who received two years of intensive preschool tutoring developed personality profiles that were significantly less aggressive, antisocial and rule-breaking than the untutored children (Heckman et al., 2013). This study is key to my model because it not only showed that experimentally induced changes in personality influence life outcomes in adulthood at age 40, but also estimated the effect size of personality compared to other contributory factors.

This study shows us that personality matters: Heckman and colleagues (2013) found that approximately 50 per cent of the crime-related treatment effect and 20 per cent of the employment-related treatment effect can be attributed to experimentally induced changes in personality development and the remainder to other causes (treatment effect means the difference in life outcomes between the children who received intensive preschool tutoring and those who did not receive it). We should note that there were sex differences. For example, personality improvements amongst tutored male participants are responsible for approximately 70 per cent of the treatment effect in the case of felony arrests at the age of 40 and approximately 40 per cent of the treatment effect in lifetime arrests at age 40. Likewise, personality improvements were responsible for approximately 20 per cent of the treatment effect in the case of employment record at the age of 40.

Personality improvements amongst female participants are responsible for approximately 65 per cent of the treatment effect in the case of felony arrests at the age of 40 and approximately 70 per cent of the treatment effect in lifetime violent crimes at age 40. Likewise, personality improvements were responsible for approximately 10 per cent of the treatment effect in the case of months in marriage at the age of 40.

Viewed in tandem with Figures 8.1 and 8.2, these data show that disadvantaged children create a burden for the criminal justice system and for the welfare state that is four times larger than the burden imposed by average individuals and that approximately half of this burden can be attributed to personality problems caused by childhood disadvantage. From this appraisal we can conclude that disadvantage-related personality problems are a key driver of blighted life outcomes and the scale of such outcomes is non-trivial.

Socialisation as a model of welfare-induced personality damage

The data discussed up to this point in the chapter suggest that a welfare state which causes many thousands of children to be born into disadvantage can cause personality damage that imposes a significant economic and social headwind on the nation. But these data only capture personality damage due to environmental factors, because the children in the Perry Preschool Project were randomly assigned to receive tutoring and thus genetic factors played no part in this set of results. Therefore we cannot obtain a full estimate of the scale of welfare-induced personality damage, both environmental and genetic. To move the argument forward, we need a more sophisticated model that integrates environmental and genetic factors in a single framework. We can do this by conceptualising the employment-resistant personality profile as a tendency to break social norms, which allows us to utilise existing knowledge concerning the process by which the norms of a society are instilled in its members. This process is known as socialisation (Clausen, 1968) and has been studied for decades. The leading theory is that an individual's level of socialisation is determined by an interaction between the size of their dose of genes for being difficult to socialise and the quality of their upbringing.

This idea was chiefly pioneered by David Lykken, whose model of socialisation goes like this:

> With the best parents and home environments, the only antisocial offspring will be those who are the most fearless, aggressive, impulsive, and so on – psychopaths with truly hard to-socialize temperaments. In the worst home environments, a large fraction of all offspring will remain unsocialized. Over the broad middle range of parental competence and environmental risk factors,

the incidence of antisocial offspring will be a product-function of parental incompetence (or indifference or parental sociopathy) and the child's innate proclivities. A complicating factor is that the worst parents are likely to contribute hard-to-socialize genetic tendencies as well.

(Lykken, 1995, p. 563)

This model might seem confusing, but it has at its heart the simple principle that children at both the low and the high extremes of the genetic spectrum are relatively insensitive to their environment. So a child with a high dose of the genes for being difficult to socialise is likely to develop the employment-resistant personality profile despite growing up in a nurturing environment that is conducive to the development of solid citizenship. Conversely, a child with a low dose of genes for being difficult to socialise is likely to develop into a solid citizen despite minimal parental interventions. In the majority of children, who carry an average-sized dose of genes for being difficult to socialise, the environment is more important. Competent parenting will convert most of these children into solid citizens whereas incompetent parenting will sway most of them towards employment-resistance.

A general point must be absorbed here, namely that there are many more genetically average children than there are genetic outliers, meaning that the childhood environment is crucial in determining the overall level of socialisation in the population. This explains why developed countries have converged on investing in schools as an essential measure for the improvement of human capital by boosting socialisation.

Unfortunately, as we saw in the experiments on the effects of intensive preschool tutoring described in Chapter 5, most of the work in socialising a child occurs before school age. This discovery has prompted leading economists to urge governments to think about more than just schooling when attempting to boost human capital and, in particular, to pay more attention to the role of the family: 'An effective skill formation policy must account for the role of the family in producing skills and motivation. Dysfunctional families produce impaired children' (Heckman & Masterov, 2005, pp. 15–16).

Returning to the theme of personality, when scores on a trait influenced by thousands of genes are plotted along a scale, 68.2 per cent

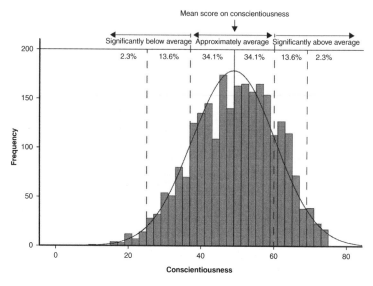

Figure 8.3   The distribution of questionnaire scores on conscientiousness in 2,532 participants from one of my own studies (dashed lines indicate one standard deviation)

of the population score near to the middle of the scale. These are the average scorers. The remaining 31.8 per cent of the population score significantly lower or higher than average. This bell-shaped pattern is known as the normal distribution and occurs in almost all frequently measured human variables, such as height or penis length. Personality data are no exception, as we see in Figure 8.3, which illustrates the normally distributed nature of questionnaire scores on conscientiousness in 2,532 participants in one of my own studies.

If we combine the statistical concept of the normal distribution with Lykken's model of socialisation, we can see that approximately 16 per cent of children are born with a significantly higher than average dose of the genes for being difficult to socialise. These children are genetic hard cases, who are relatively insensitive to their upbringing and thus have a significantly elevated risk of turning out to be employment-resistant adults regardless of whether they are neglected as children. This explains the existence of individuals who grew up in privileged, nurturing households but nevertheless turned out to be employment-resistant adults. Since employment-resistant individuals are over-represented amongst welfare claimants, we can predict that the genes for being difficult to socialise are over-represented amongst welfare claimants. This means that a welfare state which boosts the number of children born to claimants will inflict direct genetic harm on the social and economic prospects of the nation (that is, harm its human capital) by swelling the number of babies who fit into the left-hand side of Figure 8.3 due to being born with a significantly higher than average dose of the genes for being difficult to socialise.

At the other end of the scale, we can predict that approximately 16 per cent of individuals are born with a dose of the genes for being difficult to socialise that is significantly smaller than average. Although it may seem incongruous to think of them as such, these people are also genetic hard cases because they too are relatively insensitive to their upbringing. In these children, their genetic profile means they have a high probability of turning out to be solid citizens, whether or not they are neglected. This explains the existence of individuals who suffered neglect during childhood yet nevertheless turned out to be solid citizens. Thus, a welfare state that boosts the number of children born to claimants will inflict genetic harm to the human capital of the nation via a second route, namely by shrinking the number of babies who fit into the right-hand side of Figure 8.3.

Finally, approximately 68 per cent of the population are born with an average-sized dose of the genes for being difficult to socialise. This section of the population is easily swayed by their upbringing: they could go either way, towards employment-resistance or solid citizenship, depending upon whether they are neglected during childhood. As there are so many more of these children and because their personalities are so sensitive to their upbringing, the treatment of this easily swayed majority during childhood is the most important causal factor in the future development of human capital in society. Based on this analysis, I suggest that this is the mechanism by which the welfare state does the most damage to the human capital of the population, because it boosts the numbers of children with average genetic profiles who are born into disadvantaged households and who are thus at risk of being swayed towards employment-resistance by neglect.

To obtain an approximate estimate of the scale of this environmental effect of the welfare state on personality, relative to its genetic effects, consider that the UK contains approximately 63 million people at the time of writing. The normal distribution tells us that approximately ten million of these people (16 per cent) will carry a relatively low dose of the genes for being difficult to socialise, ten million of them (16 per cent) will carry a relatively high dose and 43 million (68 per cent) will carry an approximately average dose.

Government figures show that approximately 800,000 children were born in the UK in the last year, about 110,000 of them into workless households. Had the previous 15 years not seen a 50 per cent increase in welfare generosity, that latter total would have been approximately 15 per cent smaller (about 14,000 fewer children per year; Brewer et al., 2011). The normal distribution tells us that of those extra 14,000 welfare babies born per year in response to the increased financial incentives of the welfare state, about 2,240 (16 per cent) will carry significantly lower than average doses of genes for being difficult to socialise. These are the children who have a low risk of developing employment-resistant personalities regardless of their upbringing and will tend to become solid citizens, even if neglected. About 2,240 (16 per cent) will carry significantly higher than average doses of genes for being difficult to socialise. These are the children who have a high risk of developing into employment-resistant adults, regardless of their upbringing.

As a caveat, I should emphasise that this latter number is a conservative estimate, since employment-resistant adults are over-represented in the welfare-claiming sector of the population (Vaughn et al., 2010) and so babies born to welfare claimants will on average receive a larger dose of genes for employment-resistance than children born to non-claimants. However, pinning down the size of this subsidiary genetic effect is not something we have the knowledge to do at this stage, so it is safer to assume genetic parity with the rest of the population for now.

These genetic outliers are a sideshow, since the normal distribution also tells us that a far larger number of these extra babies born per year to workless families will carry an average-sized dose of genes for being difficult to socialise (approximately 9,548 of the 14,000 extra babies; 68 per cent). These are the children who are at high risk of being swayed towards employment-resistance by neglect, according to Lykken's model of socialisation. We have already seen that approximately 60 per cent of children born into households populated by employment-resistant adults will be neglected (Tonge et al., 1975) and so we can estimate that 5,728 of these easily swayed children will suffer neglect. But we can't assume that all of them will be converted into employment-resistant personalities by neglect: some might be taken into high-quality foster care, or encounter a positive role model outside the family, such as an inspiring teacher or sports coach. This brings us back to David Lykken, who concluded: 'In the worst home environments, a large fraction of all offspring will remain unsocialized' (Lykken, 1995, p. 563).

Based on the Lykken model of socialisation, his use of the phase 'a large fraction' implies a plausible conversion rate is somewhere between 50 and 100 per cent. If we split the difference with a 75 per cent conversion rate, this means that we can estimate that every year in the UK, 4,296 genetically average children (that is, 75 per cent of 5,728 of the neglected children mentioned in the previous paragraph) who have been born into workless households in response to increased generosity of the welfare state will be swayed towards employment-resistance via neglect. This is approximately twice the number of extra babies born with a larger than average dose of genes for being difficult to socialise (2,240 children). So we can see that the environmental effect of the welfare state on personality is approximately twice as large as the genetic effect, but both of them count when it comes to lowering the human capital of the nation. So we can see that by increasing the generosity of welfare benefits by 50 per cent back in 1999, the UK has acquired approximately 6,536 extra employment-resistant individuals per year $(4,296 + 2,240)$. In total therefore, we can estimate that this 50 per cent increase in welfare generosity 15 years ago has since endowed the UK with approximately 210,000 extra children born into disadvantaged families. Of these extra children, approximately 98,040 are more employment-resistant than average.

Almost 100,000 extra employment-resistant individuals created by the welfare state over the last 15 years may sound like a bad thing in principle, but in a nation of 63 million people, can such a relatively small number in practice impose a significant financial drag on society? We have already seen in Figures 8.1 and 8.2 that environmental effects alone are sufficient to cause individuals who suffered childhood disadvantage to impose a burden on society that is approximately four times greater than that of the average individual. But that fourfold burden is not suitable for producing an estimate of the absolute financial cost to society of each disadvantaged individual because, for example, they may have worse criminal records than average citizens and therefore end up having been jailed more often by the age of 40 than average individuals.

To quantify in financial terms the burden on society imposed by the extra 98,040 UK residents who possess the employment-resistant personality profile, we must first recall that under current government regulations, the most a workless household in the UK can take home in benefits is £500 per week (£26,000 per year). At an average of 2.3 people per UK household, it is reasonable to assume that each extra employment-resistant individual will cost the UK taxpayer an extra £11,304 per year in welfare benefits alone, since the prominent feature of the employment-resistant personality profile is a high risk of unemployment. For example, in Chapter 2 we saw that the study of problem families in Sheffield by W. L. Tonge and colleagues showed that only nine of the 33 problem families contained parents who had worked for more than 10 per cent of the previous three years, compared to 23 out of 33 of the comparison families.

These welfare costs take no account of any of the other costs that employment-resistant individuals typically cause to the taxpayer. Perhaps the most obvious of these is criminality. For example, Tonge and colleagues (1975) found that criminality was more than six times higher in the problem families than in the comparison families: the 66 adults in the problem group had 495 criminal convictions (446 for the men and 49 for the women) whereas the 66 adults in the comparison group had 81 convictions (79 for the men and 2 for the women).

Importantly, the higher rate of convictions in the problem group was not caused by one or two super-prolific criminals, but instead reflected a general tendency towards crime in the group as a whole: only three of the men in the problem group had no convictions (9 per cent) compared to 12 in the comparison group (36 per cent). As Tonge and colleagues matched the two groups of families on affluence, these criminality differences cannot be explained away as an artefact of differences in poverty between the problem and comparison families.

To estimate the extra criminal costs resulting from the extra 98,040 employment-resistant individuals born in the UK since 1999 due to welfare incentives, we are fortunate to be able to call upon a detailed analysis of the costs by Brand and Price (2000). This showed that 60,730,000 criminal incidents cost the UK approximately £55 billion in the year 1999/2000. This works out at a cost of approximately £934 per crime at current prices. Tonge and colleagues showed that problem family adults by the age of 30–40 had accumulated approximately seven convictions each, whereas the adults from the comparison families on average had accumulated only one conviction. Therefore we can see that crimes perpetrated by each employment-resistant individual studied by Tonge and colleagues would have cost approximately £7,000 in today's prices. This means that the criminality of employment-resistant individuals increases their per capita cost to society by about £500 per year of adulthood. If this crime cost is added to the benefits cost, we can see that each employment-resistant personality costs approximately £12,000 per year.

But welfare benefits and criminality are just two facets of the extra costs caused by employment-resistant individuals. For example, we may recall that the adults of the Sheffield problem families not only had significantly worse work and criminal records than the adults of the comparison families, but also had significantly more children and were significantly more neglectful of those children. Moreover, those children were themselves significantly more criminally inclined than the children of the comparison families: of the 55 comparison children who were over the age of criminal responsibility at the time of survey (ten years old), seven (13 per cent) had a conviction. In contrast, of the 95 children in problem families who were over the age of criminal responsibility at the time of survey, 31 (32 per cent) had a conviction.

This finding means we can say that each of the 98,040 employment-resistant individuals born in response to welfare incentives since 1999 will cost the public purse at least an extra £12,000 per year. At a national level, this allows us to estimate that the welfare-induced proliferation of employment-resistant personalities due to increased welfare generosity since 1999 is costing the UK taxpayer upwards of £1.2 billion per year.

But costs are relative and it is only when we compare the cost to society of an employment-resistant person to that of an average person that we see what a burden on the public purse employment-resistant individuals really are. For example, at the time of writing, the UK government needs to borrow approximately £120 billion per year in order to keep the nation going. If we divide that cash sum by the number of people in the UK (approximately 63 million at the time of writing), we can see that on average each person in the UK costs the public purse approximately £1,900 per year. Since our initial estimate suggests that a person with the employment-resistant personality profile costs the nation approximately £12,000 per year, we can now see that employment-resistant individuals cost the nation approximately six times as much per year compared to the average person. Note that this is likely to be an underestimate since the value for the average person includes individuals with the employment-resistant personality profile.

Cost estimates at a national level are a tricky business and so, as a sanity check, it is important to compare my estimate of the per annum cost to the nation of each employment-resistant individual to estimates by other researchers of the per annum costs to the public purse of individuals with antisocial personality characteristics. For example, including the average cost of welfare, medical care, juvenile corrections, police time, legal expenses, trial costs, probation officers and imprisonment, but not including the value of property stolen or destroyed by the antisocial individual, nor the heartache and stress that their behaviour causes to others, nor the cost of negligent parenting, Westman (1994) estimated that each individual with antisocial personality disorder in the USA costs the public purse $51,362 per year.

Westman's estimate is backed up by the results of a study of 135 persistent juvenile criminals in Minneapolis, which found that a single offender cost the public purse $239,551 over four years ($59,888 per annum; Wiig, 1995). In today's prices with today's dollar/pound conversion rate, we can see that these estimates indicate that each person with antisocial personality disorder costs the public purse approximately £48,000 per year, some 25 times as much per year as the average person (£1,900 per year) and approximately four times as much as an individual with the employment-resistant personality profile (£12,000 per year).

Viewed as a whole, these previous estimates by Westman (1994) and Wiig (1995) provide reassurance that my estimate is sensible, since we have already seen evidence in Chapter 4 that the employment-resistant personality profile represents a milder version of antisocial personality disorder and so should be less costly to the public purse, as indeed is the case. The notion that the employment-resistant personality profile is intermediate in severity between normality and antisocial personality disorder is further backed up by the study of problem families in Sheffield by Tonge et al. (1975). This showed that, despite their pervasive pattern of dysfunctional, employment-resistant behaviour, only two of the 66 adults in the problem group met the criteria for antisocial personality disorder. Reassuringly, none of the 66 adults in the comparison group met these criteria.

Conclusion

The Lykken model of socialisation means that, of the 15 per cent more children that have been born to workless families in the UK due to 50 per cent rises in welfare generosity in 1999, almost half of them will possess the employment-resistant personality profile. This occurs by a combination of environmental and genetic mechanisms, in a ratio of two to one. The financial cost to society of this welfare-induced proliferation of employment-resistant personalities is likely to be upwards of £1.2 billion per year (98,040 × £12,000), or approximately 1 per cent of overall welfare spending, which in 2014, the UK government announced is to be capped at £120 billion.

9

Further Evidence for Welfare-Induced Personality Mis-Development

Theories that are unsuitable for testing by laboratory experiments require corroboration via circumstantial evidence. This is a less satisfactory form of corroboration but it is still valuable, as Charles Darwin demonstrated by his use of circumstantial evidence to convince the scientific establishment of the validity of his theory of evolution by natural selection. Much has been made of Darwin's use of what could be dubbed 'positive' circumstantial evidence; that is, chance observations that fit the theory of evolution by natural selection (for example, the Galapagos finches). But less attention has been paid to Darwin's use of what could be dubbed 'negative' circumstantial evidence; that is, the lack of chance evidence that contradicts evolution by natural selection. For example, in the first edition of the *Origin of Species* Darwin dealt with the issue thus: 'If it could be demonstrated that any complex organ existed, which could not possibly have been formed by numerous, successive, slight modifications, my theory would absolutely break down. But I can find out no such case' (Darwin, 1859, p. 219).

In the case of the welfare trait theory, my argument hinges on the discovery that childhood disadvantage encourages the formation of aggressive, antisocial and rule-breaking personality characteristics (Heckman et al., 2013). This finding is crucial because it means that a welfare state which boosts the number of children born into disadvantaged households will also undermine the nation's stock of human capital by boosting the number of children in the population who develop employment-resistant personality profiles. To paraphrase Darwin, 'If it could be demonstrated that childhood disadvantage benefits personality formation, by encouraging the development of conscientious and agreeable personality characteristics, then my theory would absolutely break down. But I can find no such study.'

With regard to 'positive' circumstantial evidence for the welfare trait theory, most nations of the Western world have had some form of welfare state in place for approximately seven decades. If the welfare trait theory is valid, we should therefore be able to see some signs that the employment-resistant personality profile has begun to proliferate over the last 70 years or so. The chief purpose of this chapter is to summarise circumstantial evidence that fits this idea.

First, I return to a topic that was touched upon in Chapter 1, namely economic studies in Scandinavia that have explored the effect of the welfare state on work motivation, both within and between generations. We shall see that the results of these studies fit the welfare trait theory, as they show that increased welfare generosity encourages fraudulent claims and also that the willingness to defraud the welfare state increases with each generation.

These data from Scandinavia are reassuring, but it is unsurprising that they corroborate my theory since it was in part based on them. To prevent the welfare trait theory becoming just another uninformative, circular theory that is corroborated by the evidence that formed it, we need to find corroborating evidence that is consistent with the theory and yet did not inspire its creation.

We will therefore begin our escape from circularity by examining anthropological research on behaviour in small-scale, tribal societies that have existed more or less unaltered for many centuries. Such societies provide a natural experiment that can shed light on the capacity of a population's economic and social environment to shape its behavioural style – that is, its personality profile. These studies are therefore well placed to corroborate the notion presented in this book that, by altering the economic and social landscape of a nation, the welfare state has the potential also to alter the personality of its population. More specifically, if the welfare trait theory is correct, we should see signs in societies in which survival chances are disconnected from forward planning, diligence or cooperation – as is the case in the modern welfare state – that the personality profile of the population resembles that of employment-resistant welfare claimants in the Western world. Conversely, we should find that societies in which survival chances are boosted by behaving in a well-planned, diligent and cooperative manner – as was the case in Britain between AD 1100 and 1800, according to Clark (2007) – are populated mostly by individuals with conscientious and agreeable personality profiles. As we will see, this is approximately the pattern that anthropologists have found, but such research does not measure reproduction and so has limited value as corroboration for the welfare trait theory.

The true key to non-circular corroboration of the welfare trait theory is the insight that an employment-resistant attitude is just one manifestation of a general tendency to behave in an antisocial, norm-breaking manner. As we saw in Chapter 4, another manifestation of this personality profile is a willingness to have extra children in order to increase welfare income, but then to neglect those children. According to my theory, it is this latter facet of the employment-resistant personality profile that gives the welfare state its special power to alter the personality make-up of the nation by boosting the number of children who are born into disadvantaged households and who suffer personality mis-development as a result.

If it is true that the welfare state is causing the employment-resistant personality profile to proliferate, we would therefore expect workless families not only to display high rates of antisocial behaviour, but also to have more children than average – children who are then neglected. Evidence of this type has already been provided in earlier chapters by the longitudinal studies of problem families undertaken in Sheffield by W. L. Tonge and colleagues, but the sample sizes in those studies were relatively small (66 families in total) and they were completed more than 30 years ago.

What we require is a larger, more recently collected data set that can be used to provide independent replication or refutation of the findings of the Sheffield studies. Just such a data set has been collected in the UK by the Troubled Families Programme, which was initiated in December 2010 with the aim of helping families with three or more adjustment problems to turn their lives around. As we shall see, these data replicate the results of the Sheffield studies, as they show that troubled families not only display higher than average rates of antisocial behaviour, but also have more children than average families. Moreover, those children tend to be neglected. The former association is unsurprising, since unemployment and antisocial behaviour were two of the criteria used to select families for the Troubled Families Programme. However, family size was not one of the entry criteria for the programme. This means that the data from the Troubled Families Programme provide independent support for my hypothesis that the welfare state is proliferating antisocial personality characteristics by boosting the number of children born into neglect-prone households.

Continuing the theme that employment-resistance is just one manifestation of a general tendency to behave in an antisocial manner, a particularly well-documented form of antisocial behaviour is crime. This opens up a third avenue for corroboration of the welfare trait theory: if it is true that the welfare state is modifying the personality profile of the population towards greater employment-resistance, then we should not only see a reduction in work motivation from generation to generation following the introduction of the welfare state, but also find that there is a concomitant upsurge in crime as each generation passes. More specifically, because antisocial personality characteristics have a particularly strong link to criminal violence (Hodgins, 2007; Jüriloo et al., 2013), we should see an upsurge in violent crime, beginning about 15 years or so after the implementation of the welfare state, as the first generation of individuals with mis-developed personalities grow old enough to begin showing up in the crime statistics. In the final part of this chapter, I summarise evidence that supports this hypothesis.

Effects of the welfare state on work motivation

When assessing the effects of the welfare state upon work motivation, we are fortunate to be able to call upon decades of research on welfare-usage trends in Scandinavian countries. These nations have become the leaders of such research because they typically implemented a modern welfare state before most other nations of the Western world and economists therefore have been able to study its effects for longer. At the forefront of attempts to understand the effects of the welfare state on work motivation is the work of Assar Lindbeck, who, as mentioned in Chapter 1, proposed that the welfare state risks destroying itself via the erosion of norms connected to work and responsibility. In Lindbeck's view: 'The basic dilemma of the welfare state, however, is that the more generous the benefits, the greater will be not only the tax distortions but also, because of moral hazard and benefit cheating, the number of beneficiaries' (Lindbeck, 1995, p. 2).

Central to Lindbeck's work is the notion that generous welfare benefits have a delayed effect on behaviour owing to the time taken to erode the social norms of previous generations. There is some empirical support for this idea, since it has been found that generous welfare benefits weaken parents' incentives to instil work-motivation norms in their children (Lindbeck & Nyberg, 2006). A delayed negative impact of the welfare state on the functioning of society is also consistent with the welfare trait theory, which can explain it in terms of the time taken for claimants' children who have suffered personality mis-development due to childhood disadvantage to grow old enough to show up in government statistics on unemployment, crime and other key metrics of societal dysfunction. Either way, the danger of welfare-induced reductions in work motivation is clear: 'if we do not watch out for hazardous dynamics, there is a risk that the welfare state will destroy its own economic foundations' (Lindbeck, 1995, p. 2).

Basic evidence to corroborate the notion that the welfare state can erode work motivation has been provided by studies that compare unemployment rates and welfare generosity between countries. For example, Nickell (1997) investigated the effects of welfare benefits on unemployment rates in 20 OECD countries, namely Austria, Belgium, Denmark, Finland, France, Germany, Ireland, Italy, the Netherlands, Norway, Portugal, Spain, Sweden, Switzerland, the UK, Canada, the USA, Japan, Australia and New Zealand. This study showed that high unemployment was significantly associated with generous welfare benefits, as well as with lengthy/unlimited periods of entitlement.

But studies that compare unemployment rates and welfare generosity are something of a blunt instrument, since they do not directly measure work motivation and there are many other reasons why unemployment rates and welfare generosity might be connected. A more specific empirical test of Lindbeck's theory is to use self-report data on attitudes to welfare usage. For example, Heinemann (2008) used data from the European and World Values Survey to investigate associations between benefit morale and welfare generosity in 33 OECD countries. Benefit morale is a construct that reflects willingness to claim benefits to which the individual is not entitled: the more willing the individual is to cheat the welfare state, the lower their benefit morale. In four time periods (1981–1984, 1989–1993, 1994–1999, 1999–2004), there was a general increase – with a substantial time lag – in the willingness of the citizens of these nations to make fraudulent benefit claims. This trend tended to occur more strongly in more generous welfare states, such as Sweden. In order to control for age effects, Heinemann (2008) also examined differences in benefit morale between individuals from different birth cohorts who were surveyed at the same age, finding that younger birth cohorts were more willing to cheat the welfare state than older birth cohorts, even though their age at the time of survey was the same. This latter finding is especially supportive of the welfare trait theory because if the welfare state is shifting the personality profile of the population towards lower levels of conscientiousness and agreeableness, we would expect to see that young cohorts would be more comfortable than older cohorts when fraudulently claiming welfare handouts.

Subsequent studies have mostly produced similar results to those obtained by Heinemann (2008). For example, Halla, Lackner and Schneider (2010) also examined data from the European and World Values Survey, but used different statistical analyses. They studied effects of welfare generosity on benefit morale over three different time lags: short run (the effect of current generosity on current benefit morale), medium run (the effect on current benefit morale of increased welfare generosity five years previously) and long run (the effect on current benefit morale of increased welfare generosity ten years previously). They found that high welfare spending in the current period had a small positive effect on current benefit morale. In the medium run (five years) there was no effect, but in the long run (ten years) there was a significant negative effect, with a percentage point increase in welfare generosity followed ten years later by a decrease in benefit morale of approximately 0.22 points.

This finding backed up Heinemann (2008), with Halla and colleagues explaining it by suggesting that 'individuals have to experience generous welfare arrangements for quite some time until they adapt their social norm towards accepting benefit fraud, or at least considering it to be a minor offence' (Halla et al., 2010, p. 69). This explanation sees individuals as responsive to the perverse incentives of the welfare state, but with a delay in their willingness to defraud the welfare state that is caused by their need to overcome their ingrained reluctance to cheat the system. However, this result is also consistent with my theory of welfare-induced personality mis-development which explains the delayed action of benefit increases by postulating that faulty norms are acquired during childhood (for example, by observing a parent committing benefit fraud) that then make the individual more likely to cheat the welfare state a decade or so later when they themselves become old enough to start claiming benefits.

Halla and colleagues also found that, after statistical refinements which were not performed by Heinemann (2008), there were no significant differences between birth cohorts in willingness to cheat the welfare state. This finding counters the welfare trait theory, which predicts a reduction in work ethic from generation to generation due to a progressively greater frequency of individuals with the employment-resistant personality profile in each birth cohort. However, interestingly, Halla and colleagues also showed that labour-market status modulates benefit morale: unemployed individuals had a significantly lower level of benefit morale than employed individuals (approximately four per cent lower). Lower morale could be a product of unemployment, but it could also be a cause: this latter possibility is consistent with the welfare trait theory, on the basis that employment-resistant individuals are less motivated than average citizens to work for a living and so tend to be unsatisfactory employees, causing them to filter into the ranks of the unemployed at higher rates.

A recent study that could be portrayed as countering the welfare trait theory investigated the relationship between employment commitment and welfare generosity in 18 European countries (van der Wel & Halvorsen, 2015). This study used data from the European Social Survey which included the question: 'I would enjoy having a paid job even if I did not need the money.' Participants responded by endorsing one of the following options: 'Strongly agree', 'Agree', 'Neither agree nor disagree', 'Disagree', 'Disagree strongly' and 'Don't know'. The response options 'Strongly agree' or 'Agree' were coded as one and the remaining options were coded as zero, except for 'Don't know' responses, which were coded as missing.

Using responses to this question as a measure of work motivation, van der Wel and Halvorsen (2015) found that average levels of commitment to employment were high in more generous welfare states. For example, the highest levels of employment commitment were found in Norway, Denmark, the Netherlands and Switzerland, which were also the most generous nations in terms of welfare benefits. However, unlike the previously mentioned research, this was a cross-sectional study and therefore is unable to shed light on causation. For instance, the moral hazard of generous welfare benefits may be lower in countries with a high baseline level of work motivation than in countries with a weak work ethic. Furthermore, the cross-sectional study design cannot detect change in work motivation from generation to generation, which is a key part of Lindbeck's warning concerning the self-destructive nature of the welfare state.

However, the most serious criticism of this study (and much of the research in this field) is that a single, self-report question was used to measure work motivation. It would be prudent therefore to test the validity of these findings by examining whether welfare-claiming behaviour showed similar patterns to self-reported attitudes. The work of Martin Ljunge (2011) provides just such a test. First, instead of looking at changes in attitudes to welfare usage, Ljunge (2011) used data on longitudinal changes in actual welfare usage in Sweden. Second, Ljunge (2011) selected sick-benefit claims as the focus of his research because, for the first week of each spell of sick leave, the Swedish welfare state allows the individual to decide for themselves whether they are sick. Ljunge (2011) describes this system as being 'like a giant marshmallow test', since its laissez-faire design gives unconscientious individuals a free hand to defraud the welfare state by pretending they are sick when they are not. This impression is supported by previous research which showed that the number of men who reported sick in Sweden increased significantly when there was a major televised sporting event (Skogman Thoursie, 2004). The uptake of sick benefits in Sweden therefore allows objective measurement of changes in work motivation between generations.

Ljunge (2011) used data for Swedes aged between 22 and 60, randomly sampled from the 1974 population and followed for 17 years. Ljunge (2011) selected this time period because the rules governing sick leave remained constant between 1963 and 1990, with data on sick leave becoming available from 1974 onwards. This means that any changes in the usage of sick benefits over this time cannot be attributed to changes in welfare rules.

In line with the welfare trait theory, as well as the findings of Heinemann (2008), Ljunge (2011) found that younger generations of

Swedes claimed more sick-leave benefits than older generations. The effect was substantial, with each generation having approximately a one per cent higher take-up of sick benefits than the previous generation. For example, the generation born in 1920 on average claimed sick benefit in fewer than half of the years that they were in the labour force (45 per cent) whereas the generation born in 1960 had a take-up rate of almost 80 per cent, making a sick-benefit claim in eight out of every ten years of their working life.

This difference between generations in sick-benefit claims cannot be explained by health differences, since younger generations of Swedes had better health than older generations and so, if they were being honest, they should have claimed *less* sick benefit than their older compatriots. Moreover, Ljunge (2011) found that these inter-generational differences in sick-benefit claims were mirrored by differences in unemployment-benefit claims: younger generations claimed more unemployment insurance than older generations.

Ljunge (2011) then tested whether these changes in welfare usage were mirrored by attitude changes. He used data from the integrated European Values Survey and World Values Survey (EVS/WVS), focusing on data from 95 countries in five waves of collection from 1981–1984 to 2005–2006. In line with Heinemann (2008) and his own data on sick-benefit uptake, Ljunge (2011) found that younger generations of Swedes viewed it as more acceptable to claim benefits than older generations of Swedes. Furthermore, he found that this change was echoed in most of the other 95 countries studied.

Ljunge (2011) suggests that the trend for younger generations to abuse the welfare state more than older generations could be explained by increased exposure to role models who have a high take-up rate of welfare benefits. Ljunge's analysis is consistent with the welfare trait theory, but leaves unanswered the question as to what causes this increased exposure to dysfunctional role models. The welfare trait theory can explain this, on the basis that a welfare state which boosts the number of children born into disadvantaged households will increase the number of children exposed to dysfunctional, employment-resistant parental role models.

Viewed as a whole, the balance of evidence provided by these economic studies fits the notion that the welfare state is increasing the frequency of individuals with mis-developed, employment-resistant personality profiles – profiles that make them willing to defraud the welfare state. However, since the welfare trait theory was partly inspired by these same Scandinavian economic studies, any attempt to use them to corroborate it is an exercise in circularity. To begin the process of breaking this circularity, we now move on to independent evidence concerning the capacity of environmental factors to mould personality.

Cross-cultural comparison of social attitudes

Differences in social attitudes can be measured using standardised tasks that model important everyday interactions. One such task is the Ultimatum Game (UG), which measures attitudes that correspond approximately to the personality domain of agreeableness, such as fairness, generosity, altruism, unselfishness and cooperativeness. It involves two players whose identities are concealed from each other. The anonymity of the players is a key feature of the UG because it prevents their behaviour being influenced by pre-existing relationships, such as friendship or genetic kinship.

One UG player (known as the proposer) is allotted a substantial asset that can easily be divided (for example, a sum of money equivalent to two day's wages in the society in question) and is instructed to offer a part of the asset to the second player (known as the responder). The responder, who is aware of the size of offer, as well as the overall size of the asset, is free either to accept or reject the proposer's offer. If the responder accepts the offer, he or she receives that part of the asset and the proposer receives the remaining amount. If the responder rejects the offer, then neither player receives any of the asset.

The UG is a one-shot game: once the response has been made, the game terminates and the two players depart with their allotted winnings in the event of an accepted offer, or with nothing if the offer is declined. Importantly, the UG requires no work or material contribution from either player – the asset is, in effect, a free gift. This latter feature makes the UG relevant to discussions of a welfare state in which benefits are provided without requiring work in return.

The rational response in the UG is to accept any offer, however small, since something is always better than nothing from the standpoint of maximising economic gain. If this rule applied in humans, every UG offer, however mean/selfish, would be accepted. Yet scores of studies have shown that humans do not usually behave rationally in the UG. Most UG research to date has been in undergraduates from advanced nations: in this population, offers are on average between 40 and 45 per cent and offers of this size are usually accepted. Offers substantially below this value, such as 20 per cent, are typically rejected about half the time, as if to punish the proposer for being selfish (Sanfey et al., 2003). This deviation from rationality in the UG suggests that humans care about fairness and cooperation, but undergraduate students in advanced nations are not necessarily typical of the wider human population. This factor means that these early UG data were unable to reveal whether a fair-minded attitude towards non-family is universal across human cultures or whether it is shaped by local factors.

In an attempt to resolve this problem, Joseph Henrich and colleagues administered the UG to the members of 15 primitive, small-scale, mainly tribal hunter-gatherer or forager societies. This research revealed significant group-level differences between the 15 societies in attitude towards individuals from outside the family unit (Henrich et al., 2005). Whether these differences in attitude are wholly learned or also have a genetic component is unclear, but given what we know about the biological basis of personality, they are likely to be a product of both nature and nurture acting in response to the environment. More specifically, the differences in attitude between the societies studied by Henrich and colleagues seem to be shaped by the degree to which survival in a particular environment demands group-level cooperation. This idea is supported by the finding that the societies whose members care little about fairness (as evidenced by low offers being made and accepted in the UG) tend to occur in environments in which cooperation with non-family members has negligible survival value. Conversely, the societies whose members typically care strongly about fairness (as evidenced by high offers being made and accepted in the UG) tended to occur in environments in which cooperation with non-family members has major survival value.

As a caveat, these discoveries should not be interpreted as meaning that the members of small-scale societies all have the same personality profile, because there is evidence that personality outliers exist in primitive, hunter-gatherer societies, just as they do in advanced nations. For example, anthropological studies of Eskimo culture have revealed norms that are harsher than those in a typical advanced nation, as in times of hardship, the Eskimo traditionally conserved food by practising both infanticide and senicide (the killing of children and elders, respectively).

Yet evidence exists of individuals who repeatedly breach the norms of Eskimo society and, furthermore, these individuals have approximately the same personality characteristics as an employment-resistant individual in a developed Western nation such as the UK or USA (that is, who combine low conscientiousness and low agreeableness). For example, the Yupik of Northwest Alaska label unconscientious and disagreeable individuals as *kunlangeta* and describe them as follows:

> The man who, for example, repeatedly lies and cheats and steals things and does not go hunting and, when the other men are out of the village, takes sexual advantage of many women – someone who does not pay attention to reprimands and who is always being brought to the elders for punishment. One Eskimo among the 499 on their island was called kunlangeta. When asked what would have happened to such a person traditionally, an Eskimo said that probably 'somebody would have pushed him off the ice when nobody else was looking'.
>
> (Murphy, 1976, p. 1026)

The UG research by Henrich and colleagues has identified two small-scale, hunter-gatherer societies that possess particularly extreme cultural norms connected to fairness and cooperation, namely the Machiguenga of the Peruvian Amazon and the people of the village of Lamalera of Indonesia. In the UG, the Machiguenga on average offered 26 per cent of the asset to the responder and the highest offer by any Machiguenga was 50 per cent. Similarly, only one out of ten Machiguenga responders rejected an offer of below 20 per cent (Henrich, 2000). Overall, this pattern of results shows that compared to undergraduates from advanced nations, the Machiguenga possess a selfish attitude towards non-relatives, with a minimal sense of fairness, and feel little or no obligation to offer an equal share to responders. In line with this attitude, the Machiguenga had low expectations of generosity from others and seemed not to harbour any desire to punish selfish or mean proposers.

In contrast, the lowest Lamalera offer was 40 per cent of the asset, the average offer was 57 per cent and the highest offer was 90 per cent (Henrich et al., 2005). Since none of the Lamalera made a low offer, the experimenters introduced 20 sham offers ranging from 10 to 50 per cent of the asset (average 30 per cent) in order to assess the attitude of the Lamalera towards selfish proposers. Almost half of the lowest sham offers (three out of the eight offers) were rejected. Overall, this pattern of results suggests that the Lamalera are unselfish, with a strong sense of fairness. They are therefore closer in attitude to the undergraduates in advanced nations than they are to the Machiguenga, despite being hunter-gatherers like the Machiguenga.

The most likely cause of these attitude differences between the Machiguenga and the Lamalera is the environmental differences between these two societies: the Machiguenga have for centuries pursued a nomadic hunter-gatherer lifestyle – bolstered by some slash and burn horticulture – in the jungles of the Amazon basin in southeastern Peru. Due to this lifestyle, small (typically single-family) groups of Machiguenga can survive independently, without the need to cooperate beyond the family unit. Even in recent years, when the influence of missionaries and other outside agencies has caused the Machiguenga to settle in villages of approximately 300 people and turn to a largely horticulturalist existence, the Machiguenga remain almost completely economically independent at the family level (Henrich, 2000).

The people of the village of Lamalera, on the south coast of Lembata Island in Indonesia, are also hunter-gatherers but with a very different environment to the Machiguenga, since Lembata Island is poorly suited for supporting crops or game animals. Instead, the Lamalera have historically survived by hunting large sea animals, especially sperm whales (Alvard, 2011). This is accomplished using primitive technology, namely the village's flotilla of approximately 20 wooden rowing boats (known as *téna*), each typically 11 metres long and crewed by approximately 15 men who are equipped with hand-thrown harpoons. The limitations of their basic equipment mean that a successful whale hunt requires that the Lamalera behave in a highly collectivised and organised manner that cuts across family units: when whales are sighted, the village mobilises as a team in order to attempt a catch. The tightly choreographed whale hunt is directed by the boat captains, known as *lama fa*, who tend to be the most experienced and skilful harpooners.

If a whale hunt is successful, the resulting meat is shared amongst the households of the village irrespective of family relationships and including elderly and sick residents who have played no part in the hunt. Meat is also traded with other non-whaling communities nearby. The difficulty of killing and retrieving whales with primitive equipment means that only a few per cent of whale hunts are successful: despite hunting whales at near weekly intervals from May to October, the Lamalera typically catch fewer than six whales a year.

These UG studies are important to the argument in this book because they suggest that, if survival can be accomplished without cooperation beyond the immediate family, humans tend to gravitate towards a selfish, disagreeable attitude, as demonstrated by the Machiguenga. Since the welfare state permits survival without cooperation, it therefore risks encouraging claimants to develop a pseudo-Machiguenga attitude – or, as I have already dubbed it, the employment-resistant personality profile. Furthermore, because the asset used in the UG is provided for free by the experimenter, these data suggest that there is a causal link between personality and a willingness to accept handouts, because the UG results suggest that uncooperative individuals (that is, individuals with low scores on agreeableness) are especially greedy when it comes to accepting free resources. These UG data therefore bolster my argument in Chapter 2 that the welfare state filters employment-resistant individuals into the benefit-claiming sector of the population because individuals with low levels of agreeableness (the Machiguenga) are especially susceptible to the lure of unearned income. In line with this idea, studies have shown that antisocial personality characteristics are over-represented amongst welfare claimants (Vaughn et al., 2010).

A sceptic might argue that the agreeable, fair-minded attitude of the Lamalera is not a genuine example of non-family cooperation, but is actually a form of nepotism that evolved by natural selection due to close genetic relatedness between the residents of Lamalera. Due to the village's isolated location, this is plausible: for example, even though the UG game is played anonymously, the Lamalera participants in the UG might have assumed that the other player must be a relative because everyone in the village is closely related. In line with this notion, altruism between close relatives such as parents and siblings (that is, nepotism) can evolve by natural selection when the donor and recipient share many genes, as this means that the donor is effectively helping themselves (Hamilton, 1964).

But the cooperative behaviour of the residents of Lamalera cannot be explained away as nepotism because in hunter-gatherer terms, Lamalera is a relatively large settlement, which contained approximately 1,200 people at the time of the UG research. The population of Lamalera is therefore too large to be viewed as a single-family unit equivalent to a traditional Machinguenga grouping. In line with this notion, research has confirmed that close genetic kinship plays little part in the whale-hunting organisation of Lamalera. For example, no set of siblings in the village was large enough to crew even a single *téna* (whale-hunting boat), let alone the entire flotilla of 20 *téna* (Alvard, 2011).

The Lamalera whale hunters therefore provide a prime example of what is known as cultural kinship, in which a large group of unrelated individuals cooperate to accomplish a complex task (in this case, killing and retrieving a whale) that is impossible for a lone individual or a family group. Briefly stated, cultural kinship is the phenomenon that opens the door to the modern, organised world of altruistic human endeavour – of which the welfare state is, ironically, a prime example. This idea is backed up by the previously mentioned finding that modern, advanced populations (that is, undergraduates) perform similar to the Lamalera on the UG (Sanfey et al., 2003).

Viewed as a whole, these UG studies suggest that a welfare state which provides handouts without requiring work in return will encourage the development of employment-resistant characteristics by weakening cultural kinship. This analysis echoes the concerns of Scandinavian economists that the welfare state erodes work motivation by weakening work-related norms (Lindbeck, 1995), but it does not contain a reproductive component. It therefore might seem to be of little relevance to the welfare trait theory which maintains that changes in work motivation are influenced by welfare-induced differences in the number of children born to claimants and workers.

In order to make the relevant link, it is necessary to realise that these UG data dovetail with the concept of r–K selection which was introduced in Chapter 4. As we saw in that chapter, in conditions where resources are plentiful and competition for these resources is low, the optimal reproductive strategy is r selection, which entails rapid reproduction with relatively little regard to the wellbeing of the resulting offspring. Conversely, when resources are scarce and have to be competed for, the optimal reproductive strategy is K selection, which entails producing fewer offspring but nurturing them carefully so that each offspring is itself capable of competing for resources. In Chapter 4 we saw evidence that employment-resistant personality characteristics (low levels of conscientiousness and agreeableness) are associated with *r* selection whereas pro-employment personality characteristics (high levels of conscientiousness and agreeableness) are associated with *K* selection. Since the Machiguenga live in an environment in which resources are relatively plentiful (the Amazon basin) whereas the Lamalera live in an environment in which resources are relatively scarce (a small, stony island), we should expect the Machigeunga to incline towards *r* selection and the Lamalera towards *K* selection, with all the personality implications that accompany these two strategies.

The UG data obtained by Henrich and colleagues are only able to shed light on the agreeableness-related aspects of this hypothesis, but they fit it well, since they suggest that the Machiguenga are indeed significantly less agreeable than the Lamalera. In the context of this book, the welfare state can be conceptualised as simulating the Machiguenga environment in that it removes the need to cooperate with non-family in order to survive and also removes the need to care for children conscientiously. If this idea – and thus the welfare trait theory – is valid, we should see evidence that both antisocial behaviour and large, neglected broods of children (two correlates of *r* selection) are especially common amongst welfare claimants. The next section presents evidence of this type, using data from the Troubled Families Programme.

The Troubled Families Programme

The Troubled Families Programme was initiated by the UK government in December 2010, with all 152 upper tier local authorities in England being asked to identify families in their catchment area who required extra help, due to meeting three out of the four following criteria:

1. Are involved in youth crime or antisocial behaviour.
2. Have children who are regularly truanting or not in school.
3. Have an adult on out-of-work benefits.
4. Cause high costs to the taxpayer.

This initiative revealed that there were 111,574 families in England that met these criteria and could therefore be defined as 'troubled'. The entry criteria used to select families were relatively basic and so, to capture more fully the characteristics of these families, the government then asked each of the 152 upper tier local authorities randomly to select ten per cent of the troubled families in their catchment areas. The local authorities were asked to provide information on the selected families concerning 35 important variables, including employment, education, crime, housing, child protection, parenting, family size and health. Information was received from 133 of the local authorities, covering 8,447 families. In 1,048 of these families, data were available on all 35 variables, providing a comprehensive and detailed picture of their characteristics. Analysis of the data relating to these families is contained in the report entitled 'Understanding Troubled Families' that was published by the Department for Communities and Local Government in July 2014.

Overall, the report revealed that although the families had been selected on the basis of suffering three problems, on average, each troubled family actually suffered from nine problems. The unexpectedly severe magnitude of the difficulties suffered by troubled families prompted the authors to observe:

> For any family facing just one or two of the problems of the type highlighted above there is a higher risk of poor outcomes for their children. For example, truancy and parental unemployment tend to increase the likelihood of a child or young person becoming a NEET (that is a 16–24 year-old not in employment, education or training) with all the disadvantages this brings. However for troubled families, with an average of nine problems, the cumulative effect of these problems is likely to make it more difficult to get that child back into school, to tackle criminal behaviour or get a parent into work.
>
> (Understanding Troubled Families, p. 11)

The report itemised the problems faced by trouble families, with two of the most prominent problems being that 83 per cent contained a workless adult and 54 per cent of the troubled families were involved with crime or antisocial behaviour. These findings are congruent with my hypothesis that the employment-resistant personality profile is just one manifestation of a general tendency to behave in an antisocial manner. However, since unemployment and antisocial behaviour constituted two out of the four entry criteria for the Troubled Families Programme, this association is unsurprising. Of more interest in the context of this book are the report's additional findings concerning family size that were not part of the entry criteria to the Troubled Family Programme. If these characteristics cluster in a way that fits the welfare trait theory then they will provide support for it, since the entry criteria of the programme cannot be responsible for this pattern.

In short, the additional findings of the report fit the welfare trait theory closely. For example, as I outlined in Chapter 1, the central postulate of my theory is that the welfare state proliferates the employment-resistant personality profile by boosting the number of children born into disadvantaged households. For this postulate to hold true, it should be the case that troubled families, since they are particularly rich with employment-resistant personalities, will have more children than typical workless families and also that the problematic personality characteristics of the adults that cause families to be troubled in the first place are transmitted to the children. Both these points are supported by the report.

First, the report found that the troubled families on average contained 2.5 children. We have already seen in Chapter 4 that across the whole UK population there is a positive linear association between number of children and reliance on the welfare state: the greater the degree of reliance, the more children in the household (Figure 9.1).

Based on the discovery that individuals with the employment-resistant personality profile are over-represented amongst the welfare-claiming sector of the population (for example, Vaughn et al., 2010), the association shown in Figure 9.1 provides circumstantial support for the notion that the more employment-resistant an individual is, the more willing they are to have extra children in order to garner extra welfare benefits. But this finding could also be an artefact of the greater material needs of larger families, leading to greater reliance on welfare benefits for reasons unconnected to personality.

The finding that troubled families on average contain 2.5 children now becomes useful to the welfare trait theory because family size was not an admission criterion for the Troubled Families Programme, but antisocial behaviour was. Moreover, whilst not all troubled

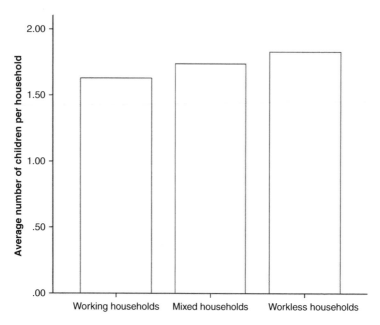

Figure 9.1   Bar chart showing the average number of children under the age of 16 in working, mixed and workless households, April–June 2013, UK
Source: Labour Force Survey Household Dataset.

families are workless, 83 per cent of them contain at least one unemployed adult. This means that the troubled families can be conceptualised as representing a subset of workless households in which the members possess particularly employment-resistant personality profiles. In line with the notion that employment-resistant personality characteristics engender a willingness to have extra children in order to increase welfare income, we would expect the troubled families to contain more children than ordinary workless families. And they do, as shown in Figure 9.2.

Second, there was a significant association between adult offending and youth offending in the troubled families: 45 per cent of families with an adult involved in antisocial behaviour also contained a young person involved in antisocial behaviour, compared to 20 per cent of families with no antisocial adults. Finally, once again in line with the notion that antisocial personality characteristics engender

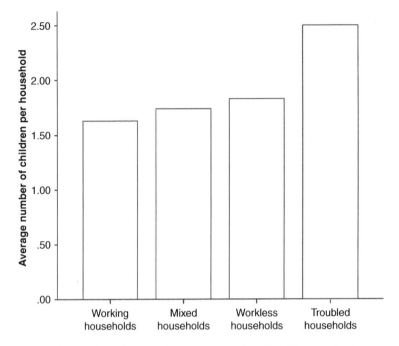

Figure 9.2 Bar chart showing the average number of children under the age of 16 in working, mixed, workless and troubled households, April–June 2013, UK

Source: Labour Force Survey Household Dataset and Department for Communities and Local Government.

a willingness to have extra children in order to increase welfare income, the report found that there is a statistically significant association between a family having more than three children and there being an adult family member with a recent criminal conviction.

None of these findings provide causal proof for the welfare trait theory, but their patterning is consistent with it, since it suggests that troubled-family status is primarily a product of employment-resistant personality characteristics in the parents/adults. Additional findings in the report reinforce the impression. For example, it shows that 29 per cent of troubled families were experiencing domestic violence, a rate that is approximately four times higher than the rate of domestic violence in the nation as a whole (seven per cent). Moreover,

23 per cent of the troubled families contained at least one child identified as being in need, due to abuse or neglect, and six per cent of the families had a child in the care of the local authorities. To put that latter number in perspective, government figures show that as of 31 March 2014, there was a total of 68,840 children in care in local authority care in the whole of England. In the UK at that time there were approximately four and half million families with dependent children: as a very rough estimate, we can therefore say that approximately one per cent of families in England have a child in care. As a result, we can see that rates of child neglect in troubled families are approximately six times higher than average.

The report also found that on average police were called to the households of the troubled families five times in the previous six months. One family had 90 police callouts in the previous six months and 21 families had more than 30 callouts in the same time frame. The extremely high number of police callouts generated by the troubled families is just one example of the high costs that troubled families impose on the public purse. These costs are detailed in a separate report entitled 'The Fiscal Case for Working with Troubled Families' that was published in February 2013 by the Department for Communities and Local Government. It concluded that the overall cost of troubled families in England to the UK government was estimated to be around £9 billion per year. Given the previous finding that there are 111,574 troubled families in England, this allows us to estimate that each troubled family costs the taxpayer approximately £81,000 per year.

This calculation is particularly interesting in the context of this book because in Chapter 8 we saw that on average each person in the UK costs the public purse approximately £1,900 per year. In 2010 there were an average of 2.3 people per UK household and so we can see that per year the average UK household costs the public purse £4,370, approximately 18 times less than the cost to the public purse of each troubled family.

However, a third government report (The National Evaluation of the Troubled Families Programme) found that the average troubled family contains more individuals than the average household (4.2 people). If we divide £81,000 by 4.2, we can see that each member of a troubled family on average costs the public purse £19,285 per year or approximately ten times more than the cost to the public purse of the average person in the UK (£1,900). From these calculations, we can see that the per-person estimate in Chapter 8 of the costs to the taxpayer of each individual with the employment-resistant personality was overly conservative: I estimated that the cost to the taxpayer of each employment-resistant individual was £12,000 per year. However, as I mentioned in Chapter 8, my estimate did not include the cost to society of paying for the care of children neglected by employment-resistant parents, whereas these new government figures do. For example, Figures 9.3 and 9.4 from 'The Fiscal Case for Working with Troubled Families' use pie charts to show how the £9 billion is spent.

As these pie charts show, approximately 41.5 per cent of the £19,285 per year that each person in a troubled family costs the taxpayer per year relates to child protection. From this we can see that my estimate of £12,000 as the annual cost of each employment-resistant individual is approximately £8,003 too low. If we add this latter figure to my estimate, it ends up as £20,003. At a mere £718 pounds more than the UK government estimate, this calculation suggests there is close agreement between these two estimates, providing reassurance that employment-resistant individuals are much more costly to society than average citizens (about ten times more costly).

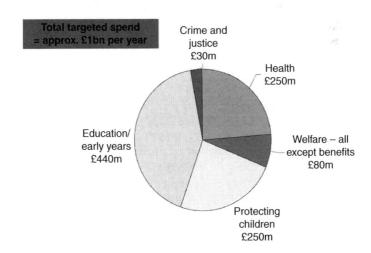

Figure 9.3 Targeted annual expenditure on troubled families
Source: The Fiscal Case for Working with Troubled Families.

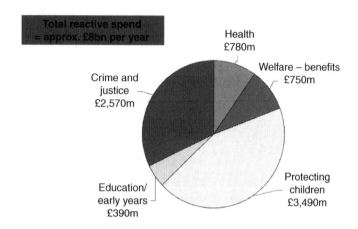

Figure 9.4   Reactive annual expenditure on troubled families
Source: The Fiscal Case for Working with Troubled Families.

As a footnote to these calculations, it should be noted that in an interview with the *Sunday Times* in August 2014, Louise Casey, the UK government's leader of the Troubled Families Programme, gave an update on the prevalence and costs of troubled families. She estimated that, in addition to the 111,574 'first tier' of troubled families, there are 400,000 'second-tier' troubled families in the UK whose problems are less severe but still significant. She estimated that the total cost to the taxpayer of all 500,000 first- and second-tier troubled families was in the region of £30 billion per year. If we refer back to Chapter 8, the number of employment-resistant individuals in the UK who exist as a result of flawed welfare policy was estimated at 98,040. At the initial per-person annual cost estimate of £12,000, this produced an extra annual cost to the public purse of approximately £1.2 billion or one per cent of welfare spending. We can now see that sum was too low: the new estimate is that employment-resistant individuals in the UK who exist as a result of welfare policy cost the public purse approximately £1.9 billion (98,040 × £19,285) or 1.5 per cent of welfare spending.

The data gathered by the Troubled Families Programme are reassuring for the validity of the welfare trait theory, yet they are cross-sectional and so do not shed light on causation. The clearest corroborating evidence of all for my theory would be data showing that the implementation of the welfare state is followed by an upsurge in a behaviour that is more common in people who possess the employment-resistant personality profile, yet is not connected to the welfare state. One such behaviour is criminality, because it is not necessarily connected to the world of work, nor is it necessarily motivated by economic gain, yet it is more common amongst employment-resistant individuals. Therefore, a convincing clue that the welfare state really is increasing the frequency of mis-developed, employment-resistant personality profiles would be the presence of an upsurge in crime following the introduction of the welfare state.

Chapter 2 introduced the research on problem families in Sheffield that was conducted by W. L. Tonge and colleagues (Tonge et al., 1975, 1981). Amongst other things, we saw evidence that the adults of the 33 problem families had personality profiles that were significantly less conscientious and agreeable than those of the adults from 33 comparison families, who were matched for location and socio-economic background. In line with the claim that low levels of conscientiousness and agreeableness constitute the employment-resistant personality profile, we also saw that the problem-family adults had significantly worse work records than the adults in the comparison families. Moreover, in Chapter 8 we saw that the problem-family adults averaged approximately seven convictions per head versus one conviction per head amongst the adults in the comparison families.

Viewed as a whole, these findings by Tonge et al. (1975) provide background support for an association between criminality, unemployment and the employment-resistant personality profile. They also fit the data gathered by the Troubled Families Programme. But they also suggest that we need to be more specific regarding which types of criminality are important. For example, Tonge and colleagues found that high levels of criminality were also displayed by some participants whose personality profiles were well-adjusted.

One of our subjects with a lengthy list of criminal convictions due to his activities as a burglar was an exemplary husband and father to his family. We were impressed by his attitude of social responsibility when he explained why he burgled only commercial premises, which he expected to be adequately insured. He avoided all private houses, even large ones 'because you never know how poor they are'. Consistency of purpose and coherence of meaning must be lacking if the diagnosis of personality disorder is to be sustained.

(Tonge et al., 1975, p. 26)

Based on this evidence, it is necessary to narrow down the type of criminality associated with the employment-resistant personality profile. Fortunately, Tonge and colleagues itemised the types of criminality perpetrated by the Sheffield families, showing that the biggest difference in type of conviction between the two family types was in criminal violence. More specifically, 8 of the 33 men in the problem families had convictions for violence, yet only 1 of the 33 men in the comparison families had a conviction of this type, a ratio of 8:1. In contrast, 20 of the 33 in the problem families had convictions for crimes of dishonesty but so did 7 of the 33 men in the comparison families, a ratio of almost 3:1. These data show that criminal violence was especially common amongst the men of the problem families, suggesting that there is indeed a link between violent criminality and the employment-resistant personality profile.

These results point to the existence of a link between employment-resistance and violent crime. The existence of this link is further supported by homicide statistics. For example, in 2007, the UK government began recording the employment status of individuals convicted of homicide in England and Wales, classifying them as employed, unemployed, retired, student and other. Table 9.1 summarises these data from 2007 until 8 November 2013 (the latest available figures), showing that unemployed individuals perpetrate more killings than individuals in all the other four employment categories combined. Moreover, given that the unemployment rate in England and Wales was approximately seven per cent during this time period, we can see that unemployed people are approximately nine times more common amongst convicted killers than amongst the general population as a whole.

These data are for England and Wales, but it should be noted that the general trend for unemployed individuals to be over-represented amongst convicted killers has also been found in other nations of the Western world. For example, Mucchielli (2004) profiled individuals who were convicted of murder in the department of Yvelines in France over the previous ten years. This study is interesting because it

Table 9.1 Employment status of individuals convicted of homicide in England and Wales from 2007/2008 to 2012

	2007/ 2008	2008/ 2009	2009/ 2010	2010/ 2011	2011/ 2012	2012/ 2013
Employed	156(29%)	121(29%)	114(27%)	120(32%)	82(26%)	55(25%)
Unemployed	311(58%)	255(60%)	265(63%)	227(60%)	205(66%)	152(69%)
Retired	8(1%)	8(2%)	9(2%)	11(3%)	9(3%)	4(%)
Student	56(10%)	36(8%)	36(8%)	19(5%)	9(3%)	9(4%)
Other	4(1%)	4(1%)	0(0%)	3(1%)	5(2%)	–
Total	535	424	424	380	310	220

Note: Figures as at 8 November 2013. Figures are subject to revision as cases are dealt with by the police and the courts, or as further information becomes available. The data for more recent years is incomplete, as cases are still going through the courts. Excludes 373 suspects whose employment status was unknown. Percentages may not sum due to rounding.

not only profiled the offenders at the time of their conviction but also attempted to trace their prior life histories. The relevant finding was that of the 122 murderers in the study, only 48 (39 per cent) were in employment at the time of the offence and of these employed murderers, only ten had consistent work records in the years prior to the offence.

These homicide data from the UK and France show that there is a significant association between criminal violence and unemployment, to the extent that unemployed people are approximately ten times more common amongst convicted killers than amongst the general population. However, because homicide is sometimes a financially acquisitive crime, some commentators might attempt to explain away this association between homicide and unemployment as a product of poverty rather than personality.

This objection is implausible because millions of people endure poverty yet are never convicted of a violent crime. Also, as we have already seen, there is evidence to show that antisocial personality disorder is associated with a high probability of both violent criminality (Hodgins, 2007; Jüriloo et al., 2013) and a poor work record (Cleckley, 1988). Nevertheless, it may be the case that on occasion an unemployed person might be driven by poverty to attempt an armed robbery and end up accidentally killing rather than merely robbing the victim. Moreover, homicide statistics do not provide data on the personality characteristics of the killers, preventing us from being sure that the causal link between violent crime and unemployment is personality.

Both these concerns are addressed by a study that profiled 336 UK males convicted of domestic violence (Gilchrist et al., 2003). This study is especially important to the topic of this book because Gilchrist and colleagues not only recorded the employment status of the offenders but also profiled their personalities. Moreover, unlike other forms of violent crime, such as mugging or armed robbery, the perpetrator of domestic violence does not benefit financially from his crime. This means that any links between proneness to domestic violence and unemployment are more likely to be a direct product of an antisocial personality profile rather than the side effect of a desire to acquire money.

The results of this study provide clear evidence for the notion that antisocial personality characteristics underpin both criminal violence and unemployment. First, Gilchrist and colleagues found that 108 of the men (47 per cent of the sample) met criteria for antisocial personality disorder. Given that epidemiology studies suggest that only around one per cent of the general population meet these criteria (for example, Coid et al., 2009), we can see that individuals with antisocial personality disorder are almost 50 times more common in these offenders than amongst the general public. Second, in line with the finding that individuals with antisocial personality disorder are over-represented amongst the unemployed sector of the population (for example, Vaughn et al., 2010), Gilchrist and colleagues found that 60 per cent of their subjects were unemployed. As the rate of unemployment in the UK in 2003 was approximately five per cent, we can see that unemployed men are almost 12 times more common amongst this group of convicted abusers than amongst the general population.

Since I earlier defined the employment-resistant personality profile as a mild form of antisocial personality disorder, these data gathered by Gilchrist and colleagues suggest that a rise in the frequency of employment-resistant personalities due to the implementation of the welfare state will indeed trigger a rise in violent crime. As I mentioned in the introduction to this chapter, we should find that the onset of a welfare state is followed some 10–15 years later by a rise in criminal violence, as the first generation of personality-damaged welfare babies grow old enough to begin swelling government statistics for violent crime. This evidence has special importance because no other personality theory to my knowledge can explain changes in criminal violence via this pattern of timing in relation to the onset of the welfare state.

There are many indices of criminal violence, but homicide statistics are regarded by criminologists as the most reliable index of trends in criminal violence, because killing another human has been regarded as a serious crime for millennia and so is more likely to show up in historical crime statistics than other types of violence. As Steven Pinker documented so brilliantly in his recent book *The Better Angels of Our Nature* (Pinker, 2011), homicide rates have been declining across the Western world for centuries – except for a mysterious upswing that began a decade or so after the end of the Second World War and continued until the 1990s. The causes of this upswing in homicide across the Western world has not yet been conclusively explained, opening the door to the possibility that it might be related to the welfare state, since the same era saw the widespread implementation of welfare legislation in advanced nations. Bearing this in mind, we will now look in more detail at homicide trends before and after the implementation of the welfare state in the UK, whilst acknowledging that the introduction of the welfare state is just one event that happened in this period – others may also have an influence.

The British welfare state evolved over centuries but began in its modern, cradle-to-grave form in the late 1940s (Timmins, 2001). This means that if the welfare trait theory is correct, in the UK we should find an upswing in criminal violence that began in the late 1950s/early 1960s, as the first generation of personality-damaged welfare babies reach the age of criminal responsibility. Figure 9.5 plots homicide rates in England and Wales for each census year from 1901 to 2011 and appears to support this hypothesis by showing that homicide rates in England and Wales began a steep upswing in 1961which continued to the mid-1990s before dipping down again. This recent dip in homicide seems to counter my theory, since the welfare state was still in place. But it can explained in part by modern medicine's increased capacity to save the lives of assault victims (for example, studies in the USA have shown that homicide rates in the late 1990s would have been up to three times higher if victims

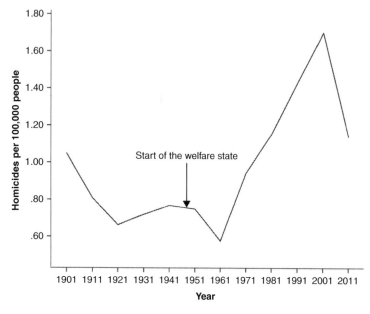

Figure 9.5   Homicides in England and Wales between 1901 and 2011
Source: Office of National Statistics.

of assault were treated with the medical technology of 1960; Harris et al., 2002).

The rise in homicide rate over time that is shown in Figure 9.5 is backed up by statistical testing: there is a statistically significant positive correlation between homicide and year, which means that 40 per cent of the variance in homicide rates is accounted for by the year. Since most other nations in the Western world show a similar trend in homicide (for example, Pinker, 2011) and they also tended to implement modern welfare states in the aftermath of the Second World War, evidence of this type appears to back up the welfare trait theory.

However, whilst this correlation is reassuring, since the absence of statistically significant correlations that fit the welfare trait theory would set alarm bells ringing about its validity, the presence of such correlations does not provide conclusive proof that the welfare trait theory is valid, because correlation does not imply causation. The

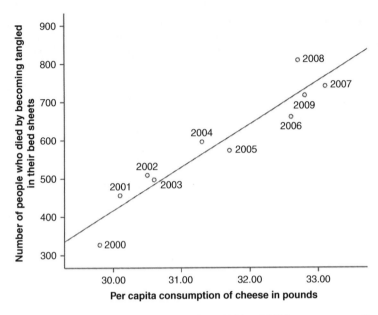

Figure 9.6 The relationship in the USA from 2000 to 2009 between per-capita consumption of cheese and deaths due to tangled bed sheets
Source: Centers for Disease Control and Prevention and US Census.

blunt truth is that, if we go fishing in large datasets, we can find statistically significant correlations that support any theory we wish to dream up but are, in reality, spurious. Or, stated another way, visually impressive and statistically significant correlations can occur by coincidence. This is perhaps best illustrated by visiting the website that mines US government datasets for spurious correlations in order to show just how misleading correlations can be (www.tylervigen. com). In Figure 9.6, I have plotted some US government data which show there is a statistically significant positive correlation in the USA between the annual per-capita consumption of cheese and the number of people who die each year after becoming tangled in their bed sheets. This correlation is extremely strong, explaining an impressive 89.7% of the variance between the two variables, yet is completely spurious because there is no sensible causal mechanism that can explain why eating cheese should cause death by tangled bed sheets.

In contrast, the statistically significant positive correlation between levels of cigarette smoking and rates of lung cancer that was first demonstrated in the 1930s (for example, Müller, 1939) is not spurious because there is a sensible causal link between the two variables, namely the carcinogenic properties of cigarette smoke. What these considerations mean is that the use of correlations in science is a two-stage process: first we need to use statistical techniques to prove that a correlation exists between two variables. Second we need to use our common sense to determine whether there is a causal mechanism that can reasonably explain the statistical connection between the variables or whether that statistically significant correlation is merely a coincidence. In the case of this book, we have a sensible causal mechanism which can explain the statistically significant correlation in Figure 9.5 between the onset of the welfare state in the late 1940s and the upsurge in homicide in the early 1960s, namely the welfare trait theory. But that is still not sufficient, since if we try to corroborate the welfare trait theory with correlations that we then corroborate via the same theory, we risk falling into the trap of circularity.

To make sure the welfare trait theory is not guilty of circularity, we need to take a broader view of the scientific literature. Most importantly, since few theories ever emerge in total isolation, if the welfare trait theory is valid, the scientific literature should already contain theories created by other scholars that point in approximately the same direction. And it does. For example, as was mentioned in Chapter 4, the economic historian Greg Clark has already published a book – *A Farewell to Alms* – that argues cogently for the notion that differential reproduction can shape social norms via personality changes, much as I argue in this book.

But Clark's book concerned the origins of the Industrial Revolution and does not address the welfare state, nor the apparent shift towards a greater frequency of violent crime that occurred in the nations of the Western world around 1960. In regard to this, we are fortunate to have at our disposal the work of the criminologist Manuel Eisner, who is a leading authority on the causes of the upswing in criminal violence that hit the Western world around the year 1960. After surveying a wide range of data, Eisner concluded that this upswing was caused by a shift in the *Lebensführung* of the Western world (Eisner, 2008). This is a German term popularised by

Max Weber that represents the way of life that a society regards as good or correct. *Lebensführung* has been translated into English as lifestyle, but Eisner finds this an inadequate representation, maintaining that '*Lebensführung* or conduct of life refers to a much wider cultural script encompassing work, politics, beliefs, education, and individual character. These models of conduct of life become reinforced and stabilized through institutions such as schools, families, the church, and bureaucracies' (Eisner, 2008, p. 290).

According to Eisner, prior to the mid-twentieth century in the Western world there was 'an emphasis on self-control as an ideal of personality; domesticity and familialism as guidelines for private life; and respectability as the yardstick for public appearance' (Eisner, 2008, p. 303). Eisner believes that the upswing in criminal violence that began in the late 1950s/early 1960s was a result of a shift away from these values of self-control, domestic duty and respectability that he viewed as causing the reductions in crime witnessed in the previous centuries. Furthermore, Eisner identifies a causal factor which links the welfare trait theory to the shift in the *Lebensführung* of the Western world. That factor is socialisation.

As you may recall, in Chapter 8 we saw how a person's scores on conscientiousness and agreeableness represent the effectiveness of their socialisation as a child and young adult. The work of David Lykken has shown us that a person's level of socialisation is determined by a combination of nature and nurture: the higher a baby's dose of genes for being difficult to socialise, the better the quality of parenting they require in order to grow into a socially well-adjusted and economically productive adult (Lykken, 1998). If we now return to Eisner's work, we can see that he blames the shift in *Lebensführung* towards greater criminal violence that occurred around 1960 partially on a change in patterns of socialisation. For example, he wrote that:

the major shifts in levels of interpersonal criminal violence over the past 160 years were associated with broad changes, across Europe, in shared cultural models of what constitutes a desirable and good 'conduct of life'. These are said to influence levels of interpersonal violence through their effects on patterns of socialization as well as by affecting expectations about adequate interaction in daily situations, especially in public space.

(Eisner, 2008, p. 290)

So what we need now to tie the work of Eisner to the theme of this book is a specific mechanism to explain how a welfare state could alter patterns of socialisation. This need brings us full circle because, as I mentioned in Chapter 1, my answer is that the welfare state alters patterns of socialisation by boosting the number of children who are born into disadvantaged households and who suffer personality mis-development as a result. This difference in reproduction is crucial to my argument because, as we have already seen, the personality profiles of welfare claimants are on average less well socialised than employed citizens (for example, Vaughn et al., 2010) and lack of socialisation impairs parenting competence (Cleckley, 1988).

The favoured reproductive status of the welfare claimants therefore means that their offspring will not only be less well socialised on average than offspring of employed citizens, but also as every generation passes they will be proportionately more numerous. As they proliferated in the years following the introduction of the welfare state, I argue that these inadequately socialised young people spread a culture of impulsive, irresponsible behaviour, culminating in the soaring crime rates of the 1960s, 1970s and 1980s. Eventually, by the 1990s, the nations of the Western world realised that the easy-going 'Dixon of Dock Green' law-enforcement practices that had been adequate up until the 1950s were no longer fit for purpose. As a result, they hardened their policing procedures, and gradually (along with advances in trauma medicine) helped to stem the rise in homicides (as shown in Figure 9.5).

As a caveat, it is important to acknowledge that Eisner (2008) argued that the sheer rapidity of the change in criminality indicates that it has a strong cultural component that does not map directly onto the concept of personality traits as a product of nature and nurture. In response, I suggest that the focus of the welfare trait theory on differences in reproduction and child socialisation between claimants and employed citizens should not be allowed to overshadow the purely environmental effect of the welfare state on the behaviour patterns of adults that has been demonstrated by economic studies. As mentioned in the introduction, these studies show that when the welfare state becomes more generous, the personality profile of the population becomes more willing to break societal norms (Heckman, 2008).

Applied to Eisner's demonstration of a shift in the *Lebensführung* of the Western world towards greater criminal violence from 1960 onwards, I suggest that these economic studies point to two rather simple explanations as to how the implementation of the welfare state can also temporarily raise the level of criminal violence in adults whose personality profiles are already formed: first, I suggest a role for social learning – learning from others – which allows an attitude or behaviour to spread quickly through a population, as a form of local tradition. Anecdotal examples of such an effect are readily found in human populations, such as the rapid spread of football hooliganism amongst developed nations in the 1970s and then its equally rapid decline in the 1990s. The power of social learning to cause rapid changes in behaviour has been proven formally via studies in chimpanzees that show it provides 'a high speed "second inheritance" system that interacts with genetic inheritance to enrich behavioural evolution' (Whiten, 2014, p. 178).

Second, I suggest that the welfare state also alters behaviour by an even simpler mechanism, namely that, by providing claimants with an income without requiring work in return, it gives them the option of sleeping late in the day and staying awake at night. In the case of claimants who happen to possess pro-social personality characteristics, this change would not affect crime: they might spend their extra time by cultivating an innocuous hobby. But in individuals who possess antisocial, predatory urges, the welfare state opens a Pandora's box of opportunities for nocturnal criminality by allowing them to sleep in late during the day and thus have plenty of energy to hunt for victims under the protection of darkness. This idea receives circumstantial support from Eisner's work, since he found that the upsurge in criminal violence that took place in the Western world from the 1960s to the 1990s was not a result of increased infanticide or domestic violence (both of which seemed to decline in frequency), but was primarily driven by a rise in violence inflicted on young men in public places by other young men who were usually strangers (Eisner, 2008).

Conclusion

The welfare trait theory dovetails with the work of criminologists, who have found that there was an upswing in criminal violence in the Western world from about 1960 to 1990 that was caused by a reduction in the value placed upon self-control, duty and respectability. This reduction in solid citizen values corresponds to the pattern of personality change predicted by the welfare trait theory. This is of course a retrospective interpretation and does not prove the welfare trait theory, but it is what we would expect to see if the welfare trait theory is correct.

10
What Next?

In the first chapter I listed three alternative narratives for the future of the welfare state, which were as follows:

1. The welfare state should be retained without change.
2. The welfare state should be abolished.
3. The welfare state should be amended to take account of personality.

As this book demonstrates, I believe the balance of the evidence favours the third narrative. In this final chapter, I will therefore make some basic suggestions as to how the welfare state could be amended so that it looks after the unemployed but does not warp the personality profile of the population towards greater employment-resistance. Richard Dawkins provided a pointer back in 1976 when he showed, using the rubric of evolutionary biology, that reproduction must be disconnected from subsistence if the welfare state is to be sustainable in the long run. Dawkins' disconnection suggestion is crucial because, as we have seen during the course of this book, it will reduce the capacity of the welfare state to shift the average personality profile of the population towards employment-resistance. It achieves this not only by preventing the proliferation of children carrying a larger than average dose of the genes for being difficult to socialise, but also, more importantly, by reducing the number of genetically average children who are swayed towards employment-resistance by being born into disadvantaged households, where they are at a higher than average risk of personality mis-development.

But the big question in policy terms is how to accomplish this disconnection? As we saw in Chapter 6, in 1976 Richard Dawkins suggested in *The Selfish Gene* that welfare benefits should be conditional upon claimants utilising contraception. Dawkins' suggestion would no doubt be effective but, since 1976, we have discovered that welfare claimants voluntarily limit their reproduction if the welfare state no longer makes it worth their while financially to have extra children (for example, Argys et al., 2000). This discovery means that I do not advise mandatory contraception. Instead I suggest that disconnection of reproduction from subsistence should be achieved by adjusting welfare generosity until the average number of children born to claimants matches the average number of children born to non-claimants.

In the UK, the effects on reproduction of such an amendment to the welfare state can be monitored because, as we saw in Table 4.1, the government already records the number of children born into each of three levels of welfare dependence. Figure 10.1 shows these data

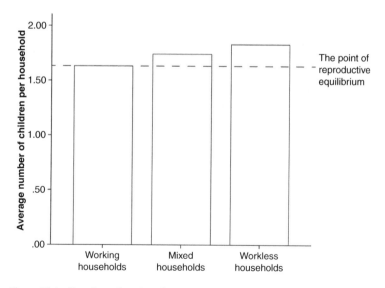

Figure 10.1   Bar chart showing the average number of children under the age of 16 in working, mixed and workless households, April–June 2013, UK
Source: Labour Force Survey Household Dataset.

as a bar chart. When thinking about these data, the crucial variable to bear in mind is the average number of children in working households (the left-hand column in the bar chart), because this provides an approximate baseline measure of the average level of reproduction that can be sustained by citizens who are not reliant on the welfare state for their survival.

The data shown in Figure 10.1 indicate that the level of welfare generosity that no longer endangers the personality profile of a population is whichever level causes mixed and workless households to have the same number of children, on average, as working households – what could be dubbed 'the point of reproductive equilibrium' (indicated by the dashed line). Therefore, my specific policy suggestion is that welfare generosity should be gradually reduced until mixed and workless households have, on average, the same number of children as working households. The importance of reducing generosity gradually is that it allows the effect of welfare generosity on reproduction to be tracked in a systematic manner and also means that claimants will have plenty of time to get the message that the government will no longer allow children to be used as tools to gain extra welfare benefits.

At first glance this policy suggestion might seem absurd as we have already seen that the risk of developing the employment-resistant personality profile is increased by childhood disadvantage (Heckman et al., 2013). Reduced welfare generosity would therefore seem likely to increase disadvantage amongst the children of claimants and thereby proliferate the employment-resistant personality profile, with dire prospects for all concerned. However, we saw evidence in Chapter 4 that employment-resistant individuals have a tendency to spend their welfare benefits on unnecessary purchases such as electronic gadgets and luxury chocolates, instead of using the money to improve the lives of their children (Tonge et al., 1975). This discovery suggests that fluctuations in the generosity of benefits do not make much difference to the quality of life for the children of claimants: they tend to be neglected regardless of household income.

More generally, reduced welfare generosity might seem likely to harm society by increasing inequality. However, as noted by James Heckman in his 2013 lecture at the British Academy, increased redistribution of wealth via an expanded welfare state (as happened in the USA in the mid- to late 1960s and early 1970s during the so-called

War on Poverty) does not cause significant improvements in long-term measures of inequality such as intergenerational mobility. Based on the personality data summarised in this book, I suggest this is likely to be at least partly because the same unconscientious attitude that increases an individual's risk of ending up unemployed and claiming welfare will mean that increased welfare generosity won't produce lasting improvements in their circumstances, because that extra money won't be managed conscientiously.

Returning to the theme of this book, if welfare generosity is reduced and the point of reproductive equilibrium is achieved, welfare claimants will no longer be a reproductively favoured group and thus the welfare state will no longer proliferate the employment-resistant personality profile. Of course, reaching reproductive equilibrium merely prevents the proliferation of employment-resistant individuals by reducing the proportion of children who are born into disadvantaged families. There is a separate, moral issue, which is whether it is right that the welfare state should encourage the birth of *any* children into disadvantaged households, given that they tend to suffer miserable lives and also, as shown by the Troubled Families Programme, tend to impose a significant per capita burden on the public purse.

This is, of course, just one of many moral concerns generated by the welfare state: for example, it is plausible that working alongside colleagues of different cultural backgrounds aids integration and that the welfare state, by removing the need to work for a living, is perpetuating cultural divisions. The welfare state might also reduce the effort that children put into their school work, since it guarantees them with an income in the event that their school grades are too low to gain them employment. Similarly, a welfare state that pays benefits to claimants irrespective of whether they have a criminal record is likely to sap the motivation of citizens to refrain from crime. The welfare state might also affect family structure since, by providing a safety net to pay for the raising of a woman's children in the event of abandonment by their father, it may cause contemporary women to be less focused than women in earlier eras on finding a conscientious and agreeable mate who will stick around and help raise their children. This raises the ironic and tragic prospect that state benefits are increasing the risk that children will miss out on a far more important benefit, namely a loving and supportive father.

These moral issues may or may not turn out to be important, but they are a matter for the philosophers amongst us: the aim of this chapter is instead to attempt to understand why Dawkins' advice to disconnect reproduction amongst welfare claimants from subsistence has been ignored. Dawkins suspected a deliberate political motive: 'Individual humans who have more children than they are capable of rearing are probably too ignorant in most cases to be accused of conscious malevolent exploitation. Powerful institutions and leaders who deliberately encourage them to do so seem to me less free from suspicion' (Dawkins, 1976, p. 126).

Dawkins' theory that existing welfare policies have been deliberately designed to encourage reproduction amongst claimants is striking, but I suspect the real explanation for flawed welfare policies is more mundane. I think that the governing elite in such key domains of society as politics, media, academia and the law – what we might dub 'the intelligentsia' – tend to live in leafy, affluent neighbourhoods and also tend to work in jobs that are interesting, prestigious and well paid. Therefore, the notion of someone opting out of work to live on welfare benefits must seem incomprehensible to them. I work in academia and therefore could be counted in the ranks of the intelligentsia. But I have a somewhat different perspective to most of the intelligentsia because, as I mentioned in Chapter 1, my scientific career was preceded by several years of low-paid work (for example, two and half years labouring in a clothing warehouse) as well as spells of unemployment during which I claimed benefits. Furthermore, my adverse financial circumstances have meant that for the last 12 years I have lived in one of the most disadvantaged neighbourhoods in the UK where I have seen first-hand the corrosive effects of well-meaning but flawed welfare policies upon social functioning.

This prolonged experience of life at the base of the economic pyramid has given me an admiration for the welfare state, yet also an understanding of just how tempting the prospect of £26,000 per annum in handouts can be if it means one no longer has to endure decades of repetitive, boring and physically exhausting labour. Indeed, the extent of this temptation is apparent when we consider that £26,000 per annum is more than twice the annual take-home pay of a person working full time on the UK minimum wage (approximately £11,752 per annum at the time of writing).

Whilst I cite the geographical, financial and social detachment of the intelligentsia as a reason for their tendency to design self-destructive welfare policies that erode work motivation and increase the number of children born into disadvantaged households, I am not seeking to blame them. I am merely saying that the intelligentsia are not the right people to design welfare policy. As support for this argument, I can point to the fact that political leaders in the Western world tend to come from privileged families and often move straight from education into the corridors of power, having spent little, if any, time living and working in ordinary neighbourhoods. Like all stereotypes, there are notable exceptions to this rule, but at the time of writing it applies to the leaders of all the major political parties in the Westminster parliament.

Nor am I the only person to have noticed the detachment of the intelligentsia. For example, George Orwell observed: 'This is the really important fact about the English intelligentsia – their severance from the common culture of the country' (Orwell, 1941, p. 48). More recently, the former policeman and author Stuart Davidson made similar, if more tongue-in-cheek, observations about the English judiciary:

> I'm sure lots of you, like me, are kept awake at night by the idea that some of our prisons are overcrowded. It's certainly been worrying Lord Chief Justice Phillips of Worth Matravers lately.
>
> Recently, his Lordship suggested that offenders should only be sent to jail 'as a last resort' and that they should really be rehabilitated in the community.
>
> I think they should be rehabilitated chez Phillips, where Lord Phillips can develop a better understanding of what persistent acquisitive criminals are really like while Lady Phillips (nee Christylle Marie-Thérèse Rouffiac) keeps an eye on the family silver...I've no idea where the LCJ's houses are (he's probably got several), or what they're like, but I'll hazard a guess. They will be imposing and beautiful pads in low crime areas. They will have walls around them and plenty of open ground that burglars have to cross before they get to the alarmed and well-made windows. He'll probably have a dog or two, and possibly a live-in house-keeper. The local nick will know exactly where he is and they will

be on tenterhooks in case they get a call to get out there (if he hasn't got a panic button or some sort of direct comm-link). His neighbours will be charming people with diverse interests, large cars and lots of antique furniture. If he encounters muggers, burglars or general ne'er-do-wells (outside his professional life) it will only be because of extreme carelessness on his part. He certainly won't be glassed in the back garden of the King's Head for brushing the arm of an unemployed yob who has drunk nine pints of Stella.

My question is this: when it comes to deciding how criminals should be dealt with, why should we trust Lord Chief Justice Phillips of Worth Matravers?

(Davidson, 2011, pp. 10–11)

I have included this quote not only to back up Orwell's claim that the English intelligentsia are out of touch with ordinary life, but also because it provides a second illustration of the knock-on effect of flawed welfare policy on other areas of life. The topic of this book is not penal reform, but one theme that I will mention in this final chapter is the idea that welfare legislation, because it meddles with reproduction, has the potential to cause economic headwinds for society that may not be immediately obvious. For example, based on the link I showed in Chapter 9 between the employment-resistant personality profile and violent crime, if the intelligentsia really are serious about reducing prison overcrowding, then instead of sparing criminals from prison, they should help to shrink the problem at source by urging the cessation of welfare legislation that increases the number of children born into disadvantaged households.

Based on the assumption that welfare legislation in developed nations reflects the attitudes of the intelligentsia that created it, it would seem that the intelligentsia generally believe that supporting a few freeloaders is a price worth paying for protecting unemployed people from starvation. Unfortunately for the intelligentsia, if the welfare trait theory is correct, it will only be possible for them ignore the problem of growing numbers of people with the employment-resistant personality profile for a decade or two. This is because, as we saw earlier in this book, the employment-resistant profile is associated not only with being work-shy but also with antisocial behaviour; if the welfare state continues to boost the number of children born into disadvantaged households, the intelligentsia will eventually get a rude surprise once the employment-resistant sector of the population becomes sufficiently numerous to invade genteel neighbourhoods, as happened briefly during the London riots of 2011.

The problems that occur when the employment-resistant personality profile becomes widespread are also mentioned in Stuart Davidson's book *Wasting Police Time*. In this brilliantly observed book, which I quoted from earlier in the chapter, Davidson describes his experiences during several years working as a policeman in the English midlands town of Burton-upon-Trent up until 2007. During his duties, Davidson observed the negative effects on the quality of life for innocent people, especially children, of the employment-resistant personality profile.

More specifically, in many of the households that Davidson visited, there are echoes of the households of the problem families studied by Tonge and colleagues in Sheffield in the 1970s, in that the adult residents have plenty of free time (because they are unemployed) yet do not spend that time wisely, on such worthwhile activities as cleaning their residence or looking after their children properly:

> In the small hours, I had to go and see an 18-year-old girl who'd had an argument with her boyfriend. He'd stormed out and she was frightened he was going to come back and attack her.
>
> She lived in a grubby flat, behind a flimsy wooden door with a cheap Yale lock and screw holes where the old one had been before it was kicked off in an earlier row. Inside the detritus of a disordered life lay everywhere; bedsheets, children's clothes, toys and sweet wrappers strewn throughout the place, a couple of photographs of the kids on the walls and an overflowing bin in the kitchen next to a cat bowl full of Whiskas. In the corner of the living room was a television, with DVD and CD players and a Nintendo Gamecube alongside. A stack of DVDs, CDs and games were shoved behind the telly. The dirty walls were painted pink and the local authority, as part of its environmental drive, had put in double-glazed windows. There were no books and no dining table.

The whole place smelled catty, stale and unaired.

The girl – like so many who spend their lives catering to the whims of the moment – had been out on the town that night. She had left her kids with her boyfriend, and that had been at the bottom of the row. He was not the father of the children and had taken umbrage when she came home, late and smashed out of her face. He restrained himself from delivering the beating he doubtless felt she deserved, but she feared his restraint wouldn't last forever.

'He had a right go at me,' she said, still drunk, and clearing a pile of unwashed children's clothes away so I could sit down. 'I don't want him here anymore.'

The children were well-behaved and dressed in dirty pyjamas. It was 3am and they had been up for hours. They were eating crisps and staring at me with dark-rimmed, saucer eyes. A wave of depression came over me, as it always does whenever kids are involved. There was nothing I could do about the young woman's situation because she had not been the victim of a real crime. (he hadn't actually beaten her up)

But I started talking to her.

'This isn't great is it?' I said. 'Your kids up at this time of night, the police here. Never mind this idiot, you need a bloke with a job, someone who can provide for you and the kids. He hasn't got a job, has he?'

'I'm going to college myself soon,' she said. I've heard this a hundred times before.

'He's no good for you, though, is he?'

'I know that,' she said. 'We've broken up twice before. But this time it's for real. He's not coming back in here, no way.'

If I had a pound etc. etc.

'Have you ever thought about getting married? Finding someone to take you on, make a commitment to you, that sort of thing?' I said.

She said she was only eighteen and, therefore, too young to marry. I looked at the children; I wanted to point out the obvious, but refrained. Instead, I said, 'Do you get any help looking after the kids?'

'My sister comes round sometimes,' she said, drifting off. There wasn't much else I could usefully say, or do, so I left.

Davidson's conclusion after his visit to the young woman goes as follows: 'It had been a profoundly miserable experience, and one experienced by every street copper all over the country, all the time: young mums, bringing up children in relative squalor, with no aspirations and no ability to see further than the next few hours.' Critiquing Davidson's analysis of this event from a scientific perspective, it is interesting to see how similar it is to the finding by Tonge and colleagues that problem families in Sheffield suffered from a lack of foresight, which you may recall went as follows:

This is a curious set of values. It adds up to a complete failure to plan for long-term action. It takes forethought to do all that these families failed to do: to take out motor insurance and TV licence, to accumulate household comforts, to limit family size; and education is above all a long-term endowment insurance. This is a style of life which shuts its eyes to the future.

(Tonge et al., 1975, p. 117)

Despite being separated by more than 30 years in time, as well as by geography and professional experience, Davidson's conclusion and that of the Sheffield researchers both point squarely to a lack of foresight as underpinning this form of dysfunctional existence. Supporting Einstein's view that science is just an extension of everyday thinking, Davidson has replicated the finding of Tonge and colleagues even though he did not have their scientific resources and training and was not (presumably) aware of their work.

Even more interestingly, Davidson then backs up the theme of this book by identifying a causal link between the welfare state and the mis-evolution of personality towards employment-resistance:

Like so many others, she had been soft-soaped by welfare agencies anxious to preserve the independence of the girl and her ability to make 'informed choices'. The problem is that the choices they make are, almost invariably, the wrong ones, and the result of all this is the systematic neglect of young children and the growth of our underclass.

(Davidson, 2011, p. 32)

This evidence from Davidson and others like him is anecdotal rather than experimental, but it is an important sanity check for the argument in this book because it demonstrates a convergence of opinion from different sources, professional backgrounds and locations, all of them saying that personality and the welfare state are connected, and not in a good way.

The nightmare scenario of the employment-resistant personality profile becoming the norm across the entire nation due to welfare-induced personality mis-development is only a scenario. It may happen or it may not, but my point is that unless we address this issue scientifically we won't know either way. What I seek is a society in which we help our children to climb the stairway of human capital rather than pushing them down it. As James Heckman and colleagues have shown, one way to do this is to provide disadvantaged children with intensive preschool tutoring. As we have seen in this book, another way is to adjust the generosity of state benefits so that they no longer increase the number of children born into disadvantaged households. Since one disadvantaged child is one too many, I'll end this book with a question: why not do both?

References

Alvard, M. (2011). Genetic and cultural kinship among the Lamaleran whale hunters. *Human Nature, 22,* 89–107.

Argys, L. M., Averett, S. L., & Rees, D. I. (2000). Welfare generosity, pregnancies, and abortions among unmarried AFDC recipients. *Journal of Population Economics, 13,* 569–594.

Barrick, M. R., Mount, M. K., & Judge, T. A. (2001). Personality and performance at the beginning of the new millennium: What do we know and where do we go next? *International Journal of Selection and Assessment, 9,* 9–30.

Bedford, R., Pickles, A., Sharp, H., Wright, N., & Hill, J. (2014). Reduced face preference in infancy: A developmental precursor to callous-unemotional traits? *Biological Psychiatry,* DOI: http://dx.doi.org/10.1016/j.biopsych.2014.09.022.

Beveridge, W. H. (1942). *Social insurance and allied services.* London: HMSO.

Blumer, D., & Benson, D. F. (1975). Personality changes with frontal and temporal lobe lesions. In D. F. Benson & D. Blumer (Eds.), *Psychiatric aspects of neurologic disease* (pp. 151–170). New York and London: Grune & Stratton.

Bogg, T., & Roberts, B. W. (2004). Conscientiousness and health behaviors. *Psychological Bulletin, 130,* 887–919.

Boisjoli, R., Vitaro, F., Lacourse, E., Barker, E. D., & Tremblay, R. E. (2007). Impact and clinical significance of a preventive intervention for disruptive boys: 15-year follow-up. *British Journal of Psychiatry, 191,* 415–419.

Bonczar, T. P. (2003). *Prevalence of imprisonment in the US population, 1974–2001.* Washington, DC: US Department of Justice, Office of Justice Programs, Bureau of Justice Statistics.

Bouchard, T. (1994). Genes, environment, and personality. *Science, 264,* 1700–1701.

Boyce, C. J., Wood, A. M., Daly, M., & Sedikides, C. (9 February 2015). Personality change following unemployment. *Journal of Applied Psychology.* Advance online publication. http://dx.doi.org/10.1037/a0038647.

Brand, S., & Price, R. (2000). *The economic and social costs of crime.* London: Home Office.

Bredy, T. W., Humpartzoomian, R. A., Cain, D. P., & Meaney, M. J. (2003). Partial reversal of the effect of maternal care on cognitive function through environmental enrichment. *European Journal of Neuroscience, 18,* 571–576.

Brewer, M., Ratcliffe, A., & Smith, S. D. (2011). Does welfare reform affect fertility? Evidence from the UK. *Journal of Population Economics, 25,* 245–266.

Brickner, R. (1932). An interpretation of function based on the study of a case of bilateral frontal lobectomy. *Proceedings of the Association for Research in Nervous and Mental Disorders, 13*, 259–351.

Broadhurst, P. L. (1960). Experiments in psychogenetics: Applications of biometrical genetics to the inheritance of behaviour. In H. J. Eysenck (Ed.), *Experiments in personality. Vol. 1 Psychogenetics and psychopharmacology* (pp. 1–102). London: Routledge & Kegan Paul.

Broadhurst, P. L. (1969). Psychogenetics of emotionality in the rat. *Annals of the New York Academy of Sciences, 159*, 806–824.

Broadhurst, P. L. (1975). The Maudsley reactive and non-reactive strains of rats: A survey. *Behavior Genetics, 5*, 299–319.

Campbell, F., Conti, G., Heckman, J. J., Moon, S. H., Pinto, R., Pungello, E., & Pan, Y. (2014). Early childhood investments substantially boost adult health. *Science, 343*, 1478–1485.

Campbell, F. A., Pungello, E. P., Burchinal, M., Kainz, K., Pan, Y., Wasik, B. H., & Ramey, C. T. (2012). Adult outcomes as a function of an early childhood educational program: An Abecedarian Project follow-up. *Developmental Psychology, 48*, 1033–1043.

Campbell, F. A., Ramey, C., Pungello, E. P., Sparling, J. J., & Miller-Johnson, S. (2002). Early childhood education: Young adult outcomes from the Abecedarian Project. *Applied Developmental Science, 6*, 42–57.

Campbell, F. A., Wasik, B. H., Pungello, E. P., Burchinal, M., Barbarin, O., Kainz, K., Sparling, J. J., & Ramey, C. T. (2008). Young adult outcomes from the Abecedarian and CARE early childhood educational interventions. *Early Childhood Research Quarterly, 23*, 452–466.

Caspi, A., Wright, B. R. E., Moffitt, T. E., & Silva, P. A. (1998). Early failure in the labor market: Childhood and adolescent predictors of unemployment in the transition to adulthood. *American Sociological Review, 63*, 424–451.

Chambers, S. P. (1964). Education and industry. *Nature, 203*, 227–230.

Clark, G. (2007). *A farewell to alms.* Princeton, NJ: Princeton University Press.

Clausen, J. A. (Ed.). (1968). *Socialization and society* (pp. 131–181). Boston: Little, Brown.

Cleckley, H. M. (1988). *The mask of sanity* (5th ed.). Augusta, GA: Emily S. Cleckley.

Coid, J., Yang, M., Ullrich, S., Roberts, A., & Hare, R. D. (2009). Prevalence and correlates of psychopathic traits in the household population of Great Britain. *International Journal of Law and Psychiatry, 32*, 65–73.

Costa, P. T., Jr., & McCrae, R. R. (1992). *Revised NEO Personality Inventory (NEO-PI-R) and NEO Five-Factor Inventory (NEOFFI) professional manual.* Odessa, FL: Psychological Assessment Resources, Inc.

Cunha, F., Heckman, J. J., Lochner, L., & Masterov, D. V. (2006). Interpreting the evidence on life cycle skill formation. In E. Hanushek, & F. Welch (Eds.), *Handbook of the economics of education* (pp. 697–812). Amsterdam: Elsevier.

Daly, M., Delaney, L., Egan, M., & Baumeister, R. (2015). Childhood self-control and unemployment throughout life: Evidence from two British cohort studies. *Psychological Science, 26*, 709–723.

Damasio, A. (1994). *Descartes' error: Emotion, reason, and the human brain*. New York, NY: Putnam.

Darwin, C. (1845). *Journal of researches into the natural history and geology of the countries visited during the voyage of H.M.S. Beagle round the world, under the Command of Capt. Fitz Roy, R.N.* London: Murray.

Darwin, C. (1859). *The origin of species by means of natural selection*. London: Murray.

Davidson, S. (2011). *Wasting police time: The crazy world of the war on crime*. Cheltenham: Monday Books.

Dawkins, R. (1976). *The selfish gene*. Oxford: Oxford University Press.

Deary, I. J., Johnson, W., & Houlihan, L. M. (2009). Genetic foundations of human intelligence. *Human Genetics, 126*, 215–232.

Dennett, D. C. (1996). *Darwin's dangerous idea: Evolution and the meanings of life*. London: Penguin.

Digman, J. M. (1990). Personality structure: Emergence of the five-factor model. *Annual Review of Psychology, 41*, 417–440.

Dijkstra, P., & Barelds, D. P. (2009). Women's well-being: The role of individual differences. *Scandinavian Journal of Psychology, 50*, 309–315.

Dilger, W. C. (1962). The behavior of lovebirds. *Scientific American, 206*, 88–98.

Dobzhansky, T. (1950). Evolution in the tropics. *American Scientist, 38*, 209–221.

Einstein, A. (1936). Physics and reality. *Journal of the Franklin Institute, 221*, 349–382.

Eisner, M. (2008). Modernity strikes back? A historical perspective on the latest increase in interpersonal violence (1960–1990). *International Journal of Conflict and Violence, 2*, 288–316.

Endicott-Davies, D. R., Barrie, A. N., & Fisher, M. W. (1996). Differences in the hiding behaviour of new-born red deer and hybrid 1/4 Père David's × 3/4 red deer calves. *Animal Science, 62*, 363–367.

Eysenck, H. J. (1947). *Dimensions of personality*. London: Kegan Paul, Trench and Trubner.

Eysenck, H. J. (1952). *The scientific study of personality*. London: Routledge and Kegan Paul.

Eysenck, H. J. (1968). *Eysenck Personality Inventory*. San Diego: Educational and Industrial Testing Service.

Eysenck, H. J., & Broadhurst, P. L. (1964). Experiments with animals: Introduction. In H. J. Eysenck (Ed.), *Experiments in motivation* (pp. 285–291). Oxford: Pergamon.

Faure, J. M., Val-Laillet, D., Guy, G., Bernadet, M. D., & Guémené, D. (2003). Fear and stress reactions in two species of duck and their hybrid. *Hormones and Behavior, 43*, 568–572.

Figueredo, A. J., Vásquez, G., Brumbach, B. H., Schneider, S. M., Sefcek, J. A., Tal, I. R., Hill, D., Wenner, C. J., & Jacobs, W. J. (2006). Consilience and life history theory: From genes to brain to reproductive strategy. *Developmental Review, 26*, 243–275.

Fisher, R. A. (1930). *The genetical theory of natural selection*. Oxford: Clarendon.

Flynn, J. R. (1994). IQ gains over time. In R. J. Sternberg (Ed.), *The encyclopedia of human intelligence* (pp. 617–623). New York: Macmillan.

Francis, D. D., Szegda, K., Campbell, G., Martin, W. D., & Insel, T. R. (2003). Epigenetic sources of behavioral differences in mice. *Nature Neuroscience, 6,* 445–446.

Friedman, H. S., & Martin, L. R. (2011). *The longevity project: Surprising discoveries for health and long life from the landmark eight decade study.* London: Hay House, Inc.

Galton, F. (1883). *Inquiries into human faculty and its development.* London: Macmillan.

Geary, D. C. (2005). *The origin of mind: Evolution of brain, cognition, and general intelligence.* Washington, DC: American Psychological Association Press.

Gilchrist, E., Johnson, R., Takriti, R., Beech, A., Kebbell, M., & Weston, S. (2003). Domestic violence offenders characteristics and offending related needs. *Findings No. 217.* London: Home Office.

Goldberg, L. R. (1993). The structure of phenotypic personality traits. *American Psychologist, 48,* 26–34.

Goodwin, R. D., & Friedman, H. S. (2006). Health status and the five-factor personality traits in a nationally representative sample. *Journal of Health Psychology, 11,* 643–654.

Gray, J. A., & McNaughton, N. (2000). *The neuropsychology of anxiety: An enquiry into the functions of the septohippocampal system* (2nd ed.). Oxford: Oxford University Press.

Halla, M., Lackner, M., & Schneider, F. G. (2010). An empirical analysis of the dynamics of the welfare state: The case of benefit morale. *Kyklos, 63,* 55–74.

Hamilton, W. D. (1964). The genetical evolution of social behaviour. I, II. *Journal of Theoretical Biology, 7,* 1–52.

Hanscombe, K. B., Trzaskowski, M., Haworth, C. M., Davis, O. S., Dale, P. S., & Plomin, R. (2012). Socioeconomic status (SES) and children's intelligence (IQ): In a UK-representative sample SES moderates the environmental, not genetic, effect on IQ. *PloS One, 7*(2), e30320.

Harlow, J. M. (1868). Recovery from the passage of an iron bar through the head. *Publications of the Massachusetts Medical Society (Boston), 2,* 327–346.

Harris, A. R., Thomas, S. H., Fisher, G. A., & Hirsch, D. J. (2002). Murder and medicine: The lethality of criminal assault 1960–1999. *Homicide Studies, 6,* 128–166.

Hart, B., & Risley, T. (1995). *Meaningful differences in everyday parenting and intellectual development in young American children.* Baltimore: Brookes.

Hart, S. D., Cox, D. N., & Hare, R. D. (1995). *Manual for the psychopathy checklist: Screening version (PCL:SV).* Toronto, ON, Canada: Multi-Health Systems.

Hathaway, S. R., & McKinley, J. C. (1940). A multiphasic personality schedule (Minnesota): I. Construction of the schedule. *Journal of Psychology, 10,* 249–254.

Heckman, J. J. (2006). Skill formation and the economics of investing in disadvantaged children. *Science, 312,* 1900–1902.

Heckman, J. J. (2008, July). *The viability of the welfare state*. Paper presented at the World Justice Forum, Vienna, Austria.

Heckman, J. J. (2013). *Giving kids a fair chance*. Cambridge, MA: MIT Press.

Heckman, J. J., & Kautz, T. (2014). Achievement tests and the role of character in American life. In J. J. Heckman, J. E. Humphries, & T. Kautz (Eds.), *The myth of achievement tests: The GED and the role of character in American life* (pp. 3–56). Chicago: University of Chicago Press.

Heckman, J. J., & Masterov, D. V. (2005). *Skill policies for Scotland* (pp. 119–165). Princeton, NJ: Princeton University Press.

Heckman, J. J., & Rubinstein, Y. (2001). The importance of noncognitive skills: Lessons from the GED testing program. *American Economic Review*, 145–149.

Heckman, J. J., Humphries, J. E., & Kautz, T. (2014a). Who are the GEDs? In J. J. Heckman, J. E. Humphries, & T. Kautz (Eds.), *The myth of achievement tests: The GED and the role of character in American life* (pp. 139–170). Chicago: University of Chicago Press.

Heckman, J. J., Humphries, J. E., & Kautz, T. (2014b). The economic and social benefits of GED certification. In J. J. Heckman, J. E. Humphries, & T. Kautz (Eds.), *The myth of achievement tests: The GED and the role of character in American life* (pp. 171–267). Chicago: University of Chicago Press.

Heckman, J. J., Humphries, J. E., & Mader, N. S. (2010). *The Ged* (No. w16064). National Bureau of Economic Research.

Heckman, J. J., Pinto, R., & Savelyev, P. A. (2013). Understanding the mechanisms through which an influential early childhood program boosted adult outcomes. *American Economic Review, 103*, 2052–2086.

Heinemann, F. (2008). Is the welfare state self-destructive? A study of government benefit morale. *Kyklos, 61*, 237–257.

Henrich, J. (2000). Does culture matter in economic behavior: Ultimatum game bargaining among the Machiguenga. *American Economic Review, 90*, 973–980.

Henrich, J., Boyd, R., Bowles, S., Camerer, C., Fehr, E., Gintis, H., ... & Tracer, D. (2005). 'Economic man' in cross-cultural perspective: Behavioral experiments in 15 small-scale societies. *Behavioral and Brain Sciences, 28*, 795–815.

Hodgins, S. (2007). Persistent violent offending: What do we know? *The British Journal of Psychiatry, 190*, s12–s14.

Hogan, R. (2011, July). *Psychology and economics: The origins of employability*. Keynote lecture presented at the 15th Conference of the International Society for the Study of Individual Differences, London, England. https://www.youtube.com/watch?v=cRxrzG0qp7o.

Hume, D. (1739). *A treatise of human nature*. London: John Noon.

John, O. P., Caspi, A., Robins, R. W., Moffitt, T. E., & Stouthamer-Loeber, M. (1994). The 'little five': Exploring the nomological network of the five-factor model of personality in adolescent boys. *Child Development, 65*, 160–178.

Jokela, M. (2012). Birth-cohort effects in the association between personality and fertility. *Psychological Science, 23*, 835–841.

Jokela, M., Alvergne, A., Pollet, T. V., & Lummaa, V. (2011). Reproductive behavior and personality traits of the five factor model. *European Journal of Personality, 25*, 487–500.

Jokela, M., Hintsa, T., Hintsanen, M., & Keltikangas-Järvinen, L. (2010). Adult temperament and childbearing over the life course. *European Journal of Personality, 24*, 151–166.

Judge, T. A., Higgins, C. A., Thoresen, C. J., & Barrick, M. R. (1999). The big five personality traits, general mental ability, and career success across the life span. *Personnel Psychology, 52*, 621–652.

Jüriloo, A., Lauerma, H., Holmalahti, T., Tyni, S., Aarnio, J., Viitanen, P., ... & Vartiainen, H. (2014). Psychopathic traits in a representative sample of Finnish male prisoners. *Nordic Journal of Psychiatry, 68*, 117–122.

Kautz, T., Heckman, J. J., Diris, R., Ter Weel, B., & Borghans, L. (2014). *Fostering and measuring skills: Improving cognitive and non-cognitive skills to promote lifetime success*. Paris: The Organisation for Economic Co-operation and Development (OECD).

Kell, H. J., Lubinski, D., & Benbow, C. P. (2013). Who rises to the top? Early indicators. *Psychological Science, 24*, 648–659.

Le Bon, O., Hansenne, M., Amaru, D., Albert, A., Ansseau, M., & Dupont, S. (2013). Assortative mating and personality in human couples: A study using Cloninger's Temperament and Character Inventory. *Psychology, 4*, 11–18.

Lesch, K. P., Bengel, D., Heils, A., Sabol, S. Z., Greenberg, B. D., Petri, S., Benjamin, J., Muller, C. R., Hamer, D. H., & Murphy, D. L. (1996). Association of anxiety-related traits with a polymorphism in the serotonin transporter gene regulatory region. *Science, 274*, 1527–1531.

Lindbeck, A. (1995). Hazardous welfare-state dynamics. *American Economic Review, Papers and Proceedings, 85*, 9–15.

Lindbeck, A., & Nyberg, S. (2006) Raising children to work hard: Altruism, work norms, and social insurance. *Quarterly Journal of Economics, 121*, 1473–1503.

Liu, D., Diorio, J., Day, J. C., Francis, D. D., & Meaney, M. J. (2000). Maternal care, hippocampal synaptogenesis and cognitive development in rats. *Nature Neuroscience, 3*, 799–806.

Ljunge, M. (2011). Increasing demands on the welfare state? Trends in behavior and attitudes. *CESifo Economic Studies, 57*, 605–622.

Lykken, D. T. (1995). Fatherless rearing leads to sociopathy. *Behavioral and Brain Sciences, 18*, 563–564.

Lykken, D. T. (1998). The case for parental licensure. In T. Millon, E. Simonsen, M. Birket-Smith, & R. D. Davis (Eds.), *Psychopathy: Antisocial, criminal and violent behavior* (pp. 122–144). New York: Guilford Press.

Lynam, D. R., Caspi, A., Moffitt, T. E., Raine, A., Loeber, R., & Stouthamer-Loeber, M. (2005). Adolescent psychopathy and the big five: Results from two samples. *Journal of Abnormal Child Psychology, 33*, 431–443.

MacArthur, R. H., & Wilson, E. O. (1967). The theory of island biogeography. *Monographs in Population Biology, 1*, 22.

Macmillan, M. (2000). Restoring Phineas Gage: A 150th retrospective. *Journal of the History of the Neurosciences, 9*, 46–66.

Maller, J. B. (1933). Vital indices and their relation to psychological and social factors: A study of the 310 health areas of New York City with reference to birth rate, deathrate, juvenile delinquency, school progress and intelligence. *Human Biology, 5*, 94–121.

Markowe, M., Tonge, W. L., & Barber, L. E. D. (1955). Psychiatric disability and employment I. Survey of 222 registered disabled persons. *British Journal of Preventive & Social Medicine, 9*, 39–45.

Martin, L. R., & Friedman, H. S. (2000). Comparing personality scales across time: An illustrative study of validity and consistency in life-span archival data. *Journal of Personality, 68*, 85–110.

Matthews, G. (2008). Reinforcement sensitivity theory: A critique from cognitive science. In P. J. Corr (Ed.), *The reinforcement sensitivity theory of personality* (pp. 482–507). Cambridge: Cambridge University Press.

McCrae, R. R., & Costa, P. T. (2008). The five-factor theory of personality. In O. P. John, R. W. Robins, & L. A. Pervin (Eds.), *Handbook of personality: Theory and research* (3rd ed., pp. 159–181). New York: Guilford Press.

Milligan, K. (2005). Subsidizing the stork: New evidence on tax incentives and fertility. *Review of Economics and Statistics, 87*, 539–555.

Mischel, W. (1958). Preference for delayed reinforcement: An experimental study of a cultural observation. *The Journal of Abnormal and Social Psychology, 56*, 57–61.

Mischel, W. (1968). *Personality and assessment*. New York: Wiley.

Mischel, W., Shoda, Y., & Peake, P. K. (1988). The nature of adolescent competencies predicted by preschool delay of gratification. *Journal of Personality and Social Psychology, 54*, 687–696.

Moffitt, R. A. (1998). The effect of welfare on marriage and fertility. In R. Moffitt (Ed.), *Welfare, the family and reproductive behaviour: Research perspectives* (pp. 50–97). Washington: National Academy.

Moffitt, T. E., Arseneault, L., Belsky, D., Dickson, N., Hancox, R. J., Harrington, H., Houts, R., Poulton, R., Roberts, B. W., Ross, S., Sears, M. R., Thomson, W. M., & Caspi, A. (2011). A gradient of childhood self-control predicts health, wealth, and public safety. *Proceedings of the National Academy of Sciences, 108*, 2693–2698.

Mouse Sequencing Consortium (2002). Initial sequencing and comparative analysis of the mouse genome. *Nature, 420*, 520–562.

Mucchielli, L. (2004). Demographic and social characteristics of murderers and their victims: A survey on a Department of the Paris region in the 1990s. *Population, 59*, 203–231.

Müller, F. H. (1939). Tabakmissbrauch und Lungencarcinom. *Zeitschrift für Krebsforschung, 49*, 57–85.

Murphy, J. M. (1976). Psychiatric labeling in cross-cultural perspective. *Science, 191*, 1019–1028.

Neumann, C. S., & Hare, R. D. (2008). Psychopathic traits in a large community sample: Links to violence, alcohol use, and intelligence. *Journal of Consulting and Clinical Psychology, 76,* 893.

Nickell, S. (1997) Unemployment and labor market rigidities: Europe versus North America. *The Journal of Economic Perspectives, 11,* 55–74.

Office for National Statistics (2014). *Childbearing of UK and non-UK born women living in the UK – 2011 Census data.*

O'Neill, J. A., Bassi, L. J., & Wolf, D. A. (1987). The duration of welfare spells. *The Review of Economics and Statistics, 69,* 241–248.

Organ, D. W. (1988). *Organizational Citizenship behavior: The good soldier syndrome.* Lexington, MA: Lexington Books.

Organ, D. W., Podsakoff, P. M., & MacKenzie S. P. (2006). *Organizational citizenship behavior: Its nature, antecedents, and consequences.* London: Sage Publications.

Orwell, G. (1941). *The lion and the unicorn: Socialism and the English genius.* London: Secker and Warburg.

Panksepp, J. (1998). *Affective neuroscience: The foundations of human and animal emotions.* Oxford: Oxford University Press.

Perkins, A. M., Cserjesi, R., Ettinger, U., Kumari, V., Martin, N. G., & Arden, R. (2013). Personality and occupational markers of 'solid citizenship' are associated with having fewer children. *Personality and Individual Differences, 55,* 871–876.

Pianka, E. R. (1970). On r- and K-selection. *American Naturalist, 104,* 592–597.

Pinker, S. (2011). *The better angels of our nature: Why violence has declined.* New York: Viking.

Plomin, R., DeFries, J. C., McClearn, G. E., & McGuffin, P. (2008). *Behavioral genetics* (5th ed). New York: Worth.

Podsakoff, P. M., MacKenzie, S. B., Paine, J. B., & Bachrach, D. G. (2000). Organizational citizenship behaviors: A critical review of the theoretical and empirical literature and suggestions for future research. *Journal of Management, 26,* 513–563.

Poropat, A. E. (2009). A meta-analysis of the five-factor model of personality and academic performance. *Psychological Bulletin, 135,* 322.

Provençal, N., Suderman, M. J., Guillemin, C., Massart, R., Ruggiero, A., Wang, D., … & Szyf, M. (2012). The signature of maternal rearing in the methylome in rhesus macaque prefrontal cortex and T cells. *The Journal of Neuroscience, 32,* 15626–15642.

Prüfer, K., Munch, K., Hellmann, I., Akagi, K., Miller, J. R., Walenz, B., … & Pääbo, S. (2012). The bonobo genome compared with the chimpanzee and human genomes. *Nature, 486,* 527–531.

Reynolds, A. J., Temple, J. A., Robertson, D. L., & Mann, E. A. (2001). Long-term effects of an early childhood intervention on educational achievement and juvenile arrest: A 15-year follow-up of low-income children in public schools. *Jama, 285,* 2339–2346.

Sanfey, A. G., Rilling, J. K., Aronson, J. A., Nystrom, L. E. & Cohen, J. D. (2003). The neural basis of economic decision-making in the ultimatum game. *Science, 300*, 1755–1758.

Schmidt, F. L., & Hunter, J. E. (1998). The validity and utility of selection methods in personnel psychology: Practical and theoretical implications of 85 years of research findings. *Psychological Bulletin, 124*, 262–274.

Schweinhart, L. J., Montie, J., Xiang, Z., Barnett, W. S., Belfield, C. R., & Nores, M. (2005). *Lifetime effects: The High/Scope Perry Preschool study through age 40.* Ypsilanti, MI: High/Scope.

Shoda, Y., Mischel, W., & Peake, P. K. (1990). Predicting adolescent cognitive and self-regulatory competencies from preschool delay of gratification: Identifying diagnostic conditions. *Developmental Psychology, 26*, 978.

Schofield, T. M. (2013). On my way to being a scientist. *Nature, 497*, 277–278.

Skogman Thoursie, P. (2004). Reporting sick: Are sporting events contagious? *Journal of Applied Econometrics, 19*, 809–823.

Smallwood, J., Ruby, F. J., & Singer, T. (2013). Letting go of the present: Mind-wandering is associated with reduced delay discounting. *Consciousness and Cognition, 22*, 1–7.

Specht, J., Egloff, B., & Schmukle, S. C. (2011). Stability and change of personality across the life course: The impact of age and major life events on mean-level and rank-order stability of the big five. *Journal of Personality and Social Psychology, 101*, 862–882.

Spector, T. (2012). *Identically different: Why you can change your genes.* London: Weidenfeld & Nicolson.

Stouffer, S. A., Guttman, L., Suchman, E. A., Lazarsfeld, P. F., Star, S. A., & Clausen, J. A. (1950). *Studies in social psychology in World War II: Vol. 4. Measurement and prediction.* Princeton: Princeton University Press.

Swallow, J. G., Carter, P. A., & Garland Jr, T. (1998). Artificial selection for increased wheel-running behavior in house mice. *Behavior Genetics, 28*, 227–237.

Tellegen, A., Lykken, D. T., Bouchard, T. J., Wilcox, K. J., Segal, N. L., & Rich, S. (1988). Personality similarity in twins reared apart and together. *Journal of Personality and Social Psychology, 54*, 1031.

Terman, L. M. (1915). The mental hygiene of exceptional children. *The Pedagogical Seminary, 22*, 529–537.

Timmins, N. (2001). *The five giants: A biography of the welfare state.* London: Harper Collins.

Tonge, W. L., James, D. S., & Hillam, S. M. (1975). *Families without hope: A controlled study of 33 problem families (No. 11).* Headley [for the] Royal College of Psychiatrists.

Tonge, W. L., Lunn, J. E., Greathead, M., & McLaren, S. (1981). *A follow-up to the adult sons and daughters of Sheffield problem and comparison families originally reported by Tonge, James and Hilliam in 1975.* London: Social Science Research Council.

Trut, L. (1999). Early canid domestication: The farm-fox experiment foxes bred for tamability in a 40-year experiment exhibit remarkable transformations that suggest an interplay between behavioral genetics and development. *American Scientist, 87,* 160–169.

Turkheimer, E. (2000). Three laws of behavior genetics and what they mean. *Current Directions in Psychological Science, 9,* 160–164.

Turkheimer, E., & Waldron, M. C. (2000). Nonshared environment: A theoretical, methodological and quantitative review. *Psychological Bulletin, 126,* 78–108.

Turkheimer, E., Haley, A., Waldron, M., d'Onofrio, B., & Gottesman, I. I. (2003). Socioeconomic status modifies heritability of IQ in young children. *Psychological Science, 14,* 623–628.

Tuvblad, C., Grann, M., & Lichtenstein, P. (2006). Heritability for adolescent antisocial behavior differs with socioeconomic status: Gene–environment interaction. *Journal of Child Psychology and Psychiatry, 47,* 734–743.

US Department of Health and Human Services, Centers for Disease Control (1989). *Health status of Vietnam veterans volumes I–V.*

van der Wel, K. A., & Halvorsen, K. (2015). The bigger the worse? A comparative study of the welfare state and employment commitment. *Work, Employment & Society, 29,* 99–118.

Vaughn, M. G., Fu, Q., Beaver, D., DeLisi, M., Perron, B., & Howard, M. (2010). Are personality disorders associated with social welfare burden in the United States? *Journal of Personality Disorders, 24,* 709–720.

Verweij, K. J., Yang, J., Lahti, J., Veijola, J., Hintsanen, M., Pulkki-Råback, L., ... & Zietsch, B. P. (2012). Maintenance of genetic variation in human personality: Testing evolutionary models by estimating heritability due to common causal variants and investigating the effect of distant inbreeding. *Evolution, 66,* 3238–3251.

Vinkhuyzen, A. A. E., Pedersen, N. L., Yang, J., Lee, S. H., Magnusson, P. K. E., Iacono, W. G., ... & Wray, N. R. (2012). Common SNPs explain some of the variation in the personality dimensions of neuroticism and extraversion. *Translational Psychiatry, 2,* e102.

Weaver, I. C., Cervoni, N., Champagne, F. A., D'Alessio, A. C., Sharma, S., Seckl, J. R., ... & Meaney, M. J. (2004). Epigenetic programming by maternal behavior. *Nature Neuroscience, 7,* 847–854.

Westman, J. C. (1994). *Licensing parents.* New York: Insight Books.

Whiten, A. (2014). Animal behaviour: Incipient tradition in wild chimpanzees. *Nature, 514,* 178–179.

Whittington, L. A. (1992). Taxes and the family: The impact of the tax exemption for dependents on marital fertility. *Demography, 29,* 215–226.

Whittington, L. A., Alm, J., & Peters, H. E. (1990). Fertility and the personal exemption: Implicit pronatalist policy in the United States. *The American Economic Review, 80,* 545–556.

Wigger, A., Loerscher, P., Weissenbacher, P., Holsboer, F., & Landgraf, R. (2001). Cross-fostering and cross-breeding of HAB and LAB rats: A genetic rat model of anxiety. *Behavior Genetics, 31,* 371–382.

Wiig, J. K. (1995). *Delinquents under 10 in Hennepin County.* Minneapolis: Hennepin County Attorney's Office.

Wright, C. H., & Lunn, J. E. (1971). Sheffield problem families, a follow-up study of their sons and daughters. *Community Medicine, 126*, 301–307.

Yang, J., Loos, R. J., Powell, J. E., Medland, S. E., Speliotes, E. K., Chasman, D. I., . . . & Teumer, A. (2012). FTO genotype is associated with phenotypic variability of body mass index. *Nature, 490(7419)*, 267–272.

Index

A Farewell to Alms (Clark), 57, 59, 61,
 170
Abecedarian Project, 90–4
aggressive personality, 2–3, 26, 32,
 80, 90, 108–9, 129–30, 140
agreeableness
 benefit claims, 145
 changes in society, 57, 62, 64
 concept, 9–10
 degree of heritability, 116
 effect of motivation, 30–2
 employment difficulties, 18–19
 employment-resistant personality
  profile, 112, 122–3, 163
 face value, 89
 family environment, 47, 121
 functional difference, 11–12
 Gage's case study, 20–4
 juvenile delinquency, 55
 occupational performance, 27,
  36–9
 personality measurement, 25–6,
  35, 44–5
 preschool training, 52
 selective-breeding programmes,
  105, 107
 self-control and, 29, 49
 socialisation patterns, 171
 Ultimatum Game (UG) data, 149,
  153, 155
 unemployment risk, 40–2, 53
antisocial behaviour
 childhood disadvantage, 2–3, 140
 childhood self-control, 50, 52
 employment-resistant personality
  profile, 33, 60, 71, 138–9,
  142–3, 181
 family environment, 121, 130–1
 fear of destitution, 32
 GED recipients, 41

 parental inattention, 85–6
 preschool tutoring, 80, 90, 129
 socioeconomic status (SES), 120
 troubled families, 155–8
 UK and US population,
  comparison, 60–2
 violent criminality, 165–6, 173
 welfare claimants, 153, 155
antisocial personality disorder, 33,
 60–1, 71, 138–9, 165–6

Better Angels of Our Nature, The
 (Pinker), 167
Big Five dimensions of personality.
 see agreeableness;
 conscientiousness; extraversion;
 neuroticism; openness to
 experience

Chicago Longitudinal Study (CLS),
 94–5
childhood disadvantage
 criminal records, 136
 employment-resistant personality,
  3–4, 117, 177
 human capital debate, 2, 140
 Perry Preschool Project, example,
  123–30
 personality mis-development, 144
childhood self-control, 29, 48–9,
 51–2, 65–7
children, number of
 childhood self-control, 65–7
 in disadvantaged households, 2,
  54, 57, 116, 124, 140, 142,
  148, 157, 172, 180–2, 185
 family/household type, 158–9,
  176–7
 household income, 63
 neglect-prone households, 143

197

children, number of – *continued*
    social class, 59
    unemployed adults, 72–3
    welfare claimants, 58, 74–5, 79,
        98, 123, 133, 154, 176
claimant reproduction
    British Cohort Study (BCS)
        participants, 66–7
    comparison families, 59, 76–7
    modern theory, 65–71
    National Child Development
        Study (NCDS) participants, 66
    pre-welfare eras, 69, 72
    problem families, 58–9, 76–7
    r-K selection theory, 55–7
    welfare era, 71–8
comparison families
    criminality, 136–7, 164
    impoverishment, 59
    mother's protectiveness, 77
    personality analysis, 25–6, 113–14
    socio-economic background, 163
    unemployment, 113
    work records, 19, 27, 76, 86
conscientiousness
    benefit claims, 145
    changes in society, impact on, 57,
        62, 64
    concept, 9
    degree of heritability, 116
    differences in laziness, 106
    employment difficulties, 18–19
    employment-resistant personality
        profile, 40–2, 53, 112, 151,
        163
    face value, 89
    family environment, 47, 121
    functional difference, 11
    Gage's case study, 21–4
    human reproduction, 68–9
    juvenile delinquency, 56
    level of motivation, 31–2
    Machiguenga environment,
        151–3, 155
    occupational performance, 27,
        29–30, 35–9, 122–3

    personality measurement, 25–6,
        44–6
    preschool training, 51–2
    selective-breeding programmes,
        105, 107
    self-control, 49
    socialisation, 171
    contraception, 2, 4, 58, 74–5, 99,
        103, 176
    criminal violence, 6, 33, 143, 164–7,
        170–1, 173–4
    cultural kinship, 154

disadvantaged households
    genetic profiles, 133, 175
    moral concerns, 178
    number of children, 2, 54, 57, 124,
        128, 140, 142, 148, 157, 172,
        180–2, 185
    uneven exposure, 120
domestic violence, 159, 166, 173
Dunedin Study, 42, 47–50, 53, 65, 76

employment-resistant personality
    profile
    agreeableness, 112, 122–3, 163
    antisocial behaviour, 33, 60, 71,
        138–9, 142–3, 181
    childhood disadvantage, 3–4, 117,
        177
    conscientiousness, 40–2, 53, 112,
        151, 163
    criminality, 163–4
    mis-evolution of personality,
        184–5
    nightmare scenario, 185
    violent crime, 164
    welfare claimants, 3, 32–3, 53, 98,
        112, 122–3, 141, 153
    welfare state, 18, 32, 79, 153–5,
        157, 163
English intelligentsia, 180–1
environmental effects, 5,
    86–7, 115–16, 118–20, 134–6,
    172
extra welfare benefits, 157, 177

extraversion
concept, 8
personality measurement, 25–6,
34–5, 44
positive emotion, 10

family cap, 73–4
family environment, 93, 119–21
Fiscal Case for Working with
Troubled Families, The, 160–1

Gage, Phineas (case study), 20–4
general educational development
(GED) test, 28–9, 33, 41, 83
general intelligence, 27
genetic influences
level of foresight, 100
natural selection, 97–8, 102
selective breeding, 97–8, 103,
105–7, 109, 111–12
genome-wide complex trait analysis
(GCTA), 117–18

homicide, 164–5, 167–8, 170, 172
household income, 72, 74, 76, 177
human capital, 1–3, 6, 18, 45, 80–1,
131, 133, 135, 140, 185

impulsive/irresponsible behaviour,
26, 172
IQ score, 24, 27, 42–3, 48, 50–3, 89,
91–3, 120

job performance, 7, 11, 19, 27, 34–6,
41
juvenile delinquency, 55–6, 138

laziness, 106–7, 116
Lebensführung, 170–1, 173
London riots 2011, 182

middle-class households, 42, 120–1
Montreal Longitudinal Experimental
Study, 95–6

The National Evaluation of the
Troubled Families Programme
(government report), 160
natural selection, 12, 65, 97–8, 102,
140, 153
nepotism, 153–4
neuroticism
childhood self-control, 49
concept, 10
personality measurement, 25,
34–5, 44
selective breeding, 105
non-human animals, 5, 81, 103, 109,
112

openness to experience
concept, 8
intellectual abilities, 10–11
personality measurement, 25, 44
organisational citizenship behaviour
(OCB), 36
Origin of Species (Darwin), 97, 140

parental inattention, 81–3, 85–6
Perry Preschool Project, 87, 89–93,
123–30
personality-damaged welfare babies,
166–7
personality development
child neglect, 81–7
family environment, 121
genetic basis, 5
life outcomes, 129
occupational performance, 27–38
state altruism, 3
personality mis-development, 6–7,
76, 79–80, 83, 98–9, 122–4, 129,
142, 144, 172, 175, 185
poverty, 58–9, 73, 80, 83, 137, 165
prefrontal brain injury, 18–20,
18–22, 22–4, 24, 26, 40–1
preschool tutoring, 80, 87–8, 90, 93,
124–6, 128–9, 131, 185
privileged families, 4, 180

problem families
    concept, 113
    criminal violence, 164
    personality characteristics, 24–7
    poverty, 59
    psychological characteristics,
        18–19
    welfare payments, 77
    work records, 76, 86
    see also Sheffield problem families
        (case study)
Project CARE, 93–4

questionnaire
    employability dimension, 38
    online, 8
    personality scores, 19–20, 23, 25,
        34, 41, 55, 68–9, 71, 132
    self-report, 7, 25, 44, 84
    social behaviour, 95
    workplace performance, 35

reproduction
    developed countries, 57
    employment-resistant personality
        profile, 56
    offspring care, 54, 154
    personality and, 14, 65–71, 170,
        172
    unrestrained, 99–100, 102
    welfare and, 4, 71–8
rule-breaking personality, 2–3, 33,
    80, 90, 129, 140

selective-breeding experiments
    Maudsley reactive rats, 103–5
    Russian domestication
        programme, 107–11
    work ethic in mice, 106–7
self-control
    Dunedin Study data, 50–1
    during childhood, 29–30, 65–7
    hybrid construct, 42
    lack of, 53
    levels, 48–9, 52, 76
    values of, 171, 174

Selfish Gene, The (Dawkins), 2,
    98–100, 103, 176
Sheffield problem families (case
    study), 100, 103, 137
socialisation, 51, 130–2, 135, 139,
    171–2
socio-economic status (SES), 3, 41,
    47, 51, 68, 120
super-prolific criminals, 136

Terman Study, 42–5, 47, 49–50, 53
Treatise of Human Nature (Hume), 11
Troubled Families Programme,
    142–3, 155–73, 178

unemployed citizens
    antisocial behaviour, 142, 157
    childhood disadvantage, 127–8,
        144
    claiming benefits, 56, 148, 178–9
    demoralising effects, 123
    *Employment-Resistant Personality
        Profile*, 33, 40–1, 45, 53,
        70, 136, 146, 163–4, 175,
        181
    homicide data, 165
    levels of reproduction, 72
    Perry Preschool participants,
        example, 90, 124–6
    problem families, 86, 113, 156,
        158, 182
    violent crime, 166
US Earned Income Tax Credit (EITC)
    scheme, 74

Vietnam Experience Study (VES),
    69–71
violent crime, 129, 143, 164–7, 170,
    181

War on Poverty, 177
Wasting Police Time (Davidson), 182
welfare benefits, 4, 24, 33, 45, 56,
    73–6, 100–1, 135–7, 144, 147–8,
    157, 176–7, 179

welfare claimants
'employment-resistant' personality
profile, 3, 32–3, 53, 98, 112,
122–3, 141, 153
children of, 4–5, 73, 82, 86, 134
effects of self-control, 52
lack of socialisation, 172
personality profiles, 17
reproduction strategies, 54–5, 58,
72, 74, 102
welfare generosity, 6, 58, 73–4, 112,
134–5, 137, 139, 141, 144–6,
176–8
welfare incentives, 76, 128, 137
welfare legislation, 29, 74, 98–9, 102,
109, 167, 181
welfare policies, 52, 179–80
welfare state
childhood disadvantage, 79–97,
116
claimant benefits, 54–7, 59, 65,
67–9, 72–3, 77–8
criminal violence, 166–7, 173
employment-resistant personality
profile, 18, 32, 79, 153–5, 157,
163
homicide, 170
personality mis-development, 122,
124, 128, 130, 133–5, 140–3,
184
personality, impact on, 1–7,
12–13, 15–17, 40–54
reproduction effects, 176–8, 182

selective-breeding effect, 103
socialisation pattern, 172
UK model, 101–2
unnatural, 99
work motivation effects, 143–9
welfare trait theory
antisocial behaviour, 143, 155,
157, 181–2
benefit claims, 145–6, 148
childhood disadvantage, 140–1
criminal violence, 167, 173–4
degree of heritability, 116
employment-resistant personality
profile, 6
family environment effects, 121
homicide, 170
human capital, role in, 45
personality and reproduction,
67–8, 142
principle of evolution, 12
socialisation, 171–2
troubled-family status, 159, 162
validity, 14–16, 168
welfare-induced personality
mis-development, 112, 122
work motivation, 144, 154
work motivation, 6, 30, 32–3, 141,
143–4, 146–7, 154, 180
Work Opportunity Reconciliation
Act, 73
Working Families' Tax Credit
(WFTC), 74–5
workplace performance, 4, 35–7

Druck: KN Digital Printforce GmbH · Schockenriedstraße 37 · 70565 Stuttgart